From the STREETS to the RING:
A SON'S Struggle to Become a MAN

Teddy Atlas

and Peter Alson

ANNIVERSARY
35

HarperCollins books may be purchased for educational, business, or sales promotional use. For information, please write: Special Markets Department, HarperCollins Publishers, 10 East 53rd Street, New York, NY 10022.

Designed by Lovedog Studio

Library of Congress Cataloging-in-Publication Data
Atlas, Teddy.
    Atlas : from the streets to the ring: a son's struggle to become a man /
Teddy Atlas and Peter Alson.—1st ed.
        p.   cm.
    ISBN-10: 0-06-054240-3
    ISBN-13: 978-0-06-054240-5
    1. Atlas, Teddy.   2. Boxing trainers—United States—Biography.   3. Boxing—United States—
History.   I. Alson, Peter.   II. Title.

GV1132.A78A3   2006
796.83'092—dc22
    [B]   2005052104

06   07   08   09   10   WBC/RRD   10   9   8   7   6   5   4   3

To my wife, Elaine, thank you for giving me the two best things in my life. To my children, Nicole and Teddy III, thank you for giving me two reasons to never again close the door on things like faith and love.

CONTENTS

ATLAS

NOT ALL BRUISES ARE BLACK AND BLUE

O F ALL THE PEOPLE WHO HAVE AFFECTED MY LIFE, and influenced the choices I've made, none has been more important than my father.

Dr. Theodore Atlas, Sr., was legendary around Staten Island. A Hungarian Jew, originally from the Bronx, he was the kind of doctor that doesn't exist anymore. He wore a bow tie and a rumpled old raincoat and he drove an old wreck of a car to go on his house calls. He traveled all over the island, taking care of people, no matter what time of the day or night. If his patients couldn't afford to pay, he didn't charge them, and when he did charge them, the most it would be was about five dollars. Sometimes they paid him with pies or cookies. In the 1970s, when I was a teenager, my mother started calling him Columbo, after the character in the TV show, because of the way he dressed and because he always seemed distracted and preoccupied.

Besides his medical practice, my father somehow found time to found and build two hospitals, Sunnyside and Doctor's Hospital. He also built over a hundred houses on Staten Island, including the two we lived in—a small one-family home, and, later, a larger Colonial that he built across the street—plus some Winn-Dixies and condos down South. Think of it: here was a doctor who owned a crane and bulldozer, and on Sundays, to relax after spending an eighty-hour week practicing medicine and taking care of people, he bulldozed the empty lots on the hill where we lived so he could build houses. He even built the sewer system for the whole neighborhood.

Because my father poured all of his time and energy and feeling into his work, my mother and I and my four younger siblings, Tommy, Meri, Todd, and Terryl, often felt shortchanged—if not consciously at least in our hearts. Maybe it was easier for him to express emotions toward his patients than his family. I don't know. Even today, I run into people who were patients of his, and they all talk about how compassionate he was with them. But at home it was hard for him to show anything. He considered emotions a sign of weakness. I remember one time we were in the car and he made fun of us kids for crying over something. He started going "Wahhhh!" in this loud, mocking way. After that I never cried again, even many years later at his funeral.

Of all the kids, I was always his favorite, which made for an odd kind of tension in the house. In some ways it was like we were two families. One family was my mother, Tommy, Terryl, Todd, and Meri. The other family was my father and me. It wasn't as if I didn't have to work hard for his attention. I did. I showed an interest in science because he liked science. I'd get him to take me out on house calls with him, because that way I could be with him and spend time with him. You have to understand, this was a man who left the house every day at six-thirty or seven a.m. and came home at ten-thirty or eleven p.m. Any time that I got with him was time that I had to steal. He never asked me to go with him. I just went. Occasionally, he would get a call in the middle of the night, and I would hear the phone and wake up. By the time he was coming out of his room and down the stairs, I was sitting there, ready to go. He would tell me to go back to my room, but sometimes he would give in and let me go with him. I remember going with him on New Year's Eve once, around 1964 or '65, for a maternity case. I must have fallen asleep in the doctor's waiting room. At midnight, one of the nurses woke me up. They were all pouring soda and champagne, saying, "Your father just delivered the first baby of the New Year." Half-asleep, I joined the celebration, knowing that it was a special thing to be there, even if my father's full attention wasn't focused on me.

My mother, Mary, suffered from my father's inattention more than any of us. She was Irish and very beautiful. She'd been Miss Staten Island in 1940. Part of the prize that went along with the honor was a screen test in Hollywood. But her mother, my grandmother Helen Riley (called Gaga—the nickname I'd given her when I was young), had refused to let her go. "That's for tramps," she said. Who knows what direction my mother's life would have taken if she had gone? I'm sure she thought about that over the years. My mother was the complete opposite of my father: very social, talkative, outgoing, used to getting attention, and with a fondness for nice things. My father, meanwhile, was driving around in jalopies and wearing shoes until there were holes in them, caught up in his own world, and his very different concerns.

When my brother Todd died at the age of five, it pushed us all further apart. With some families it might have helped draw them closer; not with ours. Todd had been born retarded and with an enlarged heart, and my father, who read all the medical journals and was always up on all the latest procedures, felt that open-heart surgery, which was relatively new at the time, could help him. It was the kind of thing where if nothing was done, Todd would die by the time he was sixteen. So my father made the decision that he should have the operation, and he was there in the operating room watching when Todd died on the table.

Years later, a woman named Sally Cusack told me that her daughter's baby had gotten sick later that same day, and my father had gone over to their house and treated the baby. When Sally Cusack found out that her daughter had called my father, she was upset. She said, "You called Dr. Atlas? Didn't you know his son died today?" Her daughter was devastated. "I didn't know," she said. "He came and he never said a thing." That was my father to a tee. *He never said a thing.*

My mother was devastated by Todd's death, and she held it against my father that he had pushed for the operation. In the aftermath, she had what I would now call a breakdown. For a while she was even taking a blanket down to Todd's grave site and sleeping there. Truthfully, I don't remember much about that time. But I think about the irony of it: how in our family, where feelings were neglected, this kid, my brother, had an enlarged heart, and it turned out to be a death sentence for him.

There was a period after Todd died when my brothers and sister and

I lived with relatives and friends. It was around that time that my mother's drinking really became a problem. It probably wouldn't be fair to lay the blame for her drinking on Todd's death or my father's neglect, since alcoholism ran in her family, but those things certainly didn't help.

Ten o'clock on a Wednesday. I'm in my room, doing homework. From downstairs comes a scream.

"You bastard. You don't even care."

I hear the sound of dishes being broken. I close my eyes, wishing it would stop. It keeps going, the yelling keeps going, the crash of dishes. Finally, a door slams, and there is silence. I go out of my room and down the stairs. My father comes out of the kitchen, looks at me.

"Dad?"

"It's okay. Go back to your room."

He walks past me and up the stairs. I stand there for a moment, then go into the kitchen. The entire floor is covered with broken dishes. The overhead cabinets are open. I get some paper shopping bags out of the drawer by the sink and start picking up shards of china and crockery. By midnight, the kitchen is spotless. I've cleaned up all the evidence.

The next day in school, I don't say anything to my friends. I don't want anyone to know. It's better if I keep it inside.

BY THE TIME I WAS IN MY LATE TEENS, I WAS STARTING TO get into trouble. At Curtis, the public high school, I was a decent student and I played on the football team. But I got into fights. I was an angry kid. I had this rage inside me that I didn't understand. Nobody in my family was getting what they wanted or needed. We were just splintered, all going off in our own directions.

My father was extraordinary in so many ways, but he had been led by his own difficult childhood to keep everything bottled up inside, and it had become his code, his sense of how everyone should be. This was a guy who stayed up all night reading books, who read so much he broke blood vessels in his eyes when he got older, but who only read nonfiction because he considered fiction a waste of time. (Not that he didn't believe in the imagination or think about what was possible. It's just that he was of the opinion that going into places that didn't exist was, for the most part, a luxury and a weakness. The world was what was in front of you, and everything else was frivolous.)

His own father had committed suicide. He never talked about it, and I didn't know about it until much later, when my mother told my wife. From what I was able to learn, my grandfather was a gambler, and my grandmother threw him out of the house for gambling and then he hanged himself.

I'm sure my father held that against my grandmother in some ways, but at the same time he respected her. She was a tough woman. She had three sons and she told each of them what he was going to be when he grew up. "Theodore, you're going to be a doctor. Eugene, you're going to be an orthodontist. Reynold, you're going to be an engineer." And each of them became what she'd told them they'd become.

My father once told me a story about how he was driving in a car with his mother to the hospital to see Eugene, the middle brother, who was undergoing an emergency appendectomy. My father was driving fast, and the roads at that time were mostly dirt. The car went around a curve and the door swung open and my father's mother fell out. He didn't even realize it at first. When he finally did realize it and went back to get her, she didn't act the way most women would act. She got up out of a ditch and brushed off the dirt. When she opened the door of the car all she said was, "Theodore, are we lost?"

This was what formed him. He was a guy who, if you talked about certain things and he thought it was wasteful, he would tell you. He'd say, "You're talking in too many words." In a way he was almost like a machine. No emotions, just principle and action. He suppressed all his emotions, and he got very uncomfortable when anyone else, any one of us, expressed ours. He couldn't handle it. The frustration of trying to get emotion out of a man like that was maddening. It was in part what drove my mother to drink. And me to do the things I did.

I was in my teens when I started hanging out with the kids down the hill in Stapleton, which was a rough section of town. There were housing projects down there, a needle park where all the drug dealers hung out, and plenty of ways to get yourself into trouble. I was still trying to get my father's attention, but in a different way than when I'd gone out on house calls with him, a much angrier way.

I don't know if he was aware of the extent of it, but I was cutting school a lot. For a while he used to force me to get up in the morning, and he'd drive me to school before he went to work. Maybe he didn't have the time or the patience to be a real parent and get involved in a more active way. He thought that if he made me go, the rest would take care of itself. He didn't understand there was more to it. He didn't understand that as a parent it took more than throwing a glass of water on your son in the morning when he didn't wake up. He should have known that something was wrong on a deeper level. As a doctor he certainly knew that he had to do more than inject medicine into a patient; that he had to take time to talk to people, to help them recover. But as a parent, he just didn't get that.

Halfway through my senior year, in 1974 or 1975, I stopped going to school entirely. I dropped out. I was hanging around with the Sullivan brothers down in Stapleton. I'd met Genie Sullivan first. He was about my age, with the Irish gift of gab, and funny, always making people laugh. One time, he and I stole these little manila envelopes from a stationery store and filled them with oregano, then stood on the corner, selling them as nickel bags of marijuana. We were so stupid we stayed on the same block for hours, until eventually some of the guys we sold them to came back. I mean, we were standing there three hours later *in the exact same spot,* and this car full of Puerto Rican guys drove up, and the driver threw the manila envelope in Genie's face. "Who you guys think you're fucking with?" Genie, who knew I was there backing him up— and by then I'd already developed something of a reputation as a street fighter—smiled and said, "What's the matter? It wasn't any good? Don't you know you have to put it *on* the sausage before you cook it?" These guys went crazy. One of them got out of the car and came at me. I wound up decking him. We were just lucky they didn't have guns.

Later on, I got to be friends with Genie's brothers. There were five of them altogether, and they kind of adopted me. Even though they were screwed up in various ways, drugs and alcohol and other things, they were a family, they were together. I wasn't seeing the problems, I was just seeing that they were a family. Over time, I got really close to Billy Sullivan, who was about eight years older than me, twenty-five or twenty-six, and who had a wife named Linda and two young kids in Jersey. Billy was a skinny guy and a sharp dresser, very charismatic and likable.

He knew his way around. He taught me stuff like craps and blackjack. He had all the odds down, knew all the numbers, and I was impressed by that. We'd play craps with guys in the street. Billy was also a very good pool player—I was pretty good, but he was very good—and we'd go into bars and hustle money that way.

There were other things that drew me to him. He had a good singing voice. I loved to hear him sing "Under the Boardwalk." We'd be in a bar, and I'd play it on the jukebox and get him to sing along with it. I'd say, "Sing, Billy," and he would. He got a kick out of the fact that I liked his singing. If anyone in the bar didn't appreciate it as much as I did, I'd tell 'em, "You better start clapping and smiling or else get the fuck out."

I looked up to Billy. When I think about it now, I can see he was giving me something I wasn't getting at home, a kind of interest and attention that I was starved for. He wasn't just a criminal, either. There was this other side to him. He coached a Little League team in Stapleton, and he asked me to come down and watch. So I went one day, and there he was, standing in the third base coaching box, wearing a uniform, talking to the kids. When he saw me, he winked. I'll never forget that. It had an effect on me, seeing him in that setting, watching him with those kids. Of course, he had to play the tough guy, too, so he said to me, "I wish there was a line on *this* fuckin' game."

MY FATHER AND MOTHER KNEW I'D DROPPED OUT OF school, but they didn't say anything to me about it. Things were tense at home. I was heading in a bad direction and they knew it—or sort of knew it—but they weren't doing anything or saying anything. Anyway, I stayed away from them as much as I could. For a while, I crashed in Jersey with Billy and his wife and kids. His wife was pretty and blonde, but the marriage was up and down. He was robbing and stealing, and he had lots of bad habits on top of that: chasing women, drinking, and gambling. There was a pretty Spanish girl about my age with big breasts who was babysitting their kids. Billy wanted to bang her, but it was too difficult with his wife in the house, so he told me I should. I actually did wind up messing around with her. I think he got a kick out of that. I mean, he seemed like a cool, tough customer, but on the inside he was just a wounded kid who needed someone like me looking up to him.

I recognized that about him, even at the time, because I identified with him. Most of the things Billy did were self-destructive. He never really hurt anyone else.

WHILE I WAS STAYING IN JERSEY WITH HIM, WE BROKE INTO a place in the middle of the night and robbed it. Billy always had some scheme or plan. "All we have to do is break through this cinder-block wall and we'll be in the back room of the store where they keep the night's receipts." So there we were in this back alley with all these tools—screwdrivers, crowbars, the wrong kinds of tools, really—trying to hack and chisel our way through this wall. It took hours. At one point, Billy whacked my hand with a slap hammer and it started to swell up. When we finally crawled through this minuscule hole we'd made, it was like a scene from a movie—we were in the wrong place. It was a grocery store. But fuck it, we robbed it anyway. We took food and soda, and I guess they had a little bit of money, too. I mean, I don't even remember what we got, but we got something. Billy was always deep into the bookies, always on the run from them. I gave him my share of our take so he could pay them off.

The really funny part is that the cops actually tracked us down the next day and questioned us about it. They didn't think we did it, but they thought we might know something. They said, "Whoever did it, they were professionals, because they bypassed the wires in the wall without setting off the alarm. That's why we know it couldn't be you fuckin' idiots." When they left, I said to Billy, "There were wires in the wall? You didn't tell me there were wires in the wall." He was dying laughing. "That cop was looking right at your swollen hand saying no way we could possibly have done it—and we're the fuckin' idiots?"

ONE NIGHT, BILLY GOT A GUN AND WE DECIDED TO ROB A bar in Stapleton. It wasn't really as premeditated as that sounds. We were just looking to do something, and that's what we settled on. I didn't even know why I was doing this stuff. Billy knew what he was doing. He was robbing a bar. Me? I was just trying to fit in with him. I saw him as someone who cared about me, and I wanted to show him that I was worthy. Anyway, we went to this bar on Bay Street, and we were there for a while, drinking, playing pool in the back room, and plotting our next move. This is what I mean; it wasn't even a plan. We were just trying to figure out what we were gonna do. We knew we wanted to do something.

"Should we rob this fucking joint or what?"

"It's still early. Let 'em get a little more cash in the till, make it worth our while."

While we were discussing it, this guy Robert Holder showed up, picked up a pool cue, and joined us. I knew him a little. His brother Dallas had been involved with wiseguys, got arrested, then flipped and ended up going into the Witness Protection program. This was back in the days when the Witness Protection program wasn't as full as it is today. Now it's like the Holiday Inn; you can't get in. But in those days, it meant something. It was like, wow, the guy fucking disappeared. He ratted out the wiseguys and now he's gone. Anyway, Billy let this guy Holder know what we were doing, that we had a gun and we were going to rob the place. I don't know what he was thinking, because this guy, whose brother was a rat, didn't even particularly like Billy.

When Holder went off to the bathroom, I said, "What the hell are you doing?"

"Ahh, it's okay," Billy said. "Don't worry about it. C'mon, I'll buy you another drink."

It was screwed up. If you're going to rob a place, you should rob it.

Twenty minutes later, we were still bullshitting around when the cops came in. We were in the back room, they were in front, but we could see them checking people out, looking around, moving in our direction.

"That motherfucker," Billy said. "He gave us up."

"You sound surprised."

"Shit! The gun."

"Give it to me."

"They're gonna nail us, Teddy."

"Give me the gun." In that moment, Billy looked very weak to me. Just a scared kid. I reached into his waistband and took the gun. I could see he wasn't going to be able to handle going to jail.

"What are you doing?" he said, but he didn't try to stop me.

When the cops came into the back room, they frisked me and found the gun. They wound up running us both in and taking pictures, fingerprints, the whole bit. My bail was set at five thousand for the gun charge, but they let Billy out on his own recognizance.

Here's the crazy thing: My father bailed me out the next day, and two nights later, I was down in Stapleton again, looking for trouble. I mean really looking. I hooked up with another friend of mine this time, a guy named John, who'd been a football player and was a big, tough bastard bent on his own mission of self-destruction. John had been stabbed at a New Year's party and lost a kidney, and he was poisoning his remaining kidney with as much liquor as he could drink. The basic plan for the night was for us to make some money, but as I say, there were obviously underlying issues driving each of us that we were too disconnected from ourselves to recognize.

We started out in Teckie's Bar on Gordon Street, across the street from the projects. Teckie's was one of our regular hangouts, just a small neighborhood drinking bar with a shuffleboard machine and a pool table. There was a friend of mine there, a guy named Nipple, who had a gun, and I just came straight out and told him to give me the gun.

"What are you gonna do?"

"I need it," I said.

There was no question, the idea of giving me his gun made him nervous. I made a lot of people nervous at that point in my life, because they knew whatever I did, I would really do. I was dangerous. I wasn't a bad kid, but I was dangerous because I was righteous about what I was doing. I thought what I was doing had a purpose to it, though I doubt I could have said what it was then—or at least I'd have been wrong.

"Come on, give me the gun."

"Teddy, I don't know. . . ."

"Just give me the goddamn gun."

John had this car, a brown Plymouth Roadrunner that he had totaled seven or eight times and was always hauling into the body shop. After I got the gun from Nipple, we went outside and climbed into John's car. A bunch of people followed us out, sort of like a send-off; it was clear we were embarking on something. I rolled down the window, and in a moment of drunken bravado I shot the gun into the air. Later on, Nipple told me that as we drove off he remarked to everyone, "Well, they're not coming back." It didn't exactly make him Nostradamus.

For a while we just drove around. It was strange—we wound up on Richmond Terrace, where my father grew up. You think of these things afterward. Did it mean something? Was it a piece of a puzzle? It's hard to think it was just coincidental. Anyway, there was a bar down there; it was closed. I don't know what time it was, but it must have been past three in the morning.

"You want to go in?"

"Yeah, let's go in."

There was a window shaped like a triangle. I put my sleeve over my hand and punched it in, then crawled through the opening, cutting my chest on one of the jagged edges of broken glass. We were terrible criminals. I mean, total amateurs. John was too big to get through the window, so he stayed outside while I poked around in the dark.

"You find the cash register? Is there any money in there?"

"Yeah, they left a box full of fucking money."

"At least get us a bottle of scotch."

I grabbed a bottle of Johnny Walker and crawled back out. John guzzled a quarter of the bottle right there on the curb, then got back behind the wheel of the Roadrunner. We drove around a while more, finally stopping at a Hess gas station.

In those days, they had these cement capsules for the attendants to put the money in, these concrete tubes right on the fuel island, next to the pumps. It was a security thing. They put the money in there, and that way they wouldn't get robbed. But this was a weekend night; they'd been busy, and the capsule was so full of money that it was almost spilling out of the slot at the top. So we were standing there, the attendant had the hose in his hand, pumping our gas, and I was plucking twenty-dollar bills out of the top of this thing. I wasn't even trying to hide what I was doing, and John was acting all silly, cracking up because I was so calm and blatant about it. At some point, the kid who was pumping gas noticed. Today, when I think about it, I feel bad for a kid like that, but at the time I was in a different place. I didn't have those feelings for anybody. Anyway, I just gave this kid a look, you know, a don't-fuck-with-me look, and he decided not to pursue it, at least not directly. Instead, he headed off into the office, where there was a phone.

"C'mon, Teddy, we gotta blow this place. He's calling the cops." John yanked the nozzle out of the gas tank and threw it on the ground while it was still pumping. It snaked around, squirting gas all over the place.

I plucked a couple more bills out of the capsule, then got into the car; John already had it started up. The kid saw us and came running out of the office to stop us. I started getting out of the car to confront him, and he ran back inside. Okay. I shut the car door, and we were about to leave again, and again he came running out. It was slapstick stuff. This time I took the gun and aimed it at him. He stopped dead in his tracks and hit the deck like he was already shot. He was scared out of his mind. I raised the gun and shot it into the air. Except he didn't know; he was facedown and whimpering.

Half an hour later, John had nearly finished off the bottle of Johnny Walker. We were cruising along Victory Boulevard when he picked up a cop car in the rearview mirror. They were a block behind us. He immediately got all panicky.

"We're fucked, man. We're fucked, Teddy."

"Just keep driving."

"Maybe we should make a run for it."

"Just keep driving. They don't have their light on."

"Yeah, you're right."

We went a ways like that, maybe a couple of miles, far enough to begin to think maybe it was just a coincidence, because they weren't doing anything. Then we came over this ridge at the far end of Victory Boulevard, and any idea we had that we were in the clear exploded in a blaze of what felt like a hundred headlights pointing right at us.

Lined up in a phalanx on the street, maybe three hundred yards ahead, was a roadblock of ten police cars.

"Holy shit!" John said in this high, terrified voice. "Oh fuck!"

"Shut up."

The cops had their doors winged open, and they were crouched down with guns and rifles drawn. Over the PA they were shouting, "Stop the vehicle!"

John slammed on the brakes. We skidded to a stop, the car fishtailing. By now there were cop cars behind us, too, the one that had been following us and some others.

"Don't move! Put your hands where we can see them!"

It was strange. I felt very calm. My thoughts were clear. I should have been like John, scared and shaky, but I wasn't. I had the gun in my waistband, and I knew what was going to happen. I started to think of where to put the gun, where to hide it. These were seemingly rational thoughts, though in reality, given the danger, they were not. At first I thought I'd put the gun in the visor. I started to raise it, but I could actually hear the rustle of the cops' guns and their uniforms; I could hear their nerves like strings being wound on a guitar. Over the PA, one of them shouted, "Don't fucking move! We will shoot if you move!" I must not have listened at first, because they kept screaming, "Do not move! We will shoot!" John was saying, "Teddy, listen to them, for Chrissakes! Listen to them!" Something penetrated, because I stopped moving my hands up. Instead, I bent forward and threw the gun under the seat, and again heard that rustle of movement and nervousness. It's amazing that they didn't shoot. I always tell the fighters I train that motion relieves tension. If you don't move, you go to this place where your muscles control you, instead of the other way around. And that's what I was hearing. All this motion. The sound of these cops trying not to go to that place.

In the next moment, they rushed the car. Hands reached in and pulled us out, throwing us to the ground. One of them cracked me on the head with his fist. Another one said, "Where is it?"

I didn't answer, so they started taking the car apart, yelling, "Where the fuck is the gun?" They took the seats out and put them on the sidewalk. They still couldn't find it. I was just lying there, hoping against hope they wouldn't find it but knowing they would.

It must have been a good five minutes before I heard one of them shout, "I've got it!" It turned out the trigger of the gun had hooked on a spring under the car seat. It was hanging from the bottom of the seat. The miracle was that when the spring caught the trigger, the gun didn't go off. If that had happened, well, that probably would have been the end of this story.

As if getting arrested for a second felony in two days wasn't bad enough, I was also being charged with attempted murder because of that shot I'd fired into the air at the Hess station. It was crazy. I hadn't been shooting at that kid. But that was the charge.

At the station house, the cops took me into a back room and began working on me. "A kid like you from a good family, going off to prison, it's a real shame."

As far as they were concerned, there was only one hope for me. If I could supply them with some info on a gun ring they were investigating, maybe the judge would go easy on me. In the space of a couple of days they'd twice nailed me with guns, so they thought I must know something. In fact, I did. I knew the names of some of the wiseguys who were involved in the ring, just from hanging around the kinds of people I was hanging around with. I said, "Are the guns you're interested in thirty-eights?" And when I said that, all the detectives perked up and drew their chairs closer.

"What did I tell you?" one of them said to the rest.

"No, the reason I'm asking," I said, "is because I don't know anyone selling thirty-eights."

It was a stupid show of smart-ass bravado, and they didn't appreciate it. One of them hit me so hard he knocked me off my chair. "You think you're funny? You're a tough guy?"

Later on, they shoved a piece of paper in front of me. It was a signed statement they'd gotten from John. And another one from Billy, from two days earlier. "Your pals put everything on you. They said it was all your idea, that you got the guns and decided what to rob. Nice friends you got." At first I refused to look at the statements, but they were smart, they kept moving away, turning their backs, and I would take a peek, and see the signatures. They kept working on me, trying to use it. They let me know they were releasing John, that he'd made bail. (His bail was much lower than mine because he didn't have the prior arrest like I did.) "He's going home, and you're going to Rikers, where you're gonna get fucked up the ass by niggers. That doesn't piss you off? You want to just let him get out this way? This guy who was supposed to be your friend?"

I knew they were trying to manipulate me, but at the same time what they were telling me was true. It made me realize how weak people are, and how you can't assume that someone is your friend. Everyone has to be tested. That didn't mean I was going to give up any information to them. From my perspective, that wasn't an option. It didn't mean that I was stronger than John or Billy. It was just that if you didn't think there was a choice, then there wasn't any temptation.

In a way, I had learned about accountability from my father. The most vivid lesson had come after a fight I'd gotten into where my head was split open with a tire iron. I'd gone to his office, and there were twenty people waiting outside. When the nurse saw me, she took me right in to see him. My father looked at me and said, "He can wait with everyone else." It was three hours before I got in to see him; I bled all over the waiting room floor. The nurse offered to administer novocaine, but my father said, "No, he doesn't want that. If he's going to live like this, he should know the way this kind of life feels." He put fifteen stitches in my head without using painkillers.

What I'm trying to say is that in my way of looking at the world, which came in large part from him, it was better to do without the thing that eased your pain, without the novocaine, or signing a statement, or whatever it was. If you were going to do something, you went in understanding the ground rules. I didn't understand something in which there was a buckling rule.

The next morning, John got released and I got sent to Rikers. They set my bail at forty thousand dollars. The news of the arrest was all over the front page of the Staten Island paper. I guess it goes without saying that it was a major embarrassment for my father. I'd finally gotten his attention, but not in a good way. He was furious and refused to pay my bail. My mother wasn't happy either. All the same, she didn't want her son in jail. So she did what a mother does. She said to my father, "Either you put up the house as collateral for his bail or I'm leaving you."

But it was several weeks before he gave in. In the meantime, I got sent off to Rikers Island.

GREEN ACRES, HERE I COME

THE OLD BLUE DEPARTMENT OF CORRECTIONS BUS rumbled through the streets of Queens, bumping over potholes. I was handcuffed to a kid who had an Afro the size of a beach ball. Every time we stopped for a red light, the other prisoners on the bus would yell out the windows at girls walking by. "Yo, mama! You looking fine, baby. You wanna gimme some of that?" It was amazing to me that some of the girls actually responded. This wasn't a city bus or a sightseeing bus. It was a prison vehicle full of rough-looking thugs and criminals on their way to jail.

At one point we passed in front of a Chinese restaurant on Eighteenth Avenue. A delivery boy was locking his bicycle to a parking meter.

"Fuck, look at this mothafucka," the kid next to me said. "That's the mothafucka who got me locked up." Suddenly he was yelling out the window, the veins in his neck popping. "Yo, Wuk Du, you mothafucka! I'm gonna come back and fuck you up! I'm gonna kill you and bury your ass in a bowl of rice!"

Everyone on the bus cracked up. I thought, *These are the people I'm going to have to live with now.*

The thing about being on that bus was that you knew it was just a prelude to something worse—that it wasn't going to be just a bus full of these guys once you got to Rikers; it was going to be a whole world of them.

I began daydreaming that I was a kid again, going out on house calls with my father. I remembered the way, when it was real cold out sometimes, he'd leave me out in the car waiting for him, and say, "If it begins to get too cold in here, you can start the engine up," even though I knew he didn't really mean it. He was eccentric about some things—like he'd shut the engine off and coast down hills just to save gas—so I was reluctant to take advantage of his offer. I'd be freezing my ass off and afraid to turn the key, thinking, *Is it cold enough? Am I cold enough?*

I guess I thought about a lot of things on that bus ride to Rikers. I knew my father was a proud man. He wasn't going to show that he was bothered by what I was going through. In his eyes, I had done what I had done and should be accountable. On some level, even though I was only eighteen years old, I understood that. Still, it was nearly impossible not to wish that I had a family that loved me the way I'd seen families love each other in the movies. I had to keep reminding myself that I didn't have that. Not because I was on this bus going to Rikers, but because I didn't have it, period.

The kid in front of me started singing that Lou Rawls song that was on the radio at the time, "I'll See You When I Get There." It had always been a happy, upbeat song. Suddenly it was something else entirely.

> *I said I might have to run all the way*
> *Because the bus might be slow today*
> *I've been thinking about you all day long*
> *And I just can't wait to get home*

The trip to Rikers seemed to take hours, and yet once we were on the bridge to the island, water on each side of us, it was ending much too quickly. On the other side of the bridge, we went through the gates, and drove past a number of buildings to the youth facility (known as the Youth Educational Facility), where we began the first step of a long processing routine in which we were shuttled from one station to another like cattle. Finally, I got stripped down and had my ass cheeks spread and searched, then was handed a set of plain blue clothes and was taken to my cell. That's when the cold reality of where I was hit full force, walking past all those other cells, hearing the shit they were yelling at me. I was scared. Nothing makes you feel more alone than prison. At the same time, I realized that as much as I didn't want to be there, I had to be sure I recognized that I *was* there. That it was real. To think or act otherwise was dangerous.

It's funny what the mind can do, though. I mean, once they put me in this five-by-eight-foot cell, with a barred window the size of a postage stamp, I realized that if I stretched up and craned my neck, I could see and hear the planes taking off and landing at LaGuardia Airport. It's almost cruel that they put a prison right next to an airport that way. Watching those planes, I began to imagine that I was on one of them. I actually made a deal with whoever, with God, I guess, that if I could be on one of those planes that I would accept that the plane was going to crash. I would take the chance. At first I thought I was the only one having thoughts like that. I thought it was a form of weakness. But then I thought, *If I'm having these thoughts, other people must be, too.* I couldn't be the only one. It was a revelation. In the mess hall, in the yard, these guys would try not to let on that they had been having these thoughts, the same way that fighters try not to let on that they're having thoughts that scare them. Of course, everyone has them. When I came to realize that, it helped me put my fears into perspective. It's one of the things that I've used ever since, and that's helped me to become a good trainer.

Rikers Island had a reputation for being a rough place, and it was. Any place where kids spit razor blades out of their mouths to cut you is not a real great place. These other prisons, like Attica and Sing Sing, were tough, but the youth facility at Rikers was more dangerous because it was all young kids who were angry and lost, and not—even in criminal ways—directed yet. They were dangerous the way I was dangerous. They didn't know why they were so full of anger, so full of hatred. They were still groping, trying to eliminate certain fractured feelings in themselves in whatever way they could; whereas the older guys in those other places had a better sense of themselves, were more practical, knew how to do their time. Older guys didn't need to stab you to show they weren't afraid. A kid in Rikers might stab you just to avoid facing something else he might be feeling.

Early on, I made it clear that I would stand up for myself. This guy who was six feet and a mean-looking motherfucker came up to me in the rec area and let me know he wanted my sneakers. I can't remember exactly how he phrased it, but I knew what he was asking and what it meant. I knew what it would lead to. I didn't even say no. I just went after him. I knew that if I didn't, it wouldn't stop there. I knew that after the sneakers it was going to be my dignity he would try to take, my soul. Some people might feel that it would be easier to avoid the confrontation, to give up the sneakers. In the ring, I see fighters quit or give up all the time because it feels at that moment like it's the easiest option. I always tell them the easiest thing is actually to make a stand. The act of fighting, of facing what you have to face, in reality lasts only a few minutes. Otherwise, you have to deal with and live with the consequences forever. And that's much harder. So I went after this guy, and it really didn't matter who got the best of who—though I think I got in more shots than he did before the guards broke it up. The point was, I was standing up for myself. That was what was important. After that I was pretty much left alone.

Even though I kept to myself at Rikers, there was one guy there I made a connection with, a chaplain there, Brother Tim McDonald, who was a Franciscan friar they called the Brother of the Rock. He knew my uncle slightly, and he kept an eye on me from the day I got there. I didn't know, but he was watching through a one-way mirror when they brought me in, and he came and saw me the next day.

Now I know that the Catholic religion has taken a big hit in the past few years, but this guy was the real deal, what a guy like that is supposed to be. He was a big, burly Irishman, and when he shook hands with you, he tried to break your hand. That was the way he showed you that he was in charge. I knew right away he was telling me very clearly, "This is my place." But he was solid, and there weren't many things in there that were solid. Or outside of there, either, for that matter.

He already had all my records. He said, "You belong in here, Teddy. You're a dangerous person."

He wasn't saying, "You poor thing. I can see you're really a sensitive person deep down." Not that I wouldn't have wanted to hear a little bullshit. I'm no different from anyone else that way. But I appreciated that I wasn't hearing it, that maybe somewhere down the line I could hear some other stuff from him that connected to something real, and that I would be able to trust that what he was saying had meaning. It was another lesson that I would incorporate into my career as a trainer. I would tell fighters under pressure the truth, even though they didn't want to hear it, because I knew they needed it and would know the difference. The ones who were going to make it would actually want to hear it, would know that they could trust it—both the criticism and the praise.

That first Sunday, I went to chapel, and afterward Brother Tim stopped me and said, "Why'd you come to church?"

"I wanted to go to mass," I said.

"No, you didn't. You came because you wanted to show me you were a good guy and get my approval."

He was right. He had a way of puncturing your pretenses that made you trust him. He was teaching me things about human nature.

"So how are you doing?" he asked. "Are you all right? You need to make a phone call?"

Everything in prison is a kind of currency. He was using the fact that he had a phone in his office that I could use to further build trust and let me know that he cared. With other guys, he might use the currency of the phone for something else. If there was someone he saw who shouldn't have been in Rikers or who couldn't defend himself, Brother Tim would go to the guy who ran the quad, the inmate with the most juice, and he'd make a deal with him. He was smart. He'd say, "Look, I don't want this kid bothered," because he knew the kid would be raped otherwise. He'd say, "I'm going to let you make five calls a week," and the guy would make sure that nobody bothered the kid.

Of course, it didn't always work. He said to me on more than one occasion, "Teddy, some people travel through here and it changes their lives. Some, it ruins their lives." There was one kid who was in for shoplifting. A frail, skinny kid, who'd slipped a couple of albums under his sweater and been caught walking out of a record store. Before Brother Tim could do anything to prevent it, the kid got raped. It was terrible. The kid's bail was only fifty dollars, and when Brother Tim discovered that, it just killed him. I mean, this kid was ruined, he was never going to be the same, and for what? Fifty bucks? Brother Tim did get the kid out after that, he paid the bail—which is something he did routinely, despite the fact that he was making almost no money—but not too long after the kid got back home, he was found in the vestibule of his building, dead of a drug overdose. "Your mistakes sometimes you never get over," Brother Tim said. "I see that here."

I got out of Rikers, but I stayed in touch with Brother Tim. He lived with the Franciscan friars on Waverly Place in Greenwich Village. I'd go visit him, and take him out to eat at these Italian restaurants on Carmine or Bleecker Street. He looked like a dockworker, a guy out of *Hard Times*. He'd wear this blue wool cap, and his clothes were what was made in prison or what someone gave him. He was an orphan himself, this guy who cared about all these godforsaken unfortunates. I remember at one of these restaurants we went to, he pocketed the silverware, and then went, "Oops, guess I lost control of myself, Teddy," and put the silverware back on the table. "Gotta get out of my old habits." It was funny, but it was also like he was making a show of having been there himself; he was saying, It's easy to slip back. You have to be disciplined.

LIKE A LOT OF PEOPLE, BROTHER TIM WAS WORRIED, WHEN my father finally paid my bail and I got out, that I would slip back. It was a genuine concern. I was back home, waiting for my trial to start, and I was facing a lot of years—ten years with the two felonies—and yet even with all that going on, it didn't seem impossible that I would do something else to compound things, that I still didn't get it.

Another guy who was concerned was my childhood friend Kevin Rooney, who had won the 147-pound Golden Gloves in New York four months earlier. Like me, Kevin came from a dysfunctional family, and he'd had several run-ins with the law. In those days the cops tried to get problem kids involved in boxing in the Police Athletic League, which is where Kevin and I first got close. We were boxing in an old laundry room in a rough project called Park Hill under the tutelage of this guy Ray Rivera. It was a no-frills setup. We'd pick our rubber mouthpieces out of a glass jar by the door and then put 'em back in the same jar when we were finished. Very sanitary. But it was a good program in lots of ways. It helped kids. I mean, when you think about the fact that Kevin and I are still involved in boxing, that says a lot.

Anyway, Kevin went on to fight in the New York Golden Gloves, and during the tournament, the Hamill brothers, Pete, Brian, and Dennis, who knew Kevin's brother, introduced him to Cus D'Amato, a well-known fight manager and trainer. Cus thought Kevin could turn pro eventually, and Jim Jacobs, who was Cus's friend and business partner, offered to pay Kevin's expenses so Kevin could live with Cus in Catskill, New York, and train at his gym. It was an offer that Kevin jumped at. Now, four months later, right after I got out of Rikers, Kevin called me up. He knew there was a good chance I'd get into trouble again hanging around Staten Island, and he was trying to help me out.

"Come up here, Teddy. I'll ask Cus, but I'm sure it'll be okay with him. You can live here, train for the Gloves, and stay out of trouble while you're waiting for trial."

I could see it was a good idea. I knew myself well enough at that point to see that he was right. I brought it up with my father, and my father, to his credit, agreed to foot the bill. Fifty bucks a week for my room and board.

Sunday morning. October 1975. I'm in a train pulling into the town of Hudson, New York. Rikers seems a thousand miles away, though in reality I only got out a week ago.

The train slows and stops with a hiss. I grab my bag and get off. Kevin Rooney is standing by an old white Dodge station wagon.

"Cus is back at the house," Kevin says. We drive across the bridge through Catskill, New York, a small, blue-collar town of nineteen thousand that has seen more prosperous days. "You'll see what I'm talking about, Teddy. Every day I learn something new from him."

Kevin explains that Cus shares the house with Camille Ewald, a Ukrainian woman, who has been his companion for many years. We pull up a long driveway outside a sprawling white Victorian mansion. Cus comes out on the porch. He's heavyset, balding, wearing a red-and-white flannel shirt. He's got a wide, flat face, piercing blue eyes, and eyebrows that arch up like triangles.

"You must be Teddy," he says. "I been hearing good things about you from Rooney."

WHEN I FIRST GOT TO CATSKILL, THE ONLY PEOPLE STAY-ing at the house were Cus, Camille, Kevin, and a kid named Jay Bright. All I knew about Cus at that point was that he had managed former heavy-weight champ Floyd Patterson and former light heavyweight champ Jose Torres in the '50s and '60s, and that Kevin considered him to be a wise and great man. Approaching seventy, Cus had been out of the mainstream of the boxing world for years. As much as he could bring his knowledge and wisdom to bear on a couple of young guys like me and Kevin, it be-came clear to me that we brought something to him, too: purpose.

You have to understand, Cus, when I met him, was a little bit like one of those gunfighters who's hung up his guns and retreated from the fray to live in peace and quiet. Cus's reasons for leaving New York and the big time were complicated, dating back to when he had managed Patterson and Torres and had taken on what was then the ruling body in the box-ing world, the International Boxing Club, a corrupt, Mob-influenced or-ganization that controlled the matchmaking process. Once Cus had control of the heavyweight division, with Patterson as champ, he took on the IBC by refusing to match his fighters with any IBC-controlled oppo-nent; he also took his fight against them to court. Some saw Cus as a hero and crusader bent on cleaning up the sport; others, a bit more cyn-ically, saw him as manipulative and power hungry, not much better than the scoundrels he was fighting. Whatever the actual truth, Cus was mostly successful in his campaign: the IBC was ultimately deposed.

Although Cus prevailed, and with Patterson ruled the heavyweight di-vision for years, he also became something of a paranoid, always looking over his shoulder for his enemies. Though no one ever accused him of being greedy—in fact, he was almost unique in the boxing world in his disregard for money—Cus's involvement in behind-the-scenes maneu-vering with an eye toward improving his own fighters' lot landed him in hot water with the New York State Athletic Commission, which not only accused him of trying to control the heavyweight title, but also made pointed references to his association with Charlie Antonucci, a.k.a. Charlie Black, a known associate of the mobster Tony Salerno. When

Cus failed to appear before the commission, claiming his absence a matter of principle, his manager's license was suspended and, ultimately, revoked. Not long after, the IRS went after him over back taxes, and Cus was eventually forced to declare bankruptcy.

By the time Rooney and I showed up on the scene, Cus had been in Catskill for several years, basically in semiretirement. He'd cut a deal with local officials to rent the gym above the police station for a dollar a year in return for training some of the underprivileged, troubled kids in the area. But the truth is, training fighters at that point in his life was more like a hobby for him than a serious pursuit. Apart from the work he was doing with Rooney and a couple of kids, Kenny Zimmer and Jeff White, and an old man, Fred Sheber, who came from across the river with two or three kids every once in a while, the gym was barely active. If you believe in things like fate, or that people come together for a reason, my going up there turned out to be something like that.

Nobody—not even his detractors—would dispute that Cus was close to a genius as a trainer. He was an innovator, and came up with, among other things, the peek-a-boo style that Floyd Patterson made famous (in which the fighter holds both fists high and tucked in alongside each cheek, with the elbows and arms tight to the ribs). He also developed a punch-by-the-numbers system, each punch corresponding to a part of the opponent's body (the numbers were written in the appropriate places on a padded apparatus called a Willie that was mounted to the wall). Cus would drill us by playing tapes he'd recorded in which he yelled out the numbers in the combinations of punches he wanted us to throw.

What really separated Cus from most other trainers, though, was his focus on the mental aspect of boxing. Every night, from the moment I arrived in Catskill, we would sit around the dinner table and Cus would expound on his life philosophy as it applied to boxing, and his boxing philosophy as it applied to life. He loved to talk, but he also asked lots of questions. As he put it, "To find out what I need to do with a guy, I have to find out about his background, learn what makes him tick, keep peeling away layers until I get to the core, so that he can realize, as well as I, what is there." A lot of the ideas he talked about were things that I had already been thinking about, but maybe hadn't put into words yet.

"Fear is the greatest obstacle to learning in any area, but particularly boxing," he said one night, while we sat at the table, eating a fresh-baked apple pie Camille had made. "The thing a kid in the street fears most is to be called yellow or a coward. Sometimes a kid will do the most wild or crazy things just to show he's not scared. . . ."

I thought of the kids I encountered in Rikers, who were capable of almost anything.

"But that's all motivated by survival. If you can harness fear it can be your ally. The example I always use is of a deer crossing an open field, and suddenly his instinct tells him danger is near, and nature begins the survival process, which involves the body releasing adrenaline into the bloodstream, which in turn enables the deer to perform extraordinary feats of agility and strength so that he can get out of range of danger. That's an example of how useful fear can be to a fighter if he learns to make it his friend."

The routine in Catskill, the discipline, was good for me. We would train and do our roadwork in the morning, spend the afternoon attending to chores, mowing the lawn, cleaning, painting, feeding the dogs and birds, and then we'd go back to the gym at night and work with the bags and in the ring. At the gym, Cus would sit in this gray metal folding chair, watching us and talking to us.

"Remember, it's always good to throw the punch where you can hit him, but he can't hit you. That's the science." He didn't actually get in the ring with us very often, but he'd demonstrate what he was talking about, moving his hands to indicate. I picked up on things quickly.

There's no question that Cus was doing things for me that I'd wanted my father to do: giving me guidance, telling me the things I needed to hear, paying attention to me—things I'd been starving for. He made me feel good about myself, focusing on my strengths, not my failings. "You're loyal, Teddy. You don't rat on your friends. I like that."

Rooney and I were sparring a fair amount in the gym, and Cus was impressed by my punching power and natural ability in the ring. "You got professional potential," he told me. "You punch with the right hand as hard as any fighter I've ever had, and you got a good chin." I knew he was exaggerating, but it still felt good to hear stuff like that.

Jim Jacobs, who was Cus's best friend and a fight film historian, was going to manage me when I turned professional. Jacobs was rich, plus he had a manager's license, which Cus didn't, so that was how they worked it out: Cus the guru, Jacobs and his partner Bill Cayton the money men.

When he thought I was ready, Cus entered me in the Adirondacks Golden Gloves. I knocked out my first opponent in the opening round, and I kept knocking guys out all the way to the title. As good as things were going for me in Catskill, there was a black cloud hanging over me: My sentencing date for the robbery and gun charges was quickly approaching, and I was more than a little worried about how it would turn out.

I wasn't the only one. The specter of me doing real jail time had my mother and father fighting about me again. The lawyer my father hired, Dan Leddy, thought it could make a big difference if my father testified on my behalf. But my father refused. "He says he's not going into that courthouse to defend a son who broke the law," my mother told me. "He's so goddamn stubborn. He won't listen to me. Why don't you talk to him, Teddy? Tell him you need him."

"I'm not gonna to do that."

"But it could make a difference."

"I don't care."

"You're just as stubborn as he is."

I went back to Staten Island, trying to mentally prepare myself for the worst. On the day of the sentencing, I sat at the defendant's table with Dan Leddy. My mother was seated right behind us in the front row. My father, true to his word, didn't show up. Near the end of the proceeding, there was a commotion in the back of the courtroom. I looked around, and there was Cus, making his way in. Dan Leddy announced to Judge Rayden, a dour-looking fellow in his sixties, that we had one more person who wanted to speak on my behalf: "The defense calls Mr. Constantine D'Amato."

I'll never know how much Cus's testimony swayed the judge, but it definitely made a difference in the judge's final dispensation. Cus had charisma and he knew how to command a room. When Leddy asked him to describe the nature of his relationship with me, Cus turned to the judge, and there was a catch in his throat. He said, "Your Honor, I realize you might not know much about me, but I've spent my whole life developing young men. As a boxing manager I trained two world champions, heavyweight champion Floyd Patterson and light heavyweight champion Jose Torres.

"I've also helped a lot of other young boys straighten out their lives and build character. I know things about Teddy Atlas this court doesn't know. Things you won't find on his arrest record. This boy has character. He has loyalty. He'll hurt himself before he'll let down a friend. These qualities are rare, and they shouldn't be lost. He's made mistakes. We've all made mistakes. But I've come to know this boy, and if we lose him, we'll be losing someone who could help a lot of people."

At this point, Cus began to cry. Without wiping away the tears, he said, "Please don't take this young boy's future away. He could be someone special. Let's not lose him. Please. . . ."

Even the court officers were choked up. Despite a plea bargain that my lawyer had set up, the judge still had some discretion in the terms. He could have made things tough on me; instead, he let me off with probation on the condition that I continue living in Catskill with Cus.

Two months later, with my legal problems behind me, I fought a guy I had knocked out in the Gloves in a club fight, a tough kid named Danny Chapman. I dropped him in the first round, but he was real gutsy and got back up. I started to go after him again and felt a sudden grab in my upper back. Sharp and very painful. Though I hadn't mentioned it to anyone, my back had been bothering me more and more over the months, to the point where I couldn't go through sustained training without it tightening up or seizing up on me. So now I was in this fight with this tough guy, and I couldn't bend or dip. I was getting hit with punches that I normally would have slipped. Instead, I was just standing there, going toe-to-toe with him, hitting him but getting hit because I couldn't move.

Somehow, I won a close decision, but it was much tougher than it should have been. Of course Cus noticed. He saw that I was wincing and grimacing after every punch I threw.

"What's the matter?" he asked me afterward.

"Nothing."

"You gonna tell me or not? I can see you're in pain."

"My back tightened up."

"Where?"

"Up here. Right below my shoulders."

"Has this ever happened before?"

"Yeah, I guess so. I don't know."

Cus wanted to take me in for tests. I resisted. I knew something was wrong, I just didn't want to hear some doctor confirm it. In the end, he took me to see this guy in Manhattan who Jim Jacobs recommended. The X-rays revealed that I had scoliosis, as well as gaps in the vertebrae and a herniated disc.

The doctor was of the opinion that boxing could make my condition worse. Cus and I wound up having an argument over it on the drive back upstate.

"You heard what he said, Teddy. It's a tough break, but what are you gonna do?"

"I can take the pain. He didn't say I had to stop."

"He said you could make it worse. I won't allow it."

I sulked, and Cus let me drive in silence for a few miles.

"It's not the end of the world," he said at last. "You can still be involved in boxing."

"What does that mean?"

"I think you could be a good trainer. I've seen the way you talk to Rooney and some of the other kids. You're a born teacher."

"I'm a fighter, not a teacher."

"You can become the same type of success through your fighters. Because if you take a boy and teach him to fight from beginning to end, part of you is in him, too. So that when he fights, part of you is in that ring."

From that day on, Cus began working on me every chance he got, telling me he thought I'd make a good trainer. He really knew how to lay it on. He told me that teachers were born, not made; that I had been born with the gift, and it would be a shame if I didn't make use of that gift. Cus was very smart about people, he had very good instincts about them, and I think he really saw something in me that made him think I'd be a good trainer. At the same time, he had an ulterior motive: if I became a trainer it would serve his own purposes. He was getting older and he needed somebody to help him, an ally. Either way, I didn't want to hear it. I was still young. I wanted to fight, I didn't want to teach. The dream of being a professional fighter was the thing that was pulling me forward, keeping me directed. If I couldn't continue, then to hell with boxing and to hell with Catskill. At least that was the way I felt at the time.

THERE AND BACK AGAIN

WHEN I TOLD CUS THAT I WAS GOING BACK HOME, HE said, "You can't go. You gotta stay here. I'm responsible for you. That was the deal."

The funny thing is that despite the fact that the terms of my parole stipulated that I stay in Catskill under Cus's supervision, my parole officer, Steve Zawada, had taken a liking to me (he'd even driven up to Catskill one time to watch me box), so he didn't bust my balls or try to stop me when I decided to leave. He understood that if I couldn't fight, I didn't want to be there.

Back home, things were pretty much the same as they'd always been. My father was wrapped up in his life and his patients, my mother was still drinking, and nobody's communication skills had improved much in the time I'd been away. My father certainly wasn't happy about my situation. I was nineteen years old and a high school dropout. It was disappointing and embarrassing for him. He tried to help me out by getting me a job as a janitor at Marine Hospital, in the Stapleton section of town. I worked there for a while, but pretty soon I was back to my old ways, hanging out with the guys down in the neighborhood, doing burglaries and getting into fights.

Cus and I maintained phone contact. We'd talk every week, and he'd try to tempt me into coming back. He was crafty. He was a seed planter. Not too long after I left, he called me up and said, "I need a favor."

"What is it?"

"Rooney's fighting in the Ohio State Fair. Somebody has to go with him. I can't go, but it's an important thing for him and he needs somebody he can trust and count on. I need somebody I can trust and count on."

The Ohio State Fair was one of the toughest and most prestigious boxing tournaments in the country, on a par with the National Golden Gloves and the National AAU. Any amateur who wanted to be taken seriously had to compete there. If you wanted to fight in the Olympics, you needed to fight in the Ohio State Fair.

Cus knew how I felt about loyalty. He was basically telling me, Rooney needs you, and I need you.

I understood that he probably could have gone himself or sent someone else. But what was implied in the way he asked me was that I owed him something and I owed Rooney something, and it was true, I did. But Cus was also saying that Rooney would have a better chance to win if I was there, and even though I didn't necessarily believe that, I wanted to believe it, which Cus understood.

"Rooney's trying to make the Olympic team. You could be the difference, Teddy."

A couple of days later, I took a train to Catskill, and then Rooney and I drove the five hundred miles to Ohio, a twelve-hour ride. The cheapest accommodations were at the university, so that's where we stayed, sharing the top and bottom of a bunk bed in one of the dorm rooms.

As Rooney's trainer, I had to register him, get his medical approval in order, find out when he was fighting, and make sure he got there on time. It might not sound like much, but it was important, because if you were late you would be disqualified. When I called Cus to tell him what was going on and how we were doing, he said, "See, I told you you'd be good at this."

The fights took place outdoors on the fairgrounds. There were three fights going on at any one time in three different rings. They used a whistle in one, a bell in another, and a clang in the other, so the fighters would know when a round was over. There were hundreds of fighters milling around, all waiting for their bouts. Across the fairgrounds were the rides and food stalls, the smell of grilled hamburgers and hot dogs hanging in the air. The first day, Rooney's fight didn't start until one in the morning. I'd found out from my father that it took five hours to digest food ("Except pork," he said. "Don't eat pork, it takes longer for the body to break it down"), so I timed Rooney's meal accordingly. While we were waiting for our fight, I eavesdropped on conversations between the other trainers and fighters. There was a lot you could pick up just by listening.

About an hour before Rooney's fight, the clouds opened up and it poured. They didn't have tents over the rings, but they couldn't cancel the bouts because the schedule wouldn't allow it. The ring was slippery. The grounds had turned to mud, and the fighters' shoes were slick with mud by the time they climbed into the ring. I found plastic bags and taped them on Rooney's feet. Just before he stepped in the ring for his fight, I cut the bags off. He was the only fighter with clean, dry shoes. I told him to take small steps, bend his knees, and not move around too much. He kept his footing, won the fight, and afterward I noticed that everybody else started using plastic bags.

Following each fight, I looked at the draw, found out who Rooney had next, then dug up all I could about the guy. In the quarterfinals we fought a New York boxer I knew very well, Davey Moore, a future world champ. He had a very big rep. I called up Cus to discuss strategy. Moore liked to shoeshine—a showboat move where you drop your hands and throw a rapid flurry of punches to the midsection. Cus said, "That's good. You know what his main thing is." I had also noticed that Moore didn't bend his knees when he did it. It left him open. So I'd instructed Rooney to fire right back to his head when he tried to shoeshine. At the very least it might take it away from him.

"Call me when it's over," Cus said. "I'll be waiting by the phone."

I phoned Cus right after Rooney won the fight. He started gushing. "The Young Master," he said, "you're the Young Master." You had to hand it to Cus. He knew exactly what to say.

In the finals we fought Bernard "Bad" Mayes from the Kronk gym. Mayes was very fast, very talented. Pure speed. Lightning hands. Cus asked me, "What are you gonna do?" I said, "We gotta go to the body, take some of that speed away, some of that eagerness. Also, time him. Timing can beat speed!" Rooney would need to be very disciplined to win.

At the end of our conversation, Cus said, "Well, he's in good hands."

The fight started well for us. Rooney won the first round, but when he came back to the corner, I saw the cut he'd gotten on his eyelid was bad. Rooney had thin skin. Irish skin. It was his curse. I managed to stop the bleeding, but the ref came over—in the amateurs it's safety first—and he took a look at Rooney and waved his hands. Fight over. Boom, just like that. I didn't make a big deal. I knew that was the rule. You can do things right and it can still be taken out of your hands. The other officials came over and said great job. But it wasn't much consolation.

Back in the locker room, I cleaned Rooney's cut, took some adhesive tape and made four butterfly bandages, and taped him up. The butterflies looked good, professional. I was proud of myself for that. I'd learned from watching my father. When I took Rooney to the hospital to get him stitched, the emergency room intern even complimented me on what I'd done.

Back in Catskill, Cus saw only the positives. "You did a great job, Teddy. He wouldn't have gone that far without you."

Camille said, "See, Cus was right."

"Why? I didn't do anything special."

"No, Cus was right."

I knew what they were trying to do. I guess I didn't trust them completely, that they were thinking only of what was good for me. Or maybe I just wasn't ready yet to make a commitment to being a trainer. In my mind I was still a fighter. Whatever the case, I went back to Staten Island a few days later.

For a year I'd lived a clean, disciplined life with Cus in Catskill. Now I was sliding backward, finding out how easy it was to do that. In a way I was even more dangerous than I'd been before the year in Catskill because of the fighting skills I'd developed and honed there. I was like a walking stick of dynamite. Someone looked at me wrong, or said the wrong thing, wham, I'd go off on them.

I was running with most of the same guys from down the hill that had been around before. Despite what had happened with Billy Sullivan when we'd gotten arrested, and the fact that he had signed that statement for the cops, I wound up letting him talk his way back into my good graces. Another guy, maybe I wouldn't have, but Billy had that charm; he got me to forgive him.

*   *   *

ONE NIGHT, IN THE SUMMER OF 1977, THE TWO OF US WERE driving around Stapleton in my old red Chevy, drinking Heinekens. Suddenly, this Cadillac with tinted windows cut us off at a light. Billy hit the brakes, and his beer tipped over, sloshing on his pant leg.

"Son of a bitch!"

He gunned the Chevy hard, pulling even with the Caddy.

"Hey, jerkoff!"

He swerved in front of them and hit the brakes. They screeched and slammed to a halt. The driver of the Caddy opened his door and got out. He was a tall black kid, with a cigarette in his mouth. He took the cigarette and flicked it toward us. I was out the door of the Chevy like a shot. Before I got more than a few steps, the other doors of the Caddy swung open and four more guys appeared. Big guys.

I kept right on going, no hesitation, and dropped one of them with a straight right hand, and hit another one with a left hook. I was doing pretty good, but then the third guy hit me from the side with a blackjack. It stunned me. Before he could hit me again, I grabbed his hair and got him in a choke hold. Meanwhile, Billy was on the roof of the Chevy, brandishing a broken Heineken bottle to keep them away from him.

I threw the guy with the blackjack to the ground, and then saw the driver coming at me, saw the flash of a knife in his hand. It was this kind of knife called an 007, a flick blade. I remember thinking, *That's a double-oh-seven.* I knew that he'd have to come with a downward motion so I tried to close the distance, get inside before he could extend his arm. But I was too late. He stepped back and spun, like a matador, slashing the side of my face. The blade was so sharp, I barely felt it. I put my hand up and my fingers just went into my cheek; there was this thick, meaty flap of skin that moved, a warm, wet, syrupy goo oozing from the gash. I staggered and fell to the ground.

The next thing I knew, Billy was dragging me across the street. We were on Broad Street, right by the projects. There was this little bodega across the way. Billy took me in and laid me on the floor. I was losing a lot of blood; it was all over the place, streaming through my fingers and onto the linoleum floor. The old couple who ran the bodega were afraid. You could see it in their eyes. Billy was shouting at them to call an ambulance. The old woman found a towel and held it to my face. Almost instantly, it soaked through with blood. She got more towels. The same thing happened.

The old man was frozen, looking at me, holding the phone. Billy jumped over the counter and grabbed the receiver out of his hand. He called 911. "A cop's been shot," he yelled into the mouthpiece.

Less than five minutes later, half a dozen cop cars and an ambulance were there. I could hear a helicopter's blades beating up above. In the ambulance, on the way to the hospital, one of the cops with me said, "The kid might bleed to death before we get there." When I heard that, I was afraid to close my eyes or let go of consciousness. "My father," I mumbled. "You gotta get my father. He's a famous doctor. . . ."

They took me to Marine Hospital (now called Bailey Seton), the place I'd worked as a janitor. As they were wheeling me in, I kept saying, "Let my father do it." The last thing I remember thinking about before I lost consciousness was his schedule.

It wasn't my father who sewed me up; it was an Asian physician, Dr. Lee. It took four hundred stitches. Two hundred on the outside, two hundred on the inside. My father showed up later that night. I opened my eyes and there he was.

"How is it?" I asked.

"The cut will heal, but you're going to have a scar for the rest of your life." He looked at his hand. There were notes written on his skin. Appointments, prescriptions, phone numbers, things like that.

"I have to go," he said.

I wanted to say something to him, or have him say something to me. But neither of us seemed to know how.

"Good night, Teddy."

Later that night some of my buddies came to visit me in the hospital. Bruce Spicer, Mousey, and some other guys I knew from the corner. They were all worked up. They were gonna get the guys who had done this. I didn't care about that. I was fixated on something else entirely: the gold ring that I always wore around my neck on a chain was gone.

"Bruce, you have to find that ring," I said. "The chain must have broken during the fight."

"Teddy, it'll never be there. It's Broad Street. Forget about it." He and the rest continued talking about finding the guys in the Caddy.

"No, the ring," I said. "You gotta get the ring."

They stopped talking and looked at me. My voice was so full of intensity, all they could do was kind of shrug, like, all right, we'll go look for it.

The reason the ring had such importance to me was that it had belonged to my childhood friend Sean Timpone, who had died the year before. Sean and I had always been close; we had a real comradeship. When we were young kids, he was diagnosed with muscular dystrophy and confined to a wheelchair. I used to go take him out and wheel him around the parks in Staten Island. He loved nature and animals, and he was always reading up on various wildlife, talking about how the animals needed to be protected or they'd become extinct. Out in the woods in these parks, we'd pretend that we were seeing all these extinct animals from the prehistoric era. He loved to fantasize about things like that.

When I had left for Catskill, Sean's condition was deteriorating. Sometime during the year I was up there, I got a call from his father that Sean was in the hospital and very sick. I took the next train back. He was in Doctor's Hospital, one of the two hospitals my father founded. Even though it was past visiting hours, all the nurses knew me, and they let me in. I found Sean in an oxygen tent. He could barely talk. One of the things he had told me, after he realized that he wasn't going to be cured, was that he didn't want to die in a hospital. I put my hand underneath the tent and took his hand and began reading him this poem that Cus always gave to all of his fighters. It was called "Don't Quit," and the last couple of lines went, "You can never tell how close you are / It may be near when it seems afar / So stick to the fight when you're hardest hit / It's when things go wrong that you must not quit!"

I didn't even know if Sean could hear it, but I just kept reading the poem to him. Over and over, I don't know how many times. The next morning, someone touched me and I opened my eyes. It was Sean's father.

"Teddy, the nurses told me you've been here since last night!"

"Yeah, I guess I fell asleep."

He was amazed. He told me how much it meant to him that I was such a loyal friend. "Now you should go back home," he said. "There's nothing more you can do here."

I traveled back to Catskill, and when I got there, Sean's father called and thanked me again, saying whatever I'd said to Sean had helped, because he'd made a small recovery. "Enough so that he could come home."

"That's what he wanted," I said.

"He always hated cages," his father said.

Two days later, Sean died. His parents asked me to be one of the pall-bearers. At the funeral, they had an open casket. Sean's mother slid the ring off his finger while I was standing there—his fingers had gotten so thin in his illness that it just came right off—and she gave it to me.

That's the reason why, even with four hundred stitches in my face, I was concerned about finding that ring. I knew there was only a slim chance that my buddies would find it—I mean, a gold ring lying on the street in that neighborhood?

When they came back a few hours later, they looked grim. Then Bruce Spicer smiled and opened his palm. The ring!

"I'm as surprised as you are, Teddy. I never thought we'd find it. Not there. I mean, there was dried blood all over the street. But there it was, lying on the yellow line."

That wasn't the end of the story with the ring. A couple of months later, I was hanging on the corner with Spicer and Mousey and Ronnie Sabino. I had this big scar now, running from my scalp down to my jaw. It matched the person I was becoming. On this particular day, these guys, who weren't as rough as some of the guys I was running with, de-cided they wanted to go camping. They wanted me to go with them.

"Camping?" I said. "You gotta be kidding."

"Nah, it'll be great."

They pooled some money together, went to the army surplus store, bought sleeping bags, canteens, canned food, the whole thing. My atti-tude was, I'm not going. I'd rather go rob a delicatessen. But they dragged me along. We went to Lake Minnewaska, upstate. As soon as we got out of the car, these guys were into it. They got their hatchets out, started chopping branches, looking at their compasses, everything. "Who do you guys think you are," I said, "Grizzly Adams?"

I might have been making jokes, but what I was really thinking about was Sean, how this was really his world, how he would have loved it. It made me miss him. Meanwhile, these wackos were shooting slingshots and trying to start a fire with two sticks.

We ended up going on this long hike to the top of this mountain. It was beautiful. You have to understand, I was living a bad life, and this was the cleanest, nicest thing I'd done in a while. There was no question that if I hadn't been there, I would have been robbing places with Billy.

On the hike back, a branch hit me in the neck, and a moment later I felt my neck and realized the ring was gone.

"The ring!" I yelled.

"Oh no, not the ring again!"

These guys all knew what it meant. We looked all over the place, retracing our steps, turning over rocks, sifting through leaves. We couldn't find it. "It's gotta be here," I said. It was getting dark by then.

"Teddy," Spicer said. "We'll come back. We'll bring metal detectors. We'll find it." At last, I relented and we gave up the search. We marked the trees in the area with the hatchets, and made our way back to the car. It's hard to explain, but in some way I felt that Sean had taken the ring away from me. I know it sounds crazy, but I began to think that he was trying to tell me that he didn't approve of the way I was living. I'll never know if that was true (I never went back to look for the ring), but not long after that trip something did actually happen that wound up pushing me in a positive direction: I was approached by these two kids who asked me to train them, Joe "the Blade" Slattery and Freddie Koop.

They just came up to me one day while I was standing on the corner and said they needed someone to train them, could I do it? I thought, *Did Cus send these guys to me?* I knew Cus had never lost hope that he was going to get me to go back to Catskill to work with him. I knew he had tried with the Ohio State Fair. At the same time, I also knew it wasn't Cus actually sending these kids; that would have been a bit farfetched, even for him.

Joe and Freddie were fifteen or sixteen years old. They were both thin, but Joe, especially, was on the skinny side. He was tall, about six feet three, maybe 175 pounds, with dark hair, olive skin, and dark, melancholy eyes. The reason they called him "the Blade" had less to do with how skinny he was than with his proficiency at using the 007 flick knife—the same kind that I'd gotten cut with. He came from a messed-up family—one brother was a methadone addict and had stabbed him, another brother had hit him with a baseball bat—I mean, he was lucky to have survived. Freddie had his own problems, though not nearly as bad. They were both looking for something, I guess, some kind of structure and discipline. The fact that they came to me blew my mind. But I said yes.

I took them over to a gym in the basement of the church that was run by my old mentor from the PAL, Ray Rivera. He was the same as ever, still having the kids put their mouthpieces in the communal jar by the door. I'd been one of his toughest kids, and he had a soft spot for me. He helped me out, let us use some of his equipment, gloves and wraps, jump ropes and other stuff. This was in the springtime. A month later, the church closed the basement for the summer. I didn't consider stopping; I asked Ray if we could borrow some equipment for a few months. He had an extra pair of gloves he could spare, a pair of hand pads, and a few other things he let us have.

We trained outdoors, in Silverlake Park, near the reservoir, every day from two to five in the afternoon. Ray had been able to spare only one pair of boxing gloves, but we were okay so long as we were just working on conditioning, footwork, and technique. Once we started sparring, though, I needed another pair of gloves. Hanging on my bedroom wall, I had these gold-colored gloves that my friend Johnny "the Heat" Verderosa had worn the night he won the New York Golden Gloves. The reason he'd given them to me was that I'd helped him out when he was preparing for the finals, even though I was sick with a 102-degree fever and had to get out of bed to spar with him. My doing that had meant so much to Johnny that he tried to give me the golden gloves the *Daily News* had awarded him. Of course, I wouldn't take them. Instead, he gave me the gloves he had fought with that night. So that's what we were using.

People in the park would stop to watch us. We didn't have a ring. We were sparring on the open grass. And they would watch: old people, kids, parkies, junkies, pigeons, couples holding hands. We were oblivious to everything, caught up in what we were doing. Sometimes, at the end of the day, when it was particularly hot, we'd jump in the reservoir to cool off. We weren't supposed to—it was illegal—but we did it anyway.

One time, the cops caught us. They drove their car down across the grass. Freddie and I were near the shore, but Joe was in the middle of the reservoir, and when he saw them, his street instincts took over. He swam away from them, all the way to the other side. They drove around to intercept him. Joe turned around and swam back. They drove around again, he swam back again. Finally, they got out of the car. Joe was on the other shore, lying in the shallows, exhausted. They said, "Well, you finished or you want to swim some more laps?" It was like they knew we weren't bad; they had that soft edge to them. They said to me, "You're not going to make him do his roadwork today, are you?"

"I guess not."

"Listen, we don't wanna have to give you a summons, so don't go in the water on our shift, okay? See what time it is?"

It was a quarter to four.

"We change shifts in fifteen minutes, and the other guys don't get here right away." They were basically telling us when it would be okay to swim. They could see we were all right, that we were doing something positive.

There was one guy who walked by every day at the same hour. I never knew who he was at the time because he wasn't wearing his collar, but I found out that it was this priest, Father Murphy. Years later, after I had started becoming well known as a trainer, he told my mother, "One of the things, Mary, I always felt good about, is that I would take my evening constitutionals knowing that your son and his young charges were there to watch me."

The park was changing. There were more and more drugs around, and it wasn't as safe as it once had been. Father Murphy told my mother, "I adjusted my walks to coincide with the hours Teddy and his boys were going to be there because I knew if something happened, they'd look out for me." Every once in a while, he would stop, look, and make a comment. He'd say something like, "Keep the left up," and then continue walking.

I was a stern taskmaster. I made rules for Joe and Freddie that extended beyond our workouts. They couldn't stay out on the corner too late. They couldn't be around drugs. They couldn't drink. Meanwhile, I was going out at night, after our training sessions, and robbing people. I knew it was screwed up—I mean, I would not let these kids do one thing wrong, and yet there I was doing what I was doing.

What changed everything started one night at this low-life bar down on Bay Street by the waterfront. It was a place called Mandia's. They had a late crowd there. People would come in around one, two in the morning. Screwed-up, lost souls, the kind of people who gravitate to places like that. I guess I was one of them. I'd go there looking for trouble, and more often than not I'd find it. On this particular night, trouble started over a game of pool. I put my quarter up on the table, and when it came my turn, some asshole tried to cut in front of me. He was with two other guys. One thing led to another, and I cracked the guy with a pool ball. One of his friends hit me with a pool stick. By the time it spilled out onto the sidewalk, I had broken one guy's jaw and another guy's nose. They kind of quit at that point, and I went home.

Four in the morning at the end of what was a long night, I was in bed, half asleep, and I got a call from Billy Sullivan. "Teddy, we got big problems. Those guys that you beat up found out where you live and they're saying they're going to burn your house down."

Burn *my* house down? It was my parents' house.

"They realize they're all going to die if that happens," I said.

"I'm just telling you what they said."

"You made it very clear to them that they're going to die?"

"Yes."

"All right. You tell them they can meet me somewhere and we'll straighten this thing out."

Billy said he'd get the word to them.

Half an hour later, I drove over to Teckie's Bar on Gordon Street. When I got there, they were already there. One of them couldn't fight because his jaw was broken, but the other two were ready to go. When you were fighting two guys at once, the key thing was to nail one guy good right away, because then the other guy tended to lose a little courage. So I hit this one guy a shot before he even knew what was happening, and he went down. His head hit the ground and bounced. The other guy saw that and took off. Everyone took off. My instinct was to get out of there, too. I jumped in my car and drove off.

About a block away, I started thinking about the fact that everybody just left the one guy there on the street. His friends, everyone, they just left him. I turned around and drove back. I knew I couldn't afford to get in trouble. I was still on parole. But I went back.

At first, I tried to revive the guy. When that didn't work, I dragged him down the street and into the backseat of my car. I took him to Marine Hospital. I went into the emergency room and told them at the desk that I had a guy who was unconscious in my car and I needed them to bring a stretcher out. So they wheeled the guy in. I was about to leave when the nurse at the desk said, "Wait, you can't leave. We need some information. Where did you find him?"

"I found him on the street."

"What do you mean you found him on the street? Was he drinking? Was there a fight?"

I said, "Yeah, there was a fight. I saw guys running." I wasn't even thinking about how I must have looked. That I had bruises and marks on me. "Just do me a favor," I said. "Tell me if he came to." I was a little worried because he was still unconscious when I brought him in.

"They're working on him now. He's still unconscious. Sit down and we'll let you know."

I was uneasy about it, but I sat down. After about five minutes, I realized what was going on. I got up and ran for the door. Too late. The cops were coming in. It's not a good sign when the cops see you and say, "Hello, Teddy." It was the same pair that had arrested me in the bar with Billy Sullivan.

They handcuffed me and then brought me back inside. Meanwhile, the guy had come to, and he identified me. I knew I was screwed. The guy's orbital bone—the bone right below the eye—was fractured. They had to do surgery, take the eye out, repair the bone, and then put the eye back in the socket. With something like that, it was going to be a minimum of first-degree assault. Put that on top of my previous record, and the outlook was grim.

They put me in lockup, and a few days later I went before a grand jury, which is the step in the justice process where they ask you a lot of questions and then decide whether to indict you. My lawyer prepared me well. "Don't deny anything," he said. "You tell them you didn't want to fight, but you had to, it was self-defense. When they say, 'You've been arrested. You're out on parole,' you say, 'Yes, that's the reason I did not want this to happen.'" I did exactly what he said, and it worked (or at least I thought so until I found out what had really happened), and they didn't indict me. The DA came up to me afterward and said, "You're a very lucky guy. But you better start making some different choices in your life. Otherwise, you're going to wind up dead or in prison."

As it turned out, the real reason I didn't get indicted—and if I had, it would have changed my whole life; I would have been gone for years—was not because of anything I said in front of the grand jury. It was because the guy that I beat up changed his story. What I found out was that a couple of wiseguys, who were patients of my father, went and had a talk with the guy. They told him they'd pay his medical bills, but he better change his story. It's not like my father asked these guys to do this; they did it on their own just because of their feelings for him. After the guy changed his story, the grand jury had no choice but to throw the indictment out.

What was interesting to me was that while I was locked up, the thing I was most upset about wasn't my own plight, it was that I was letting down Freddie and Joe, that I wasn't around to train them.

The day after I was released, Joe came over to my house, ten o'clock at night. He said, "Teddy, could you come outside?" He wouldn't talk inside. I went with him. It was getting cool out. Summer was ending. I wasn't sure what was going to happen with Freddie and Joe in the fall.

"Listen, it's those guys, the ones from the bar," Joe said. "Word on the street is that they're looking to kill you."

"They don't have the balls," I said.

"They're sneaky bastards, Teddy. They won't fight with you, but they're liable to put two in you one night because they're so scared and embarrassed."

We walked down to the end of the block. "Let's not wait for them to do something, Ted." Joe reached into his waistband and pulled out a gun. "We'll go take care of them."

I didn't know how to react. You see that kind of true loyalty so rarely. For what I had done for him, he was willing to do this thing for me without even thinking about it. I know it sounds screwed up, but in my mind this was the way everyone should act. Not that people should go around killing people out of loyalty, but they should be *willing* to risk themselves. After that, it's up to the person to whom they're being loyal to protect *them*. That was how I thought about it, at least. So I made a choice. I said to myself, "I can't let him do this. I can't let Joe risk himself this way." I was his trainer, and I had that responsibility to him. That's what allowed me to get off the hook. Normally, I'd have gotten in the car, gone down there, and taken care of the problem myself. But all of a sudden, there was this other element: Joe's involvement.

I went right inside, picked up the phone, and called Cus. I could never do it before. It would have been like I was chicken, like I was running from these guys. But now it wasn't about protecting myself or my image. It wasn't about me. It was about being responsible to someone else. At that moment, I became a real trainer.

I called up Cus and said, "Do you still want me to come train fighters for you?"

Without even hesitating, he said, "Come up now." It was late at night and he said, "Come up now."

"I can't come up now. First of all, I've got two kids I've been training. . . ."

"You've been training kids?"

"Yeah. I'll tell you about it later. The thing is I can't come unless I can bring them with me."

"Bring them with you. Come up now."

"I'll come tomorrow."

And that was it. We packed our stuff, and the three of us went up there the next day.

SMOKERS

JOE AND FREDDIE COULDN'T BELIEVE THE SIZE OF the house in Catskill. It had nine bedrooms and was on ten acres of land. Here were these two kids who'd grown up poor in Staten Island, and now they were moving to this country estate. I felt like I'd accomplished something, bringing them there. There was structure to their lives now, stability, a family of sorts. Camille nourished them with delicious home-cooked meals, and Cus gave lessons in life in and out of the ring. To earn their keep, Joe did chores around the house for Camille, and Freddie got work in town as a house painter.

For me, it was a totally different experience being back. Before, I had been a fighter, with limited responsibilities—most of them to myself. Now I was running things. In the space of a few short months, the gym over the police station went from being empty most of the time to being packed morning till night. Two things led to that: one, the fact that I was in the gym every day from ten in the morning till nine or ten at night (whereas Cus had only been showing up three or four times a week for a couple of hours at a stretch); two, the arrival of Gerry Cooney, his trainer, Victor Valle, and a group of his sparring partners. Cooney was undefeated in seven fights at that point, and an up-and-coming heavyweight. His arrival on the scene, along with mine, helped create a kind of critical mass that drew others. Word got around that I was a good teacher, and that our gym was a haven for troubled kids. Suddenly, kids started showing up from all over, wanting to learn how to box.

Before you knew it I had ten fighters. Then fifteen. Then twenty. Then thirty. It was something, it really was. I was obsessed, and the energy I brought to what I was doing rubbed off on everyone else. Cus was smart. He really was a clever old bastard, and he had understood that I was someone who would be able to breathe life into him and his gym. The fact that I was doing it free of charge was icing on the cake. In fact, it was better than that, because I was actually *paying* for the privilege— or, to be more accurate, my father was paying. Cus was collecting the same fifty bucks a week off me that he had been when I was getting trained, not doing the training. "It's less money than college, Atlas," he would say. "And you're getting a better education."

It was true. More important, I was committed to something. I was responsible to something larger than myself. Every day, first thing in the morning, I was in the gym. I'd work with the pros until late afternoon, then with the amateurs in the evening. Often, after training was finished, I'd sit around with the kids, talking to them about whatever problems they might be having at home, trying to help them figure out how to deal with what were often difficult situations.

There was one young kid named Mane Moore, who came by the gym one day, then didn't show up for weeks, then came by again and disappeared again. He was a skinny kid, about eleven years old, with a shy manner, and an engaging, toothy smile that didn't show itself nearly enough—at least in the beginning. I asked some of the other kids about him. They told me his father was gone, and he and his younger brother and sister lived alone with their mother, who was very religious. They also told me that there was a bully in his school named Goo who was beating him up every day and taking his lunch money. A lot of the kids who came to me had similar home situations. It was interesting how many of them had mothers who tried to cope by leaning on religion. There's nothing wrong with it, really, but on the other hand, it wasn't helping a kid like Mane much. The fact that Mane's mother went to church and prayed a lot wasn't stopping a bully in school from taking his lunch money every day. That's why he kept coming to the gym and then disappearing. He knew he needed to do something, but he was afraid because he lacked confidence.

The next time he came to the gym, I had a talk with him. I said, "Come here. I want you to try something." I walked over to the mirror we used for shadowboxing, and Mane followed me. "Come here. I'm not going to bite you." I threw a jab toward the mirror. "Try that." I threw another jab. "Just like that."

He threw his left fist out weakly.

"That's good."

"Yeah?"

"Definitely. You got natural ability, Mane. You sure you never boxed in another state?"

"No, never."

"Tell me the truth, 'cause if I'm gonna be training you, I don't want to find out that you already got a contract with another trainer."

"I don't got no contrack."

"Good, then you got yourself a trainer."

I put out my hand, and we shook on it.

He started coming to the gym regularly after that, and I began teaching him the fundamentals: how to throw a punch, how to slip a punch, footwork, the basic stuff. After a couple of months, I decided he was ready to spar with another kid, but when the day came, he broke down and started crying. Then he ran out of the gym.

I caught up to him outside the gym door on the second-floor landing. "Come here," I said. I led him into the empty courtroom across the hall (the police station was downstairs). He was still sniffling. I put my hand on his shoulder.

"Well, it's good to see you're normal," I said.

"What do you mean, normal?"

"I mean, everybody gets scared."

"Not like me."

"No, you're just more honest than most people. You show what you're feeling. Most people try to hide it even though they actually feel the same way you do."

"They do?"

"Sure. Let me tell you something I never told too many people. When

I was a boy in school I used to get picked on by a bigger kid. He'd push me around and take my money."

"He took your money?" Mane brushed away the last of his tears with the cotton sleeve of his shirt. He didn't know that I knew all about him and Goo.

"Yeah. He was a bully, and I was afraid."

"You were afraid? But you're not afraid of nobody."

"I'm afraid all the time," I said. "That doesn't mean you would ever know it. I'm afraid of a lot of things. You *should* be afraid. If you didn't get afraid, you wouldn't be aware when danger's close by. You just have to learn how to deal with your fear."

"So what about the bully?"

"Well, one day he caught me in the lunch room by the garbage pails where the kids dump their trays. He told me to give him some money for dessert."

"Did you give it to him?"

"I didn't have it."

"So did he beat you up?"

"He tried. But I had realized something."

"What?"

"That I would feel better if I fought back."

"You fought back?"

"Yeah. It's a funny thing. You know that garbage pail where the kids would dump their lunch trays?"

"Yeah."

"The bully wound up with his head in it and his legs sticking out."

Mane wasn't sniffling anymore. He was smiling.

"Did that really happen?"

"Yeah."

"What about the next day?"

"He never bothered me after that. See, what I realized afterward was that I had always had a choice. Sometimes it takes a while to realize that. You do what you think is easiest and you don't know that there's another option. Now, I know that this has nothing to do with you, Mane, but for me, the feeling I had all those days before that happened—going home without my money and without having eaten lunch—was a lot worse than dealing with this guy for one minute. Not dealing with it meant it was there every minute, every hour, every day. I never realized that until that day. But I've never forgotten it."

I gave Mane a hug and a little pat. "Now let's go back inside the gym before they come looking for us."

That was the first of several conversations that Mane and I had in that courtroom. It was funny and strange for me to be hanging out in a courtroom given my previous experiences in one. As Mane and I got more comfortable, sometimes I would even sit in the judge's chair. After that first day, Mane would still have these little regressions, where he would get scared and start to cry, but he got better and better, until finally I could get him through a whole round of sparring without him shedding a tear or giving up.

One day, weeks later, I was in the gym training the pros, and Mane came running in. It was around lunchtime, and he'd run all the way to the gym, even though he wasn't supposed to leave the school grounds. He said, "I just had to tell you, I had to tell you, Goo ain't going to pick on me no more."

I was working in the ring with Kevin Rooney. From other parts of the gym came the thudding sound of someone hitting the heavy bag, the rat-a-tat-tat from the speed bag, the rhythmic creaking of the floorboards, and suddenly this eighty-pound kid comes running in, saying, "Goo ain't gonna pick on me no more!," and the place fell silent for a moment; then, all at once, these big, tough guys started to laugh.

Mane didn't notice or care. He was so happy he couldn't contain himself. "Goo tried to take my lunch money, and I pushed him and told him, 'No,' and he ain't going to pick on me no more."

I climbed out of the ring, went over to him, and gave him a hug. "I'm proud of you, Mane. That took a lot of guts. Now I want you to go back to school before you get both of us in trouble. I'll see you tonight."

I can't tell you how great it was to see this kid, who used to be sad all the time, happy that way.

That was the way it was with the kids. It went beyond the gym. I took them out on picnics, to the movies, we went out for pizza, because that was all part of it. That was part of their development—and mine. Some of them came to the gym because they didn't have fathers, or they came from rough situations. I recognized what it was they needed; I understood them instinctively because of things I had gone through myself. I was strict with them. I gave them discipline. But I showed them I cared, too.

When you're developing young fighters, after they reach a certain skill level, you need to find suitable opponents for them to fight so they can continue to grow. There were very few good fights for my kids in or around Catskill, so I started taking them down to the city. Cus knew this guy Nelson Cuevas who ran these Saturday night "smokers"—unsanctioned amateur boxing shows—at a club on Westchester Avenue in the South Bronx. Nelson was a former fighter of Cus's from the Gramercy Gym days. He was an interesting guy. He'd been around when Jose Torres won the light heavyweight title with Cus, but his own fight career hadn't amounted to what he'd thought it would. Now he ran the smokers, both as a way to pick up a few extra bucks on weekends (he had a day job as a construction worker with the electrical union) and also to keep his hand in the fight game. Who could say he wouldn't develop his own champion?

Cus called Nelson one day and paved the way for me to bring my kids to his place. "Teddy's doing a good job with them," Cus told him. "I want you to help him out. Take care of him."

From then on, every Saturday afternoon I'd drive my kids down to the South Bronx in an eight-year-old blue Chevy station wagon. It took two and a half or three hours, depending on traffic. The club was located in an area so rough the police didn't bother with it. There was a guy across the street, Mr. Santos, who owned a bar, and he and his people would look after my car. We'd come out at the end of the night and some of the batteries from other cars would be stolen, but my car was never touched; the people in the bar made sure nobody fucked with it. (Funny story: I began writing up accounts of the smokers for the local paper in Catskill, and the editor, a guy named Gunther, who admired what I was doing with the kids, made the mistake of offering me the use of his brand-new station wagon if I ever needed it. Well, some time later, the car I usually used was in the shop, so I took him up on his offer. Saturday came, and the kids and I went over to the paper to pick up his brand-new Ford Country Squire. Gunther had grown up in Catskill, and he was a little naive, but even so, as we were getting in his car, the reality of where we were going began to dawn on him and he got a little nervous. He said, "So I don't need to worry, do I, Teddy? I mean, where you're going isn't the kind of neighborhood where they're going to steal my hubcaps, is it?" "No, not at all, Gunther," I said, hitting the gas and waving good-bye. I turned to the kids, knowing he couldn't hear me. "It's the kind of neighborhood where they take the whole car!")

The building where the Apollo Boxing Club was located was one of the few on the block that wasn't boarded up, abandoned, or reduced to rubble. When you walked up the three flights of stairs, the stench of urine was thick. You'd see discarded needles, sometimes even a guy shooting up.

Nearing the third floor, you'd begin to hear the noise. Latin music blaring from a boom box and the din of a couple of hundred boisterous voices. It cost three dollars a head to get in, and the room was always packed to the rafters. There was a pungent aroma of cigar smoke, booze, fried food, and sweat. On the near side of the room was the ring, and on the far side a makeshift counter where they sold liquor and Spanish food: fried bananas, empanadas, potatoes in oil, canned beer, and rum in paper cups. Out a row of windows were the tracks of the el. When a train thundered by every ten or fifteen minutes, you could see the sparks shooting from the wheels and feel the building shake, that's how close it was. Families came to watch their kids and cheer. Men came to gamble and drink and talk smack. It was quite a scene, and one of the few positive things in that bombed-out neighborhood.

I was the only white guy in the place, me and some of my kids. And even though I didn't speak Spanish, Nelson wound up making me the matchmaker after a few weeks. I think he knew I'd be good at it. But it was a difficult task because there was a lot of lying going on. Everybody wanted an edge. They'd say their guy was ten when he was actually twelve. They'd say their guy had no fights when he had five fights. But you learned the code, you learned that no fights meant a kid had a minimum of three fights; one fight meant six to ten; three meant anywhere from ten to fifteen; and once they said four or more, forget it, the kid was practically a pro. So you came to understand to what degree they were lying, and you took all that into account.

From the kids' point of view, it was even rougher. They'd walk into this big room and look at the other kids and try to figure out who they'd be fighting, and they would grow up, in that way, right in front of me. They were on their way to becoming pros and they didn't even know it. Pros for the real world. Their hearts were going a million miles an hour, they were dying inside. I remember looking at one of my kids one time, and I knew he was dying. I said, "Don't worry, you can't see it." He said, "See what?" I said, "See your shirt moving up and down over your pounding heart." He looked down at his shirt, and then at me. I smiled, and when he saw me smile, he smiled back because I was telling him it was okay.

There were always mixed emotions for the kids. They wanted the glory but they were also afraid. Here they were in this madhouse with two hundred or so people jammed into the place. On some level it had the feeling of a meat market. They were just waiting for their call, waiting to be tapped on the shoulder and hear the words, "You've got a bout," because they wanted to be fighters and they dreamed of being Sugar Ray Leonard and having the chance to be on TV. At the same time they were hoping maybe they'd get the other kind of tap, the one where they would hear, "Sorry. Couldn't get you an opponent," and the knot of fear would unloosen in their stomach, and they'd be able to mutter regretfully, "Ah, too bad."

For five years, from 1977 to 1982, I did this every Saturday, leaving Catskill with them in the afternoon and getting home at three or four in the morning, knowing that if I matched them wrong, if they got beat up, I could lose them. It was a tremendous responsibility. As big as raising your own children.

There were different ways to ensure a good match. I might know the coach, or I might have seen the kid fight before. That was the best way. But there were so many new kids and coaches showing up there each week that it got tricky. You might have to go by someone else's word, and you didn't know if you could trust them. Even if their intentions were good, their judgment might not be. So you had to know who you were getting your information from. Always, in the end, I'd want to take a look at the kid if I hadn't gotten a line on him I was satisfied with. If he was a tall, skinny kid, I wouldn't take him. Most tall, skinny kids have a lot of leverage. They can almost always punch like bastards. So I'd turn them down. Then I'd watch later in the night as they knocked some guy dead, and know that I'd been right.

When it came down to it, if I still wasn't sure, I'd pull out my trump card. I'd go up to the trainer and I'd say, "Look, I have a feeling that your kid has more fights than you're saying. My kid's green. As soon as that bell rings, I'm going to know if you've been straight with me. If your kid's a ringer, two things will happen. One, my kid will have a problem, but I won't let him get hurt. I'll stop the fight. Two, if that happens, then you're going to have a problem, because I'll be on my way over to you. So think about it. We've got another half hour before this match." Twenty minutes later, Nelson would come over and say, "Teddy, Jose said he don't want to make that match." I'd say, "Tell Jose, thank you."

I was very careful with all my kids, but especially with Mane. He was so fragile. He'd come such a long way, but I still couldn't rely on him in the ring. I searched and searched for the right guy, and I finally got him, Raul Rivera, who was the same type of sensitive kid as Mane, had the same kind of confidence problems, and was similar in experience and ability. We put them in with each other, and all they did for the three rounds was grab at each other and look at the referee to break them up. Nelson had no patience. He said, "Ahhh, they're terrible, they're girls." He didn't understand where Mane had come from to get to that point. For him to just get in that ring, to last three rounds, was huge. I said to myself, "He's got to keep doing it. I've got to keep him fighting every week. And I can't take a chance with anyone except Raul."

I went to Nelson the next week and said, "Mane's going to fight again. He's going to fight with Raul again."

Nelson looked at me like I was nuts. "Again? You serious, Teddy? I'm going to throw up."

"Again," I said.

And right after they fought a second time, I went to Nelson and said, "They're fighting again next week."

"Teddy, you're killing me," Nelson said. "Nobody wants to watch this."

I said, "I do." I wound up having Mane and Raul fight six straight weeks. People couldn't believe it. Nelson thought I was insane. But I wasn't. It was working. Each time, Mane and Raul got a little bit better, and there was a little less holding, less pleading to the referee. By the sixth time, they were actually throwing punches. It was a pretty good fight. After that, I began letting Mane fight other guys, and he started becoming a fighter. Raul, too. (He actually later went on to win the New York Golden Gloves and turn professional. Nelson thought he might have found his champion—this kid he had initially wanted to give up on—but then Raul got involved in drugs. He was 10–0 as a pro, but he got involved with drugs and the street and didn't achieve what he should have. It broke Nelson's heart.)

My only real problem that first year at the Apollo was that my guys weren't getting the decisions they deserved. There was a lot of corruption. The judges were guys right out of the audience. They were all related, and they were drinking and betting and they had a stake in the outcomes. As a consequence, we were getting robbed all the time. I would tell my kids, "You're getting good experience, you're learning, you're going through the process. Even though they're robbing you, the most important thing is that you're improving. They won't be able to rob you after a while."

One thing I did to even the playing field a little was that afterward I would write up accounts of the smokers in the *Catskill Daily Mail.* I'd write these really colorful stories about the fights, and if I thought a kid really won, I'd put down that he won. The kids loved it; they loved reading about themselves. It made a difference.

At a certain point, though, I knew I had to do more than just talk or "write" the wrongs. Mane, in particular, needed to have his confidence lifted up to the next level. I went into Nelson's office one day. He was dressed in one of the colorful three-piece suits he always wore. I could see the outlines of the gun that he kept tucked in his waistband. Nelson and I had a very interesting relationship by that point. We were linked by Cus and our mutual love of boxing. He was developing his kids, and I was developing my kids, but in some ways, even though we were helping each other, we were adversaries. I said, "Nelson, tonight my guys are winning."

"I'm sure they will," he said. "They always fight good."

"No, no, you don't understand," I said. "Tonight they're *winning.*"

"I know, Teddy. They're winners, they're good kids."

"No, you're not understanding, Nelson. I'm telling you they're gonna get their fuckin' hands raised tonight. They need it, they deserve it, and I ain't gonna let you rob them tonight. Maybe it sounds to you like I'm trying to fix it, but my kids are gonna win anyway, and I just want to make sure you're going to acknowledge it."

"Sure, Teddy. I see what you're saying."

"Good, and there's another thing. . . ."

"Yeah?"

I opened my bag and took out a big trophy. It was at least three feet tall, with a gold figure of a boxer on top of it.

"Wow, that's beautiful," he said.

"Starting tonight," I said, "there's gonna be a trophy like this for the fighter of the night."

"That's great. That's a good idea, Teddy. But I can't afford a trophy like that every week."

"I'll pay for them," I said. "I'll bring one down every week and you'll give it to the fighter of the night. Tonight, it's gonna be Mane Moore."

"But the fights haven't even taken place yet."

"Tonight, Mane Moore is the fighter of the night."

"Okay, Teddy." Nelson was shaking his head.

However browbeaten he might have felt, Nelson didn't show it. Got to give him credit. After the last fight, he climbed into the ring, and took the microphone with his usual élan. "Ladies and gentlemen . . . tonight, the Apollo Boxing Club is proud to begin a new tradition. Fighter of the night. . . ."

At that point, someone handed him the trophy. I was looking at my kids. I always had them sit in one area, quiet and still, like little soldiers. When that trophy came out, you would have thought it was—forget it—a brand-new go-kart or minibike they were going to win. They were slapping each other, saying, "Holy shit, it's bigger than me!" And looking around, trying to figure out the winner. When Nelson announced, ". . . And the fighter of the night is . . . Mane Moore!," I was looking right at Mane. He couldn't even take it in. Couldn't process it.

All my kids started hitting him, whacking him on the head and on the back. Then the Spanish kids came over. At first they'd been mad they didn't get it, but within seconds they understood that something special was taking place. They joined in, whistling and cheering. Mane had fought a hell of a fight that night, so it wasn't like charity; it was real. All these kids were patting him on the back, congratulating him, and he just looked confused. One of them said, "Mane, it's you!"

He said, "What?" He looked up and he saw Nelson in the ring, holding the trophy, waiting for him. He couldn't understand it. He looked at me, and I nodded.

When he got up and stepped into the ring to accept the trophy, the whole place erupted. They gave him a standing ovation. Mane finally came out of his daze and grinned that toothy smile of his. It was worth a million trophies to see that smile. It really was.

A DEATH IN THE FAMILY

CUS HAD A THING ABOUT THE PHONE. HE DIDN'T LIKE anyone else answering it. I don't know what he was like when he was younger, but by the time I encountered him he was an old man with a number of eccentric habits and preoccupations. There were certain areas in his domain that he needed to control. The phone was one. Food was another. When the groceries came in each week, they had to be left on the kitchen counter so that Cus could supervise their transfer to the pantry and make sure that everything was in order. If Camille hadn't bought at least fifteen cans of tuna fish, an argument would ensue.

"You only got ten cans? What if we get unexpected guests?" Cus was nothing if not a creature of habit, and it was his habit to eat tuna fish for lunch every day. What that meant was that we had to have several extra jars of mayo on hand, because if we had tuna but we didn't have mayo, we might as well not bother.

This was all serious business to him. I remember putting stuff away one day, when suddenly he started yelling at me. "Not in there! Don't put it there! I'll never find it." Like if he had to look in another cabinet for something the world might come to an end.

When we actually did sit down to eat, he'd start discussing the next day's meal before we'd even finished the one we were eating. Camille was incredibly tolerant of him, although she did occasionally lose her patience. "Cus, I'm still digesting. Please. I don't want to think about what I'm going to eat tomorrow."

"But you have to think about it," he'd say. "Otherwise you might not take the meat out of the freezer in time, and then we'll be stuck with something that isn't properly defrosted."

Camille gave up after a while. You couldn't argue with Cus.

The phone was another one of his big obsessions. He had this favorite chair that he would fall asleep in. It was an old wooden chair with a high, regal back, and a brown cushion tied down to the seat. Even when Cus wasn't sitting in it, it retained his aura, and a sense that he would be back soon. The telephone sat near it, on a little table. As soon as the phone rang, Cus would pick up the receiver. He'd be dead asleep in that chair, but the phone would ring and his hand would shoot out in the middle of some dream, and snag it off the hook. His reflexes, when it came to the phone, were almost superhuman. It was rare that anyone would beat him to a call.

New kids arriving at the house were immediately made aware that his room, which was on the second floor, right across from Camille's room, was strictly off limits. No one ever saw the inside of his room. Ever. If you happened to be walking past when he was coming out, he'd open the door just enough so that he could squeeze out, and then he'd quickly shut it behind him. Of course, everyone was curious as to what the hell was in there. But that was the next thing he made everyone aware of: He had rifles in the room, and he knew how to use them.

This one time, I was downstairs and I heard the phone ring, and Cus answered. I could always tell when he was talking to my parents. His tone, especially with my father, would become uncharacteristically deferential. On this call, I knew it was my mother, and I could also tell that something was wrong. Cus handed me the receiver, looking apprehensive.

"Teddy, Gaga died," my mother told me.

Gaga was my grandmother, Helen Riley, my mother's mother, a tough old Irishwoman with an iron constitution, who'd hardly been sick a day in her life. She was eighty-eight years old, but the news of her death still came as a shock. I'd gotten closer to her as I'd grown older. She called me regularly in Catskill and sent me cards, always with a ten- or twenty-dollar bill enclosed. When I went back to Staten Island, I visited with her, and often took her to bingo.

The way my mother described it, she had been taking Gaga a cup of tea that morning on one of those occasions when my grandmother had stayed over at the house (at eighty-eight, she still lived by herself), but when my mother tried to wake her, she couldn't. "It was awful, Teddy. She was so still. I kept trying to wake her up. I just thought she was asleep."

After I hung up, Cus looked at me. "You okay?"

"Yeah."

He and my grandmother had gotten along well, and he knew how she felt about me and how I felt about her. Whenever she called me, the two of them always talked. "That Cuff is a nice fella," she'd say to me when I got on. "Gaga, it's Cus." "Yeah, I like that Cuff," she'd say. "I hope he's taking good care of you. Did you get my card? Did you get the ten dollars I sent?" "Yeah, Gaga, I got it." "Make sure you spend it on some warm under-wear." She was the typical grandmother that way. Always sending me money to buy warm underwear. Like Catskill was in Siberia or someplace.

"So you're going back for the funeral?" Cus said, even though he knew the answer.

"This afternoon."

"Don't stay too long."

"A couple of days."

Cus always got uneasy when I went home. It was a combination of things. When I was away, things at the gym ground to a halt. That was one problem. Also, he fretted that I might regress, that Staten Island would re-claim me, and I'd get sucked back into the things I had been doing.

"Hurry back," he said.

I drove down in the station wagon. There were several cars parked outside my parents' house. I had a front door key and I let myself in. Everyone was in the kitchen: my mother and my sister by the counter, laying out a plate of cookies and cake, and my father and my brother Terryl at the kitchen table. I hugged my mother, and she started to cry.

"Where's Tommy?" I asked.

"He's in his room," she said.

My uncle Frank, my mother's brother, arrived shortly. We embraced, and he said, "She didn't suffer. She just got tired finally and went to sleep."

At that point, there was certainly no reason to think otherwise. After my mother came upon Gaga's lifeless body that day, my father had rushed over from his office, joined later by a couple of guys from the

funeral parlor. He wrote up the death certificate as a cerebral hemorrhage, noting that there was a trickle of blood coming from Gaga's ear,
which was consistent with his diagnosis.

My uncle and I sat down at the kitchen table with my father and
brother. My father turned to me. "Teddy, my car got a flat tire this
morning. It's over in Concord. Would you do me a favor?"

"You want me to go fix it and bring it back?"

"Yes."

"Sure, Dad."

My father and I were getting along better than we had in a long time.
He was happy that I was doing something productive, and that I was off
the streets. He had no way of knowing that in the future I would train
champions and get paid for it. He just knew that I wasn't in Rikers. I
wasn't robbing and beating people up. That was a big improvement.

I was putting on my coat to go out when my brother Tommy came
downstairs. He looked drawn and thin, and, to be honest, a bit scary. He
had this way of looking at you with these hollow eyes—nothing really in
them, or if there was, it wasn't good. I was used to it by then, but it was
still unnerving. When we were younger (he and I were only fifteen months
apart, and some people thought we were twins), Tommy had been normal
(at least within the fucked-up parameters of our family), a bright and talented kid. Then, like me, he reached his teens, and he started getting into
trouble. When he was sixteen, he got arrested for stealing a car and was
sent off to Rikers.

I'm not sure exactly what happened to him while he was in Rikers, although I can imagine, but when he got out, he wasn't the same. He was still
facing trial. There was a chance he'd go back to prison. He and I both
moved in a world where it was necessary to put up a façade of macho
toughness. It was like, "Yeah, you go to jail, so what?" But underneath, I
could tell he was scared, just like a fighter before a fight is scared. That's why
I never say "So what" to a fighter's fear. I learned how dangerous it can be.

For Tommy, what had occurred inside Rikers coupled with his fear of
going back there proved to be too much for him. With the specter of his
trial looming, he just snapped one day. Maybe it would have happened
anyway; there was something inside his mind, and if it hadn't been one
thing triggering it, it would have been another. But maybe it never would
have happened at all. I don't know. I just know that we were sitting in the

living room one day, watching TV, and he went away. The Tommy I knew went away. I said something to him, and he didn't answer me. I yelled at him, but it was as if he didn't hear me. He was just staring straight ahead at the screen, expressionless. At first I thought it was an act. I thought he was kidding around. Everyone did—"C'mon, Tommy, cut it out"—that's how hard it was to understand something like that.

The sad thing is that when his trial did come, he won the case. He didn't have to go back to prison, to the source of his torment. But it was too late. His mind—that battle—was lost. The next thing you knew, we were taking him to doctors, to psychiatric specialists. I remember one time we were in the car, on our way to a psychiatrist, and my mother said to Tommy, "Stop faking it." I was young, but I could see she was just angry, mad at life. By that point, I knew he wasn't faking it. My mother just couldn't accept the truth. (It wasn't entirely a case of denial on her part—one psychiatrist agreed with her, actually telling my parents that he thought Tommy was faking it the same way that some kids did to dodge the Vietnam draft, a diagnosis that was dangerously wrong.)

We spent years after that dealing with the problem. Tommy was in and out of Bellevue. He was treated with drugs like Thorazine, which was new at the time, and lithium; he even underwent shock therapy. I don't think my father should ever have allowed that to happen, but he did. I'm talking about the treatments where they tie you down and zap you with high electrical voltage.

For a while my father sent him away to the Ozark Mountains, to this ranch he owned there. Tommy and my cousin Keith both went there to work on this ranch. Keith was supposed to keep an eye on Tommy, this poor sick-in-the-head kid out there in this beautiful mountain range in Missouri. It was a pretty crazy idea, when you think about it. That's what happens when you're desperate and grasping at straws. I don't think Keith was much good for him. I mean, Tommy was out there having conversations with crows and then shooting at people in cars with a rifle, and I didn't hear about Keith doing anything to stop him (not that he necessarily knew about the shooting at cars part). I only thank God Tommy didn't kill anyone while he was there.

After that, he was put back in either Bellevue or Kings County, I can't remember which. It went on for years. He'd get out, come back home, and everything would be okay for a while—at least until he stopped taking his medication and turned up walking around the streets naked or something. He was in one of the back-home periods now.

When I saw him coming down the stairs, I said, "Hey, Tommy. Do you want to come with me? I've gotta go deal with Dad's car."

He didn't answer, but when I went out, he followed me. It was cold. Tommy wasn't wearing a coat. We got in my car and I started driving.

"You okay?" I asked.

He shrugged. "Gaga died, huh?"

"Yeah. That's why I came down from Catskill."

We found my father's car a few miles away, sort of angled into the curb, as if he'd just coasted to a stop and gotten out without really paying attention to the fact that the tail end was sticking out in the street. I got the jack out of the trunk and went to work. Tommy stood there, watching me.

"Did you like Gaga?" he asked me.

"Did I like her?" It was an odd question. "Yeah . . . I liked her."

I pulled the wheel off the axle. Tommy had turned away. He was looking off in the distance at something I couldn't see.

"You want to give me a hand with the spare?" I said. He stood there, not moving. I got up and got the spare out of the trunk myself. While I slid the tire into place, I found myself thinking about Gaga, thinking it was too bad I hadn't taken her to bingo more often. I really thought I'd have the chance to spend more time with her.

When Tommy and I got back to the house, it was late afternoon and already getting dark. More people had shown up. Friends and family. Tommy went up to his room without saying anything to anyone. I went into the kitchen, and found Uncle Frank telling a funny story about the time my mother was delivered home by her date a little past the ten o'clock curfew Gaga had set. "Your mother took one look at Gaga and realized her date had better get out of there. But the poor guy didn't get it. He started to say hello to Gaga and she walked over to his car and snapped the antenna off." Everyone in the kitchen laughed as Uncle Frank finished.

I looked around, wondering where my father was. "He had to go out," my mother told me.

When the phone rang a while later for about the hundredth time that day, I answered. It was my dad. I carried the phone on its long extension cord down into the basement, where no one could listen in.

"Where's Tommy?" he asked.

"I think he went up to his room."

"Well, make sure he doesn't go anywhere."

"Dad, what's going on?"

"Is Ralph still there? Let me talk to him." Ralph Metz was my father's best friend. I went back up to the kitchen to get him.

"You're where?" Ralph Metz said, after he put the receiver to his ear. "What!" He grimaced, suddenly looking very uncomfortable. "Uh-huh. Uh-huh . . . I think you should talk to Teddy about this." He extended his arm and I took the phone back from him.

"Dad, where are you?"

"I'm at the funeral parlor."

"What are you doing there?"

"The police are on their way over to the house." I looked over at Ralph Metz, who was pale and visibly distressed. "It looks like Tommy killed your grandmother," my father said.

The mortician had found a bullet hole near her ear and called the cops. It wasn't a cerebral hemorrhage at all. The fact that my father, the legendary Dr. Atlas, had missed something so crucial and apparently obvious was puzzling. One of the detectives said, "Of course we know that you would never have intentionally tried to cover this up. . . ." But the implication was there. Faced suddenly with a very different set of facts, my father immediately understood the truth: "Let me call the house, and make sure Tommy doesn't leave," he said. There was another problem—namely, me. He knew right away that Tommy had done it, but he must have had some fears about the way I would react. That's why he asked for Ralph first. But when Ralph passed off the phone to me, he had no choice except to tell me.

"I gotta go get Tommy," I said as soon as I heard that the cops were on their way. "Get him out of here." That was my instinct. The thing my father had been afraid of.

"Wait a minute!" he yelled with a ferociousness that shook me. There was no in-between with my father. He either said nothing and kept his feelings to himself—or he exploded. "You've done a lot of things wrong in your life! Don't let this be another one!"

Maybe there was nothing worse he could have said to me at that moment. Here, I'd been up in Catskill, trying to turn my life around, and he said this thing that made me feel as though what I'd been doing didn't count, or he hadn't noticed, or didn't care. Of course, there was truth to what he'd said, too. That was why it hurt so much.

"You've screwed up a lot of things," he said. "You've hurt your family enough. Don't screw this up!"

He hung up on me, and I lowered the phone, looking at Ralph Metz. For some reason, Ralph couldn't even meet my eyes. I found out why almost immediately, as he grabbed his coat out of the closet and headed for the front door. Here was this guy, who was supposed to be my father's best friend, walking out of the house. Just abandoning fuckin' ship. *You piece of shit*, I thought. I started up the stairs toward my brother's room. Everyone in the kitchen saw Ralph leaving. They knew that it had been my father on the phone. It was clear something was wrong.

"Ralph, wait," my mother said. He was the one they focused on. The guy who was walking out the door, who knew the police were coming and didn't want to get involved.

I got to my brother's room and opened the door, and there he was, stretched out on his bed, asleep. In that moment, looking at him, I knew that my father was right, that Tommy had murdered my grandmother. I don't know why I knew that, because Tommy looked so peaceful lying there. In sleep, his handsome, square-jawed face was nearly angelic. There was no sign of torment, no way of understanding the demons inside. I stood a few feet inside the door, looking at him, knowing the police were coming, knowing that I had to make a choice. Did I wake him up, get him out of there, and worry about the consequences later? Or did I do what my father wanted?

Every instinct in me told me not to abandon my brother. At the same time I was afraid of my father. I could still hear his words echoing in my head. How I'd let everyone down in the past, and how I was about to do it again.

I don't know how long I stood there, but the next thing I knew there were loud voices, footsteps thundering up the stairs. It was too late. The door flew open behind me, four cops rushed into the room, and I was thrown aside. I could hear my mother and everyone screaming.

When I looked over at Tommy, they had him belly-down on the floor, head turned to one side, and they were slapping cuffs on him. One of the cops was holding me back, and two of them were holding him down, but somehow Tommy's eyes went right to mine, as if he knew I'd been standing there watching him all that time. There was no madness in his eyes, no anger, he was just looking at me. His older brother.

One of the cops flipped over his mattress, and there it was, a .22 rifle. They got Tommy to his feet, marched him past me, down the stairs and out the front door. I followed. The street was icy. Tommy slipped as they hustled him toward the open back door of a patrol car, but they didn't let him fall. They held him up, and then they shoved him in the backseat, a hand on his head so he didn't crack himself on the car's door frame. All the noise from the house became distant to me as I watched the cop car pull away, the light on top spinning.

After he was gone, I stood there for a couple of minutes. I didn't want to talk to anybody, so I got in my car and started driving. I was in a dangerous state of mind. I remember that I started running red lights, hoping something would happen. Logically, I knew that my brother was not well. That didn't make me feel any better about how I had acted. Everyone had a price. Mine had been my father's approval. All the things I'd gone through that time I hadn't signed that sheet the cops put in front of me—now, I was just another guy who'd signed.

I must have run fifteen or twenty red lights, pushing my foot to the floor each time I approached an intersection. If there was such a thing as it not being your time, then I guess it wasn't my time. Eventually, I wound up in Greenwich Village, outside Brother Tim's place on Waverly. I double-parked and waited for him. I knew that he left for Rikers each morning around five a.m. Sure enough, a few minutes before five, the door opened and he came out, wearing his blue pea coat and watch cap.

"Teddy, what are you doing here?" he said when he saw me. He knew it must have been something bad. It wasn't even light out yet.

I told him what had happened. He said, "Oh, my God." He put his arm around me. "I'm so sorry."

"I feel like I was supposed to do something more, like I let Tommy down," I said. I told him about running the red lights. It was tough to admit it to him, because it felt like weakness.

"Teddy, I want you to listen to me," Brother Tim said. "Sometimes there's nothing you can do for a person. It becomes more important to save yourself. You've gotten on a good track with your life. You mustn't stop now. Those kids in Catskill need you."

"But what about Tommy?"

"I'll pray for him," Brother Tim said.

Somehow the fact that I made it there that morning, that I ran all those red lights hoping something would happen and nothing did, got me past my darkest urges. At least that was the last day of that period of my life when I could act like I didn't care.

I was there in court throughout Tommy's trial, the only member of my family to attend. I watched him get sentenced to fifteen years. I also watched the powers that be in the criminal justice system stick him, in their infinite wisdom, into the prison's general population at Greenhaven prison. It was almost predictable that he wound up killing another inmate there. Too late, they put him in a prison for the criminally insane, which is where he remains to this day, having been diagnosed as a paranoid schizophrenic.

For many years after the murder and Tommy's arrest, my father didn't have any contact with him at all. It was ironic that this great doctor, who had spent his life trying to save lives, saw somebody to whom he gave life take a life. Eventually, he softened to the extent of accepting calls from Tommy, but he was never able to tell my brother that he loved him. As a doctor, he could understand his son's sickness on a scientific and intellectual level, but on an emotional level he could never fully forgive him. I remember a conversation I had with Tommy after the two of them renewed, in their very limited way, a dialogue. He said, "I talked to Dad. . . ."

"You talked to him?"

"He knows I'm sick. He understands."

"That's good. He said that?"

"Do you understand, Ted?"

"I do."

"Dad's not mad at me anymore," Tommy said. "He understands."

"All right, Tom."

"You understand, Ted?"

"Yes, Tom, I do."

"That's good."

THE PROMISED LAND

S OMETIME IN THE FALL OF 1979, CUS GOT A CALL from a guy named Bobby Stewart, who was a counselor at the Tryon reform school in Johnstown, New York. He had a twelve-year-old kid under his charge there he wanted us to take a look at. The kid's name was Mike Tyson.

Stewart, a former U.S. Golden Gloves light heavyweight champ and, briefly, a pro, was in charge of Elmwood Cottage, a disciplinary dorm where the worst kids at Tryon often wound up. Tyson, recently arrived from the Spofford Juvenile Detention Center in the Bronx, landed in Elmwood after going into a rage and beating up a kid while in one of the lower-security cottages. The violent outburst wasn't surprising to anyone who knew Tyson's background. This was a poor kid, raised in the worst section of Brooklyn, who had accumulated, by the age of eleven, a rap sheet longer than the menu in a Greek diner. What set Tyson apart from most other violent young kids his age was his freakish physical size—five feet nine inches, a muscular hundred and ninety pounds—along with a survivor's instinct for self-improvement. It's unlikely, but not entirely out of the question, that the incident that got Tyson moved to Elmwood was calculated. He had been intent on meeting Bobby Stewart from the moment he learned Stewart was a former pro fighter. The assault—premeditated or not—helped him achieve that goal.

Tyson, like a lot of kids from rough backgrounds, saw boxing as a way out. When then-champ Muhammad Ali had visited Spofford the previous year, the impact on Tyson had been huge. Seeing "the Greatest" in the flesh was exciting enough for an underprivileged kid, but even more mind-bending was to see the way the other kids and the guards reacted to him, the way they hung on his every word and smiled and tried to touch him. If that's what being the champ of the world got you, then Tyson wanted to be champ of the world. In Bobby Stewart, he saw someone who might be able to help him—if not to become a champion boxer, at least to help him improve his immediate situation and maybe gain him some special privileges.

Stewart, for his part, saw in this kid someone he might be able to help. He used boxing lessons as an incentive and a tool to get Tyson to behave better. It gives you a measure of Tyson's ambition: He was so determined to take what he needed from Bobby Stewart that, to prove to his prospective mentor that he was sincere, this supposedly uncontrollable kid became a model inmate.

When Stewart began teaching him, several things became apparent almost immediately. First, and most obvious, was that Tyson was tremendously large and powerful for his age. Second, he was a prodigiously gifted athlete with exceptional hand speed. Third, and perhaps most impressive, he was a sponge who soaked up everything Stewart threw at him and then asked for more.

After a few months, Stewart decided he needed another set of eyes to confirm that this kid was as special as he thought, so he took Tyson over to Matt Baranski's Trinity Club in Albany. Baranski had trained Stewart in his amateur career (and would later become Tyson's cut man in the professional ranks). He seconded his former pupil's assessment. The two discussed what to do next. Neither Baranski nor Stewart felt they had the time or the resources to unlock Tyson's full potential. They both knew Cus and Jimmy Jacobs (Stewart had been managed by Jacobs during his brief pro career), and they knew about the program I'd been running for kids, some of whom actually lived in the house with us. It could be a good situation for Tyson, they agreed. They should definitely try to get Cus to take a look.

Bobby Stewart made the call. "The kid's pretty good," he told Cus, "but I think I've taken him as far as I can."

Cus agreed to let them come down. He came to me and said, "I want your input, Teddy. You're the one who'll be working with him. Maybe Stewart is right and he's a special kid."

The day Stewart brought Tyson down, Cus showed up at the gym with his friend Don Shanager. I was training four of Shanager's sons, and he told me, only half jokingly, that I was the reason they weren't dead. He said he would have killed them if boxing and training with me hadn't steadied them out and calmed them down. Shanager was a transplanted New York character, a hard-drinking Irishman who did some bookmaking down in Queens and considered himself sharper than the country bumpkins in Catskill. He enjoyed being around Cus and ate up his stories, so Cus liked that. Also, Shanager was a bit of a finagler and had political connections in town, which made him potentially useful. That's the way Cus thought about things.

Anyway, it was the three of us there in the gym when Stewart showed up in the prison van—he had Tyson with him, and the kid was as impressive a physical specimen as advertised. A hundred and ninety pounds of pure muscle. It was hard to believe that he was an adolescent. In fact, when Stewart was gloving him up, Shanager said, "I gotta see this kid's birth certificate. The only way he's twelve years old is if he laid in his mother's blubber for twelve years before they discovered him." That was the way Shanager talked.

Stewart actually had documentation. The kid was twelve. You have to imagine it. I was up in the ring with them, Stewart and Tyson. Cus and Shanager were sitting in these folding seats outside the ring. Cus wore his glasses. Stewart, as I said, was a former pro fighter, with about fourteen fights. He was twenty-eight, a light heavyweight. A man. And he was in there with a twelve-year-old kid. True, the kid outweighed him by a few pounds, but he was a kid. He couldn't even get into an R-rated movie by himself. It was one thing to look imposing; there were plenty of guys with impressive physiques who could shake the bag if you let them. It was something else entirely to put the gloves on and try to deal with another fighter.

Normally, with a green kid like this, we wouldn't put him in the ring, but this was an unusual situation. It was a one-day audition, and we needed to find out about Tyson; we needed to see his character and find out some things about him that we weren't going to find out by watching him hit a bag. It was understood that if we decided we wanted to get involved, there would be no more boxing until we taught him what we needed to teach him. But for this day what made sense was to see him box.

Tyson knew this day was important. He was nervous and he wanted to impress. Stewart, for his part, had a true desire to help him. He was hoping that we'd get involved, because, let's face it, Tyson was getting out of reform school in several months, and he had no life waiting for him. If he went back to Brownsville, there was a very good chance he'd wind up in prison again, maybe a more serious prison. This was a road out, a real way for him to alter the course of his life.

When the bell rang, Tyson came at Stewart hard. He was extremely aggressive. You could see right away how strong he was. He fired shots at Stewart's ribs and stomach, and they hurt. I saw Stewart wincing. Tyson was extremely raw. His technique was crude. But there was a quickness and resolve in his attack that was unusual in an unschooled fighter. Stewart had to keep hitting him just to hold him off.

In the second round, Tyson got a bloody nose, but by then I had seen enough. Stewart was working hard as hell to keep him in his place, to keep from being overrun by this kid's power, and that told us a lot. We were professionals. We knew what we were looking at.

At the end of the second round, I looked over at Cus. He was smiling. I shouted, "Okay, that's it, that's enough!" Cus already knew I was going to be the kid's trainer, so he just sat there, watching and not saying anything, wanting to see how I handled things.

Tyson objected in that lispy voice of his, which was an octave higher then, "No, no. I'm going another round. I want another round." He was trying to show how tough he was, because he wanted to be accepted by us, he wanted to ace his audition. His life audition.

I already knew what was going to happen. I knew that I would be working with him, and it was important to establish the way things would be. I said, "That's it! Get out of the ring! Two rounds is all you're going today."

The way I said it stopped him for a moment. He didn't really want to go another round. He wanted me to think that he wanted to go, but he didn't really want to. He kept making a fuss, looking over at Stewart and saying, "We always go three rounds."

I got up in his face. "That's it, you're done! Now get out of the ring!" I wiped off his nose with a towel, and he stopped.

I was showing him that I knew he was coming back and that I knew I was going to be in charge of him. Cus always said that I was born to be a teacher—and part of it, I guess, was that I could recognize what was going on with a kid like this and know what I needed to do.

Of course, Cus was also flattering me, throwing me pieces of candy like that. He was good at it. He knew when I needed stroking. I remember one day, a year or two after this first encounter we had with Tyson, Cus and I were sitting in a lunch counter in Catskill, eating cheeseburgers. The guy behind the counter, the owner, said to me, "I saw you on ESPN the other night. . . ." I was training Rooney at the time and the fight had been on TV. Cus jumped right in. He said to the guy, "This is the Young Master. This is Teddy Atlas, the Young Master."

When we went to pay, the guy waved his hand and said, "No charge." He was a boxing fan and he wanted to buy us our cheeseburgers. Cus could have been gracious about it and just said thanks, but instead he said, "One of these days Atlas will come back here and buy this place out from under you. This is the Young Master and he's going to be rich and famous and have nothing but world champions." Meanwhile, I could barely afford a freaking cheeseburger—it was lucky the guy was treating. All the same, I walked out of that diner feeling like I already owned it and was a successful trainer of world champions. That's how intoxicating it was to hear that stuff.

So now, here we were, standing outside the ring with Tyson and Stewart and Don Shanager, and Cus turned to me and said, "What do you think?"

"Strong kid. He can learn."

"This young man can be heavyweight champion of the world," Cus said. "He might be your first heavyweight champ, Atlas."

It was extraordinary when you think about it. When you put it into words it sounds too much like some hoked-up Hollywood moment. But he actually said that. He said, "You and I will teach him, Atlas, and if this young man listens and does what we say and lets us take him there, he will be heavyweight champion someday."

Tyson soaked up Cus's words. He let himself smile a little smile. Cus was like the Al Pacino character in *The Godfather* when he sees the beautiful girl in Sicily. It was the thunderbolt. Love at first sight. He said, "We'll make arrangements when he gets paroled for him to come live with us." He turned to Tyson. "Would you like to come live with us?"

This all happened within an hour—it was incredibly fast. For someone else it might have been too fast, but really, when you think about it, what was this kid, with no real home, nothing to go back to, going to say? Especially when visions of fame and glory were dancing in his brain. So Tyson said, "Yes, live where? Your house?"

"Yes," Cus said. "How would you like that? We could arrange that. You could come live with us and become a fighter. You work hard, you could become champion of the world."

From what I learned afterward, Tyson kept saying to Bobby Stewart on their way back to Tryon, "Did you hear what he said? Did you?"

Tyson wasn't due to be released for four months or so, but Cus didn't want to waste any time. He was lazy about a lot of things—he would eat his tuna fish and watch *Barney Miller* and walk around in his bathrobe all day—but now for the first time since I'd been there, he seemed to really wake up and come to life. He said, "Okay, we've got to make sure this gets done, and he comes here to live." He enlisted Don Shanager's help, because Shanager had a friend in the county office whose approval we'd need before Tyson could be released into our custody.

Meanwhile, during the next few months, while we waited for Tyson's official release, Bobby Stewart brought him in every Monday to train with me. "This way," Cus said, "by the time he gets out, he'll already be developed to a certain point." I worked with him, showing him moves and combinations, and he'd go back to Tryon and, in every spare moment he had, practice the things I'd taught him. I heard that a couple of guards found him in his room one night past midnight, grunting and snorting as he shadowboxed in the pitch dark.

One stipulation of him being released into our custody was that he spend a couple of weekends at the house to see how it would go. During his first sleepover, we were eating dinner, and the table was crammed with food as usual because Cus, as was his way, had forced

Camille to cook too much. I'd helped her count the number of chicken legs we needed, but Cus barged into the kitchen and insisted we needed more. "I eat six," he said, "so if everybody eats six, there won't be enough."

"But nobody eats six chicken legs."

"I eat six," Cus said. "And if everybody else eats six, one person will be left with five."

"No, that's it," Camille said. "Thirty chicken legs is enough. I'm not cooking any more."

At that point, Cus went into the refrigerator and found a frozen kielbasa sausage to add to the feast. "Cook this, just in case," he said. So we had thirty chicken legs and a big kielbasa sausage, plus mashed potatoes, string beans, peas, carrots, baskets of bread, all of it served in these big, heavy dishes that weighed down the table.

Tyson was sitting there with us, his back facing the cabinets, a little overwhelmed by the contrast between this warm, bountiful dinner table and what he was used to. Everything with him was "Yes, sir" and "No, sir," and I knew it was all bullshit. In fact, later on, when he had moved in, I actually said to him one day, "Stop with the 'Yes, sir,' because in a few months you're going to be wanting to say something a whole lot less ingratiating, like 'fuck you,' but you're not going to be allowed to say that. So don't go too far in this direction, either."

He was a kid who was really the opposite of the image that built up around him later on. He grew up in a rough place and got knocked around. He had no father to look up to. He had a mother who for whatever reasons, although I don't want to pass too much judgment on her, wasn't able to raise him the way you'd want to raise a kid. And he suffered. He was made fun of and picked on by other kids, who called him "Stinky Mike" because he didn't bathe. By his own account, he avoided getting beat up by hiding between the walls in abandoned buildings—an image that has always stuck with me.

The point is, this was a kid with no self-confidence, who had this very imposing physical presence, but underneath, though he tried to project power, felt like a fraud. He was a con man and a predator, which was how he ended up in reform school. His real crimes, which very few people know about, were against old ladies. He'd go up to them in the projects when they were carrying bags of groceries and ask them in that sweet lispy voice, "Can I help you, ma'am?" Just like he was saying "Yes, sir" to me and Cus now. When these old ladies would say, "Yes, thank you, young man," he'd carry their bags into the elevator, and after the doors closed, he'd knock their teeth out and take their money. The difference was—as he was about to learn—not everybody was as gullible or weak as those old ladies.

Here at the dinner table, he was nervous. He felt that he was still auditioning because he hadn't yet gotten paroled to us. He was on his best behavior.

When Camille said, "Mike, can you please get me a fork? They're right behind you in the cabinet," he didn't react the way a normal person who was secure with himself would react. He thought that the quicker he got the fork, the more points he'd get. So he jumped up to get it, and one of his legs—and he had big, muscular legs—caught underneath the table and literally picked up that end of the table. The food—all those chicken legs and mashed potatoes and everything—started sliding off.

I had reached the point in my life in Catskill where I was able to step back a little and observe things in an almost detached way. I was noticing more and more how wacky Cus was, how he was this kind of lovable old crank. There was an odd geometry that described his relationships with Camille and me—and now Tyson (everyone else, even Rooney, was in the background). Now in the moment, with the table crashing back to the ground and dishes rattling around and nearly spilling, everyone had a different angle on what was happening. Camille was saying, "Careful, you're going to knock the table over, Mike." Tyson had his hands up, overreacting as if he'd committed a crime, going, "Oh, my God! I'm sorry. I'm sorry." Cus was saying, "Look at that power! Wow! What savage raw power!" And I was thinking, "This is weird. This kid is going to be fucking heavyweight champ." It was just a moment, but it was naked, everyone revealed in their essence, and for that reason it's stayed with me.

It was one of the only times I saw Cus not care about food. If it had been Rooney or Frankie Minicelli, Cus would have said, "Frankie, you jerk, be careful, you're going to knock that kielbasa on the floor." But with Tyson everything was different. He was Cus's way back to the big time, to the promised land.

In the end, that would be all that Cus could see.

It's funny to think about, but if Bobby Stewart had never made that phone call, a lot of things would have been different. At the very least, Cus, Jimmy Jacobs, Bill Cayton—and Tyson himself, probably— would have lost out on millions of dollars. Cus promised Stewart that he would be taken care of when Tyson became champion. But what reward or recognition did Bobby Stewart finally get for his discovery? Well, six years later, when Tyson became the youngest heavyweight champion in history, and Cus was dead, a lot of promises were forgotten. What I heard, and what Peter Heller found out in the course of researching his book Bad Intentions, *was that Jimmy Jacobs had to be badgered by Kevin Rooney before giving Stewart, his former fighter, a check for $10,000. Stewart, who had left the Tryon School by that point and become a chauffeur for a doctor, told Heller that he actually wished "they didn't give me nothing. . . . It belittled me in my own mind. Money can ruin people. I liked the kid. I did it because I liked doing it. I really cared about the kid."*

THE TRUTH
AND A LIE

I HAD A GUY TRAINING WITH ME NAMED LENNY Daniels, a 220-pound heavyweight who had played college ball at Lehigh and had a tryout with the Cleveland Browns. Lenny was in his twenties. He was strong and a good athlete. Even so, I had to be really careful letting him spar with Tyson. I had to stand in the ring with them and stay on top of them. I had to remind Tyson, "Have some respect. Do not hurt this guy."

Then he'd go ahead and hurt him anyway. Even at the age of fourteen or fifteen, Tyson was so strong and so phenomenal that he would hurt these guys no matter what. It was difficult. All my kids meant a lot to me. The thing is, I was training only a few heavyweights that I could put in the ring with Tyson, and he wasn't strong enough emotionally, he wasn't sure enough of himself, so that when I would say, "Go easy here," he would listen to me. After a round, I'd say, "I told you, don't hit them," but he'd still sneak in a hard one, and it was such a vicious, ferocious punch that he would damage these guys.

Later on, we wound up paying guys to come down. I remember one day we got this guy Melvin somebody, an older guy, a heavyweight who'd been around a long time. We paid him twenty-five dollars to spar with Tyson. All I kept thinking was, *You got twenty-five dollars but now*

you've got to go to the emergency room to get stitches, and that's going to cost
you a hell of a lot more than the twenty-five dollars.

Cus went up to Tyson on one occasion as he was getting in the ring
against another guy we'd hired, and said, even though he didn't think I
could hear him, "Make sure this guy earns his twenty-five dollars." So of
course Tyson practically knocked the guy's head off, which was what
Cus wanted. He wanted Tyson to get that confidence. Cus was Franken-
stein creating his monster—whatever the expense to other people. It told
you something for the future, though I wasn't smart enough at the time
to realize what.

The first time I took Tyson down to the Bronx with the rest of the
kids was around 1979. It was funny and at the same time predictable.
When I was setting up the night's bouts, I said, "Okay, Mike, get on the
scale." Everyone was watching as he stepped on the scale. "Okay," I said.
"Two hundred and five pounds. Zero fights. Twelve years old." I jotted
down his info. All of a sudden the other trainers were in an uproar.
"Twelve years old?"

Nelson came over. "Teddy, now you went too far! This beast, this
thing here, twelve years old! Teddy, c'mon."

I said, "Nelson, to make you happy, do you want me to put down
sixteen?"

"Sixteen. You see, I knew you were just fooling."

I said, "No, actually, he is twelve. But I knew you were going to go
crazy. So I guess I gotta put down sixteen just to appease you."

"You're saying he's really twelve?"

"That's right."

It didn't matter. It wasn't as if I'd be able to find a kid near his age to
fight anyway. We wound up matching him with a seventeen-year-old, a
Spanish kid with a big Afro who could really fight.

Tyson was spectacular, a perpetual-motion machine of relentless,
nonstop aggression. The Spanish kid was a hell of a fighter himself. He
had to be to deal with all that power and speed without getting overwhelmed immediately. In the third round, Tyson pinned the kid on the
ropes and hit him with a double left hook, one to the body, and then—
bang!—one to the head. The guy went backward and collapsed on the
bottom strand of the ropes and just sat there. He couldn't fall because of
the way he had landed against the ropes. Tyson hit him another shot.

The force of the punch snapped his head back and the water and sweat from his Afro went flying into the back of the room and smacked against the wall with a loud *thwack*. The room wasn't huge, maybe twenty feet across, but the water and sweat flew into the wall, followed by the mouthpiece, which landed six rows back. You had to see it to believe it.

Don Shanager was there that night. He didn't come too often, but I had all these kids now, and I needed someone to drive a second car. It was more than that, though. Cus wanted him there. He wanted another set of eyes to report back to him. It was a special night, Tyson's coming-out, his first real competition, and Cus wanted to hear about it from every angle.

When the fight was over, Shanager said, "I never saw anything like that. The sweat from that kid's Afro slammed against the wall. You could hear it!"

Before we got back in the cars to drive back to Catskill, I went over to Santos's bar across the street and called Cus from a pay phone. He answered on the first ring, so I knew he was sitting there in his chair, waiting. He didn't even ask about the other kids. It wasn't, "We won six fights and we lost two," the way it was on normal nights. I knew exactly where he wanted to start.

"He knocked him out in the third round. He had a good fight."

We fell into a rhythm, almost a kind of shorthand.

"This guy was a good fighter, then."

"And experienced."

"Twenty fights?"

"Between ten and fifteen."

"Older?"

"Seventeen."

Cus whistled. "And Tyson never stopped moving?"

"Perpetual motion."

"Like a heavyweight Henry Armstrong?"

"Yeah." Cus always said if you could get a heavyweight that could fight like Henry Armstrong, throwing punches nonstop, never giving his opponent a chance to breathe, you'd have a champion. Jimmy Jacobs had these old fight films of Armstrong, and the two of us had watched them with Tyson many times, analyzing Armstrong's style and discussing it. "Imagine," Cus said. "A guy that could move that quick, that could fight with that ferocity and passion. That would be a fighter. Because he'd be exciting, too." Cus never overlooked that. A champion was one thing, but combine that with excitement and you would really have something special.

When I tried to bring up how some of the other kids had done, when I said, "Greg won, too," he said, "The punch, the final punch, what was it, a left hand?"

"Yes."

"After the double left hook?"

"After that."

"When he saw he had him hurt he finished him, huh?"

"Yes."

That still wasn't enough for him. The next day, he couldn't wait to see Shanager. It was kind of like a guy wanting to hear good things about himself. All these years, he was out of the mainstream, out of the limelight, and now it was right there again, that excitement of being at the beginning of something big.

It actually kind of got to me, watching Cus with Shanager. You know how when you're a kid and you do something and you want to hear the person tell you everything good about it? Like if your parents came to your high school football game. "Did you see my touchdown run? The way I cut around that guy?" You had done it, they weren't telling you anything you didn't know, but you wanted to hear them describe it anyway. "Yeah, I saw the way you faked him out of his shoes. That was beautiful. . . . And the way you leaped over that guy at the end. . . ."

It was just human nature. "The mouthpiece landed six rows back?" "The sweat hit and you thought it was somebody slamming their hand on the wall?"

There was a purity to it, and there aren't many things in life that are pure once you get beyond childhood. So I was happy for Cus. At that point the joy and excitement over Tyson was untainted. It hadn't gone to where it was going to go. I was happy that I was training his guy and contributing. It felt good to be a part of it. That's why I would feel so betrayed later. I thought Cus appreciated my being a part of that good feeling, and that we were partners.

As far as Tyson, he understood that he had something, a quality and a talent, that made him special. He knew he was going somewhere. At the same time, he was scared, because he felt like maybe his boxing talent was all he had, and what if it wasn't enough?

Our relationship to that point was based on need more than any kind of real feeling. I was his trainer. I was important to him, maybe more important than anyone else, because Cus was too old and couldn't do what I was doing. He couldn't be in the gym every day, or go to the Bronx. I was the guy Tyson needed to prop him up when he was otherwise alone and scared. But he also had that street understanding of who had the power—so there was no real loyalty possible. Later on, he would realize that *he* was the one with the power. When he was older and more experienced, with a certain level of confidence, he would start playing both ends against the middle. But in the beginning, he was softer and weaker, and he needed me.

One of the toughest problems when you have a kid like Tyson, who can destroy other kids in the ring, is finding people to fight him. You have to get him that experience, but word gets around and nobody wants to put their kid in against him. Cus and I started paying Nelson fifty bucks, which he in turn used to get other trainers at the Bronx club to put their fighters in against Tyson. Fifty bucks—which was actually a lot of money for us—to sacrifice a kid. Here were these trainers, who otherwise wouldn't put their kid in with Tyson, and now, for fifty bucks (or some portion of that amount), they would. It was screwed up, because the kid wasn't getting the money, the trainers were, but that was the reality. We had to get fights.

We probably got twenty fights that way, which, under the circumstances, once Tyson was out of the bag, was a lot. Eventually, though, there came a night when we couldn't get anybody. To sway this one trainer who was on the fence, I said, "Make it an exhibition." I knew that an exhibition automatically put it on a different level, made it more palatable, removed some of the fear. The trainer said, "Okay. We'll put big gloves on, sixteen-ounce gloves instead of the ten-ounce, and we'll use headgear."

For me, all that mattered was that Tyson get more experience, that he get in the ring and deal with his imagination and the fear of fighting someone. As far as I was concerned, "exhibition" was just a word; other than the gloves being different, the intent was going to be the same.

Then Tyson went out there, big gloves, headgear and all, and knocked this Spanish kid out cold. It almost caused a big problem. The trainer and some other guys rushed the ring and they were angry. "Hey, he wasn't supposed to hit him!" Meanwhile, their fighter was still stretched out. Another guy vaulted into the ring and started moving toward Tyson. I jumped between them. "Where are you going?"

"This was supposed to be an exhibition."

Tyson was standing right behind me. I didn't want him to get involved, but he spoke up anyway.

"I didn't do nothing to him that he wasn't trying to do to me."

It was true. Everyone knew it was true, and it sort of stopped them. I said, "Listen, back down." And they did. They backed down.

Not too long after that there was another fight, a good fight, in which Tyson's opponent got in trouble and was hung up on the ropes much the way the kid with the Afro had gotten stuck on the ropes in that first fight. The referee tried to intervene but didn't get there in time, and *pow*, Tyson hit the kid with another shot and knocked him out.

Again, people were upset. A number of them stormed the ring and started going after Tyson. I jumped in and screamed, "I'm telling you right now, you go near him, we got a problem."

That didn't stop them. Three of them were going after Tyson, trying to get around me. I pushed one of them, and he fell down. It started to turn into a melee. It was bad. I pushed this guy because I knew what type of guys they were, and I knew that once a few of them showed some courage and got into it, I wouldn't have any control, it would get completely out of hand.

Luckily, Nelson did some quick thinking. I had grabbed one of the other guys by the shirt collar and he had me by the shirt, too. We had our fists cocked and were about to start throwing punches, and Nelson jumped in the ring and grabbed the microphone. He said, "This fight is a draw. It's a draw!"

It was the perfect move. In the streets everything is instinct and flashes of brilliance like that. Calling the fight a draw calmed everyone down. A draw meant that no money would change hands, and that lowered the temperature considerably. The guy I was holding let go of my shirt; I let go of his. Tyson and I knew who had won the fight, which was all that mattered to us. Tyson got another win, got some more confidence, and the crowd was placated.

Not long after that fight, we took Tyson out of town, up to Scranton, Pennsylvania, to fight the first white guy he fought. It turned out to be an interesting night. When you're developing a young fighter (a couple of years had gone by and Tyson was fourteen or fifteen at this point), no matter how good or talented he is, the one part of him that requires the most work, the trickiest and ultimately the most important factor in determining his future, is his psyche and his will. Whatever else he's got going for him, his mind and his will are the real ingredients of his ultimate success or failure.

Against this white kid in Scranton, I knew immediately we were in for a test. The kid was big, not very skilled, but tough. Tyson jumped all over him in the first round, coming out strong as he always did, and knocking the kid down a couple of times. Instead of staying down, though, the kid kept getting up. Tyson had never had that happen to him before; when he hit 'em they usually stayed hit. This was new. He got discouraged and started feeling tired. I could see it happening.

Tyson came back to the corner at the end of the first round and flopped down on his stool like it was the last round of a brutal fight. He had dropped the guy two times already. The guy was half out of it, almost drunk from punches, and Tyson had barely been touched. But he was exhausted. "I think my hand is broke," he said.

I knew right then that there was nothing wrong with his hand, but I had to make sure. I grabbed his glove—he was looking into space—and I squeezed real hard. He didn't react.

I said, "There's nothing broken. The only thing broken is you." I got up in his face. "You want to be a fighter? Stop the bullshit! The only thing this guy's doing is being dumb enough to get back up. Every time you hit him, you hurt him."

Tyson was looking at me. I could see a flicker of anger, which was good. "You're going to let it get to you because he keeps getting back up?" I said. I pushed him out of the corner as the bell sounded.

Tyson dropped the guy two more times in the next three minutes, but the guy kept getting up. By the end of the round, Tyson barely made it back to the corner. "I can't go on," he said.

"You can't go on?" I said. "I thought you wanted to be a fighter. I thought you had this dream of being heavyweight champion. Let me tell you something, *this* is your heavyweight title fight."

It's amazing when you think about it. You see all these big fights on HBO, but you never see these backwater bouts when a guy is on his way up, and there are these crossroads moments where if he hadn't overcome something, he'd have never made it to HBO. I said, "You bullshit artist. You've been with us all this time, saying you want to be champ, and everything's fine when you're knocking guys out. But now, for the first time, a guy doesn't want to be knocked out, a guy has the balls to get up, and you want to quit? You know what I'd be doing if I was in that other guy's corner? I'd be stopping the fight. That's how beat up this guy is, and you want to quit! Now get up, goddamn it!" I picked him up off his stool and stood him up.

He staggered out into the ring, and the two of them grabbed each other. He hit the guy again, the guy hit him. To Tyson it must have been like Sugar Ray Robinson versus Jake LaMotta, but in reality it was two big palookas. They were pawing at each other, hugging and slow-dancing, and with about twenty seconds left in the round, the guy got Tyson into the corner. I could see in Tyson's eyes what was about to happen. He was going to quit. He was going to go down. If I didn't do anything, he was going down.

I took a risk. If you go up on the ring apron, they can disqualify your fighter. I knew that. I also knew that we had amateur refs, and it was a crazy crowd, so I took a chance. I got up there. They were in the corner right by me, and I screamed, practically in Tyson's ear, "Don't you do it. Don't you fucking do it!" He hung on those last few seconds. Then the bell rang.

When we were out in the corridor afterward, on our way to the locker room, he leaned close to me and said, "Thanks." That was it. Nothing else really needed to be said.

"Listen," I said, "I'm not going to make a big thing about this. I'm only going to talk about it once. You almost did it. You almost let it happen. But you didn't. You have to learn. That's part of being a fighter. The important thing is that you didn't let it happen. If you had, it would have ruined everything. Instead of us standing here, you humbly telling me 'thank you,' you'd be crying somewhere, and you'd never be a fighter. You would have looked back and said, 'Oh, my God, I didn't have to do that.' But you would have done it. It would have been done. So you need to learn from this experience, and make sure that you never let yourself get that close to that place again."

It was a watershed moment for him, a real defining moment, because if he had quit then he might never have become Mike Tyson.

Cus was at the fight that night. It was the first time he'd seen Tyson. Obviously, he was very disappointed. He saw the power, he saw that Tyson could knock down this bigger, more mature guy who was stubborn as a boulder. But he also recognized that Tyson was still weak, that he wasn't strong mentally, and that we would have to help him get stronger.

At a certain point, if he's going to get to the top of the boxing profession, a fighter has to learn the difference between the truth and a lie. The lie is thinking that submission is an acceptable option. The truth is that if you give up, afterward you'll realize that any of those punches that you thought you couldn't deal with, or those rough moments you didn't think you could make it through, were just *moments.* Enduring them is not nearly as tough as having to deal with the next day and the next month and the next year, knowing that you quit, that you failed, that you submitted. It's a trainer's job to make a fighter understand that difference, that the parts of a fight that are urgent last only seconds; seconds during which you have to stave off the convenient excuse—"I'm too tired" or "I hurt too much" or "I can't do this" or even simply "I'm not going to deal with this." Sometimes it just comes down to not floating—just being there and understanding that if you give in, you'll hurt more tomorrow. Maybe there is no more important lesson to learn from boxing than that.

COMPLETE AND INCOMPLETE

O NE NIGHT, AFTER A SESSION AT THE GYM, I TOOK A bunch of the kids to the Jamesway Shopping Center in Catskill. It was one of those strip malls with a dry cleaner, a video rental place, and a pizzeria. I often took the kids out and did things away from boxing. We'd go to movies, have picnics, play touch football, or just hang out and talk. As I've said, I was more than just a trainer for these kids; most of them came from families where the father was dead or absent, and so for many of them I was filling that void.

When we walked into the pizzeria, I made the boys sit down in a couple of booths that were side-by-side while I went up to the counter to order. The girl behind the counter was in her early twenties and pretty. I had seen her around town a couple of times but we had never talked. She had dark hair, playful brown eyes, and a nice figure.

"So these all your kids?" she asked.

"Yeah, they're all mine," I said.

"Impressive," she said. There was a spark there right away. It wasn't like I knew I was going to marry her, but I was definitely interested.

She had sort of a provocative flirtatiousness. She was very confident, and I liked that. Even though she was working behind the counter,

I could tell she wasn't going to let anyone push her around or take an attitude with her.

I ordered a couple of pies, because I didn't have money for any more, and went back and sat down with the boys. A while later, she came over with a tray full of Cokes.

"I hope you boys are taking good care of your father," she said.

"He ain't our father," Mane Moore said, giggling.

She looked at me with a little smile. "He isn't? He told me he was."

"Naw!"

When the pizzas came out of the oven ten minutes later, I went up to the counter to get them. Hot steam was rising off the cheese. She saw me looking a little perplexed.

"What's the problem?"

"I only ordered two pizzas."

"Oh yeah? I thought you ordered three. I'll tell you what, why don't you take the extra one and I won't charge you for it."

"You don't have to do that."

"Yeah, I know. But those boys look pretty hungry."

"You sure?"

She nodded.

"I'm Teddy."

"Elaine."

She helped me carry the pizza back to the table.

"Thanks . . . Elaine."

"My pleasure." She went back to the counter.

I sat down and the boys were all staring at me, grinning.

"What?"

"You like her, don't you?"

"What are ya talking about?"

They all started laughing and giggling. I looked around the table, leveling them with a stern gaze.

"Shut up and eat your pizza, all of ya."

A few days later, I went back to the pizzeria, without the kids this time. Elaine was behind the counter again.

"Hi. Elaine, right?"

"Right."

"Listen, I wanted to ask you something. . . ."

"Yeah?" She looked amused.

"I been thinking of opening a restaurant. . . ."

"You want to open a restaurant?"

"Well, like a sports bar."

"A sports bar."

"Well, like a sports bar and restaurant."

She stared at me.

"I thought maybe you could give me some advice."

"You want advice from me."

"Yeah, you know, like how to get started."

"Maybe you should be more direct."

"What do you mean?"

"When you want to ask a girl out."

"Oh." It threw me a little that I was so transparent. "You think that's what I'm doing?"

"Actually, I thought you'd come back here sooner," she said.

I laughed. She was so cocky that there was nothing else to do. Anyway, that was how it began. I followed her advice and asked her out. One night, early on, I took her to an amateur fight show near Catskill that Tyson and the other kids were fighting in. I had never taken any other girl I'd dated to a fight—I was like my father in that way and considered it a little unprofessional—but I guess subconsciously I wanted her to know what I did. I wanted to impress her.

While she sat in the audience, I took care of the kids. I wrapped their hands and did my thing. Every once in a while I'd look over at her in the crowd. She didn't seem to mind being by herself. She understood that I was working. I could tell that she was enjoying herself, watching the fights, watching me with the kids.

I had dated a fair number of girls before her. There had been girls who liked me. One girl I even took back to Staten Island, during the holidays, to meet my mother. She was a gorgeous blonde girl but a little naive; she'd never really been outside of Catskill. I remember we took a ferry boat over to Manhattan to go Christmas shopping in the city, and there was a shoeshine guy on the boat, walking around, saying, "Shine, shine." Well, this girl started looking around, on the floor, under the benches. I said, "What are you doing?," and she said, "I'm looking for that man's dog, Shine." You can imagine what my mother thought when she heard that. She went, "Shine, huh?"

With Elaine it was different. She was quick. She kept me on my toes. Her instincts about people and situations were sharp. The first time I took her to the gym could have been awkward. There was this girl fighter I'd been training, Nadia, who liked me a bit. What had happened was that she had come to me because she was going to take the state police test, and in those days the trooper test required sparring for one round whether you were a man or a woman. Nadia asked me if I would train her and also help her lose weight at the same time—she was overweight. In a matter of months, she lost fifty pounds. I guess between that and watching me work with the kids, she started to like me a little.

It was flattering, but I didn't feel the same way about her; I did my best to keep things professional. At the same time I didn't want to hurt her feelings—I had spent a lot of time trying to build her up. One day, I got to the gym—this was after I'd started seeing Elaine—and one of my kids, Kevin Young, was waiting downstairs. He said, "I wanted to get you before you go in the gym. Nadia got here early today and she said that enough is enough. If the mountain don't come to Mohammad, Mohammad is gonna come to the mountain. She's gonna ask you out on a date tonight."

I went up to the gym. I had a couple of boxes of new gloves with me, and I put them down and started opening them up. Nadia made a beeline for me. "Hey, Boss," she said. She always called me Boss.

"Hey, Nadia."

"How you doin'?"

"Okay." I knew what was coming. To spare her feelings as much as possible, because I could see she was geared up to ask me out, I said, "Nadia, I may need you to help me out tonight. I have to get finished early. I have to go somewhere. . . ."

"Oh . . . ," she said, and I could see her sag a little. "Sure. . . ." She'd been ready to ask me out afterward and now she couldn't. If she had caught me off guard and asked me, it might have been awkward. So it was due to my kids that it didn't happen that way. They were good kids and they thought about stuff like that and looked out for people's feelings.

The next week, or the week after that, I brought Elaine to the gym. Everyone was doing their thing, getting ready for their workouts. This was before Velcro wraps, and all my fighters learned to tie their own wraps using their teeth. Elaine saw Nadia tying her hand wraps with her teeth, and she didn't know that it was actually a point of pride for Nadia. She just saw this woman struggling to tie these wraps with her teeth, and she went, "Oh, here, lemme help you," and Nadia growled at her. She actually went, "Grrrr!"

A lot of women would have been thrown, but Elaine didn't get flustered. She handled it well. Instinctively, she understood what was going on, but she didn't react the way another woman might have. She wasn't jealous or insecure. She didn't put her arm around me, and throw it in Nadia's face. She had compassion and handled herself with dignity. It was one more thing I admired about her.

Things got serious with us pretty quickly. I brought her to the house to meet Camille and Cus. She brought me home to meet her family. Her parents were Albanians who had escaped to Italy from Pristine, Yugoslavia, right after Elaine was born. When she was six, her mother and father had come to America, living first in the Bronx, then later on moving to Catskill, where they had relatives. Like most Albanians, they were a very tight-knit clan, patriarchal, observant of the old-world customs and traditions. Arranged marriages were still the norm in their culture, and after a girl got married, she would move into her husband's family's house and become basically a slave. Elaine was headstrong and independent, a bit of a rebel. I was the first man she had ever brought home to meet her parents, and I wasn't Albanian. It might have been a problem, except her father adored her and made allowances.

So things kept moving forward. It was different. She was the first girl to be allowed to eat at the house with Cus and Camille and the kids and me. I had certain privileges and standing by then, and it was clear that things with me and Elaine were serious.

It was interesting, though. Cus tried to scare her off. He was threatened. She put demands on my time, and he was worried that I would lose my focus, or spend less time at the gym. He said to Elaine, "He's got a bad temper, you know. There's a lot of things you don't know about him. He's a dangerous guy." He could have blown things—I mean, he couldn't have, really, but he thought he could have, that was his intent.

I actually think it had the opposite effect. I think Elaine saw through him in a way, and understood that if somebody was going to all that effort to scare her off, there must be something worth coveting there. Anyway, it didn't work. She didn't stop seeing me.

A few months after we began dating, my career as a professional trainer got a boost. Cus lined up a fight for Kevin Rooney with Alexis Arguello, the lightweight champion of the world, who was looking to move up to the junior welterweight division. Rooney was a welterweight, so he'd need to bring his weight down from 147 to 140. But it was an opportunity to put himself on the map. Me, too.

As I started to study tape of Arguello's fights, I began to believe that even though we were a big underdog, we could beat him. In his bout against Villemar Fernandez, I saw that a skilled boxer could give Arguello trouble. Arguello had many strengths as a fighter. He had power in both hands, and his punches were extremely accurate. But he also had weaknesses. He stood up very straight; he needed to be set to punch; and he had trouble with movement. I formulated a plan to keep him off balance that I thought could work, although it would take tremendous execution on Rooney's part. My belief that we could pull it off was so strong that it had an effect on Rooney. Of course, most of Rooney's confidence was inspired by what Cus, the *real* master, thought. When Cus thought he could win, that really had a big impact on Rooney, and on me, too.

Early on in training, Cus came to the gym to watch. When he saw what Rooney and I were working on, he said, "That's why you're the Young Master. You have a workable plan to win this fight." It made me feel good to hear him say that. Really the only thing that worried me was the weight. Rooney had never fought below 145 pounds. The positive, as Cus kept reminding me, was that Arguello was going to be fighting at a higher weight than he'd ever fought at before. So each side had something to overcome.

Training went well. If anything, Rooney came down in weight too easily. When I asked him about it, he attributed it to an improved diet. Then during a sparring session one morning, with the fight only a week away, it became obvious something was wrong with him. He was slow and weak. His face was drained of color. I stopped the workout, put cool wet towels on him, and made him drink water. It was hot in the gym, so I thought maybe that was the reason. I started asking him questions, pushing him to tell me anything he'd been doing that might have been the cause. At first he was reluctant to say anything, but then he told me that every night after training he had been going to Brian Hamill's place in Rhinebeck, New York, and sitting in Hamill's sauna. That's how he'd dropped the weight so easily.

I immediately called my father. He told me to bring Rooney to see him. We drove in to Staten Island that night. My father examined Rooney, gave him this stuff called Ensure that replaced all the nutrients and electrolytes he had lost, and also gave him a shot of B_{12}. Then he took me aside and said, "He needs to rest. His body needs to recover. It'll take time. Can you postpone the fight?"

"It's not that simple."

"You shouldn't let him fight, Teddy. You're his trainer, and it's your responsibility. You shouldn't let him fight."

We drove back to Catskill. I explained the situation to Cus. "We have to postpone the fight," I said.

"Impossible."

"Then we need to pull him out."

Cus went crazy. "We're not pulling out! Don't you dare even think about it."

We got into a big argument. I knew Rooney wasn't himself. This was a fight where there was no margin for error. We'd have to fight a perfect fight to win. Instead, we were going in knowing ahead of time that something was wrong. I had always deferred to Cus on big decisions. He was like the pope. More and more, though, I was beginning to find myself uncomfortable with some of the choices he was making.

In the end, he found a way to appease me. He was a brilliant manipulator. He turned the situation around so I could feel as if I were the one making the decision. He said, "Look, we'll let him spar in a couple of days. If you don't think he's right, then he won't fight." Rooney got back in the ring after resting a couple of days, and he definitely looked better. Not a hundred percent, but better. Still, I saw he wasn't strong. "If he's not strong, it'll be like letting him walk into the propeller of a plane," I said.

"He doesn't need to be strong," Cus countered. "That's not how this fight will be won. You've given him a plan that doesn't require strength."

That was true to a point, and it enabled me to rationalize. Still, I shouldn't have given in. Three days later, in Atlantic City, Arguello knocked out Rooney in two rounds. In the training room afterward, I watched my father examine Rooney. It felt like I had beaten him up myself. I knew I could have done something more. I'm not going to tell you that Rooney would have won if he'd been physically fit, but he would have done a lot better.

It was unfortunate that a loss like that was also the occasion of my first real payday as a trainer. My father was even more surprised than I was when I got the check for four thousand dollars. He never thought I'd make a dime. He'd been paying for me to stay at Cus's all these years, but I'm not sure he realized I was actually building a career for myself. From his point of view, the main compensation was that I was staying out of trouble. The money made him so happy that he said, "Give me the four thousand and I'll put it in the stock market and match it for you."

After I gave him the four thousand, he immediately gave me back two thousand so Elaine and I could go spend a few days in his condo in Florida. It was the first vacation I'd had in years, but I'll never forget it. Elaine had been feeling strange for a couple of days. Her clothes were tight on her and she was light-headed. She didn't tell me, but she went out and got one of those home pregnancy tests. The day she told me the results had been positive, we'd just finished breakfast. I was sitting at the table, reading the newspaper.

She said, "Teddy, I think I'm pregnant."

I looked up, not sure I had heard her right.

"I don't expect you to do anything about it," she said. "That's not why I'm telling you."

"No, no. I'm just—what do you want to do?" I knew that was a stupid thing to say, but I was still processing the whole concept, trying to take it in.

"Look, Teddy, whether you stand by me or not, I'm going to have this baby. I—"

"No, Elaine, that's not what I'm saying. I'm glad you feel that way," I said. "That's what I wanted to hear you say. I mean, that baby is a part of us and . . . and I want you to marry me. Elaine, will you marry me?"

Now she was the one who looked shocked. "Are you just asking me because of the baby?"

"You mean, would I have asked you today? Probably not today—if I had to be completely honest about it. On the other hand, I was going to ask you at some point." I looked in her eyes. "Don't you know that?"

She laughed and said, "Are you sure, Teddy?"

"More than sure."

I was, too. It's not hard making a decision to do a thing you want to do. Sometimes fate just lends a helping hand and gets you a little faster to a place you were going all along.

When I think back now about all the things that were happening in this period, it amazes me. I was already responsible to Rooney and Tyson and all the kids. Now I was getting married and had a child on the way.

Apparently, that wasn't enough. I needed more on my plate. When we returned from Florida, I heard about a nineteen-year-old Catskill kid named Jeff Amen who had driven his car off a cliff into a ravine one night and had been paralyzed from the waist down.

In a small town like Catskill, news of something like that spreads fast and hits people hard. I didn't know Jeff, but his brother J. B. had trained in the gym, and the story really affected me. Apart from the personal connection to his brother, I had all those years of watching my father take care of people. I decided to go visit him.

The morning I walked into Jeff's room at the Albany Medical Center, I found him propped up in a hospital bed, wearing a halo. I had never seen a halo before and hadn't realized that the screws actually go into the person's skull. I introduced myself. Jeff and I had never met, but he knew who I was. He had curly brown hair, a round face, and glasses, and he talked in a voice so soft I could barely hear him. From the waist down, he couldn't move.

"How you feeling? You doing okay?"

"I guess, considering I'll never walk again."

"You don't know that."

He looked at me. "The doctors don't think I will."

A nurse was passing by, and I asked her if I could take him outside. She said yes and helped me get him into a wheelchair and wrap him up in blankets.

I wheeled him out and the two of us talked a bit more as we went.

"Doctors aren't always right," I said.

"I guess sometimes they're not," he said.

I wheeled him along the sidewalk outside the main entrance. The air was freezing, but his body's thermostat had been affected by his injury, and he couldn't feel cold or heat. If you held a match to his skin, he wouldn't know the difference. I realized I couldn't keep him outside too long.

"Other people have overcome very tough things when most people thought they couldn't. You're a lot stronger than you might realize. You don't know what you're capable of if you put your mind to it."

He looked at me and I realized that his reticence was mostly self-protective. He was a small-town kid and it took him a while to get comfortable with people.

"What makes you think I'm strong?" he said.

"I can see it in your eyes. The fact that you survived to be here."

After that first visit, I started going up there regularly to visit him. Of all the people he saw, his physical therapist, the doctors and nurses, I was the only one who talked to him consistently about the idea of his walking again. He liked hearing it, but he was reluctant to tell the hospital staff that I was saying it. He thought maybe if they knew, they would say I was being irresponsible. They were all telling him that at best maybe he'd be able to use his hands and arms and be able to dress himself using sticks with hooks to grab loops on his pants.

I went there one day and they were doing his physical therapy. With a paraplegic they can't really do much, because the patient's paralyzed, so the therapist just moves his limbs, putting his arms and legs through a range of motion, to keep them from getting atrophied. After physical therapy, his social worker came by to check up on Jeff and see how his spirits were. She was a sweet, red-haired woman, and I got friendly with her. She told me stuff about spinal injuries, drew up a diagram, and showed me the location of the C4 vertebra that Jeff had injured. I found out that there was a difference between a complete severing of the spinal cord and an incomplete. Jeff's was incomplete.

I called my father and got him to explain the difference. He said, "Well, with an incomplete, there's hope. That doesn't mean that it's not as damaging as a complete. It might be, but if it's not completely severed, there's a little hope." He started explaining it to me, and then I said, "So it's like a dam in the middle of a river?" and he said, "Exactly. That's very good. It's like a dam in a river, and you don't know how long it's going to be there. It might be there forever, or it might not be. That's a very good analogy."

That was all I needed to hear. I got off the phone feeling like I had gone through twelve years of medical school and understood everything there was to understand about spinal injuries. *It's not severed. It's a dam. There's hope!*

I went to visit Jeff the next day. The physical therapist was exercising him, what she called "ranging" him. She was young and sure of herself. She picked up one of his legs, talking to him as she did, then she dropped it, boom, the leg flopping back down on the mat. It bothered me, watching that. I didn't think it was hurting him, but still it bothered me. It was like watching a butcher throw a side of beef onto a cutting block.

I said, "Jeff, I know you can't exercise. I know you can't move your legs, but how about if you tried to keep them from falling?"

The physical therapist said, "What do you mean?"

I looked at Jeff. He was lying on his stomach, but I could see him smiling. He was getting a kick out of me. "How about I hold up your leg and you don't let it drop. I know you can't actually stop it, but by trying to stop it, maybe you'll feel something."

"He can't feel anything," the therapist said. "That would mean that there would be muscular connections." This is what she'd learned in school and she was very certain of it.

I didn't know enough to argue with her. I just knew I thought what I was saying made sense to me. I knew about the dam. She was saying what she was saying, and I was thinking to myself, *It's a dam. Dam, dam, dam.*

So I had Jeff's leg in my hands, and she was talking to me, and I was holding his leg up, with my hand on his hamstring, and suddenly I thought I felt a little something. A tiny contraction. I said, "I think I felt something."

She said, "You didn't feel anything."

I said, "I don't know. I thought I did. Maybe not."

The physical therapist was disgusted with me. You could see it. "I have to leave for the day," she said. "But I don't think this is productive, talking this way. I think you should stick to things you know."

After she left, I went right back to telling Jeff about the dam. The complete and the incomplete. I said, "It's like you've got a stream and there are these beavers and—" He was looking at me like I was nuts, but he was being entertained. Here was this kid who had to lie there twenty-four hours a day getting bedsores, and this was the best shit he'd heard in a long time. I said, "It's like you've got this stream that's jammed up, and you're just waiting, because there's no water, there's nothing running, so there's no sense in doing anything. But what if the exercise was just to *think* about moving your feet."

"What do you mean?" he said.

I had learned this from my father. I said, "You know, electric stimuli gets sent from your brain to your toe, to move your toe. . . ."

"Yes?"

"You've got veins that carry blood, and you've got these other things that carry this electric stimuli." I really thought I was Ben Casey. I did. I said, "You've stopped sending those signals because you figure there's no reason to. Because Nurse Shithead tells you that you can't do it. And the doctors tell you you're never gonna do it. So you're not sending the things you're supposed to be sending. But how about if your exercise was just to send the impulse and keep hitting that mud every day, keep hitting the dam, and by sending these impulses, hitting the mud, hitting the mud, all of a sudden it gets through? See, because if you don't send impulses it won't ever get through and you might just be lying here your whole life."

This was two days before I was supposed to leave with Tyson for the National Junior Olympics in Colorado. Suddenly I had an inspiration. "Listen, Jeff," I said, "while I'm gone, you've got to try and make your toes move every day. Tell yourself, 'I'm making my toes move,' keep sending those signals."

"I'll try," he said.

"Don't give me that 'try' bullshit. Just do it. I'll make you a deal. You keep sending messages to your toes, I'll make sure Tyson wins all his fights and defends his title." This was the second year I was taking Tyson to Denver. He'd won the national amateur title the year earlier.

"That's not nearly as hard as what you're asking me to do," Jeff said. "He won every fight last time."

"All right, what if he wins every fight by knockout this time?"

"He won every fight last year by knockout."

"In the first round?"

"You're telling me he's gonna knock everyone out in the first round?"

"Are you gonna send those messages to your toes?"

So we went out there, and Tyson knocked out every guy he faced in the first round. I came back a week later, and I know this sounds too much like the movies, but I came back and Jeff was moving two toes. This guy who was supposed to be a paraplegic was moving two toes. None of the doctors could believe it.

Over the next few months, he continued to progress. Even with all the other stuff that was going on, my wedding included, I kept visiting him and pushing him. Elaine had to stay on me about taking care of wedding stuff. She did a lot of the organizing, but I had plenty of responsibility, too. In most cultures, the bride's father pays for everything; not so with the Albanians. They didn't have that tradition. All their traditions, and they couldn't have that one. I wound up cashing in some of my stocks to pay for things. I got five grand, which was basically seed money, and we found this resort ten miles outside of Catskill. It was beautiful. Elaine wound up with everything she wanted. They put up a tent, we had ice sculptures, swans, dolphins, a glass pond full of fresh shrimp. She wore a designer gown.

The people in that area had never seen anything like it around there. It was like a mob wedding. Wiseguys showed up in limos. Dennis and Brian Hamill came. Jose Torres was there. All my kids from the gym showed up. The only one who didn't make it was Tyson. His mother had died, and her funeral was the day of the wedding. So the day before, I drove him to the train station. He was wearing a new warm-up suit I'd bought him with my last fifty bucks.

We wound up having about 400 people at the wedding. It was the biggest thing they'd ever had in that area. Today, a wedding like that would cost two hundred grand. In the middle of it, I started opening some of the gift envelopes so I could pay for everything, and the guy who ran the resort said, "Don't do that. Pay me after your honeymoon."

Lots of people gave toasts, including my brother Terryl, who was my best man. But the big moment came when Jeff Amen pushed forward in his wheelchair toward the microphone. He said he had a wedding present for me and Elaine, and then he slowly got up out of the wheelchair, stood up, and walked ten steps across the dance floor before collapsing in my arms. It was incredible, it really was. There wasn't a dry eye in the place after he did that.

* * *

ELAINE AND I WENT TO SAN FRANCISCO ON OUR HONEY-
moon. We were supposed to be there nine days, but I cut it short after
three days and went back to work the corner for Tyson and the kids in
an amateur show. I regret that now, when I think about it, because the
show got canceled, but also because of the way things developed later. At
the time I thought I needed to be there. I thought my responsibility to
Tyson and Cus and the rest of the kids was more important than my
honeymoon. To Elaine's credit, she didn't complain. It was like something my father would have done, cutting short the honeymoon, just like
he never went on vacation with us, or the way he got up from dinner par-
ties in the middle because he had to be at the hospital. But Elaine was
incredibly understanding. She knew who she was marrying going in,
and for better or worse, she signed on anyway. Luckily for me.

*Elmore Leonard always talks in his novels about how tough the Alba-
nians are. Let me tell you, he knows what he's talking about. Elaine is
probably one of the toughest women I've ever known, in addition to
being one of the most loyal. This one time, after we'd left Catskill and
were back living in Staten Island, she was driving, and we were down
in the area between Stapleton and Park Hill, near the projects, when
she suddenly turned into a gas station.*

*This was the worst part of Staten Island, and we were just asking
for trouble stopping there. There was no reason to, we still had a quarter of a tank left. "Elaine, why are you going in here?" I asked.*

"Why not?" she said.

*We weren't quite arguing; I was just trying to make a point, but she
ignored me and pulled in anyway. Just as she did, this car cut her off.
I saw that there were two big guys in it. Elaine angled ahead and
barely missed clipping them. She stopped the car and got out. The
driver of the other car stuck his head out the window. "Hey, bitch.
Move your ride." Now I was going to myself, "This is why I told you
not to come in here." Elaine was outside the car, and she wasn't helping
the situation much. "Is that the way your mother taught you to talk?"
she said. That was it. The two guys got out, and there was no stopping*

things now. The guy on the passenger side said, "Your bitch has to do your talking for you?" Well, that was all I had to hear. I was out of the car, on a beeline for them. I cracked the driver, and he went down.

Then I half slid, half vaulted over the hood of the car and started fighting with the other guy. We got ahold of each other, and I drove him into the pumps, forcing him between them because I was afraid he had a knife, and I didn't want him to be able to reach for it. This wasn't far from the place I got my face cut. So I was thinking about that, I was worried about being stabbed, and I was also worrying about how long the other guy was going to be on the ground. I knew I had to take care of the passenger quickly. I was banging him and hitting him shots. And then I felt someone over my shoulder. A punch grazed me and hit the other guy. Suddenly, I heard this voice saying, "Get out of the way." It was Elaine. She reached past me and took hold of the guy's Afro, pulling his hair out. He was screaming. By now, a whole crowd from the projects had gathered round. Someone yelled, "You got a bad woman there!"

I literally had to pull Elaine off this guy. She came away with a handful of his hair. It could have been ugly with the crowd there, but they were actually on our side. I mean, they weren't doing anything, but they were saying shit, rooting us on. Anyway, we got back in the car, and were about to pull away, and the guy whose hair Elaine had pulled out said, "I'm gonna get a gun and I'm gonna come after you and kill you."

Elaine opened the car door, got out, and said, "Go get the gun now. We'll wait. Go get the gun now, so I can stick it up your ass and blow out your brains."

The crowd that was watching went crazy when she said this. The guy was all puffed up, angry and embarrassed, and someone yelled, "Ain't you learned your lesson yet, fool?"

We finally left, and I said to Elaine, "What the hell were you doing? I told you not to go in there." But she totally ignored me. She was looking at her nails and going "Ooh." Very ladylike. "Ooh, that's disgusting." And she started pulling some of the guy's hair out from where it had gotten stuck under her nails. I'm telling you, my wife is one of the toughest people I've ever met. She really is.

WORDS AND
ACTIONS

ELAINE AND I TOOK A GROUND-FLOOR APARTMENT IN a two-family house outside of Catskill; the rent wasn't high, but it was more than I had been paying at Camille and Cus's. Money was obviously more of a concern with a baby on the way. The strange thing was that although I knew Tyson had an enormous future—I'd been training him for almost four years, and understood better than anyone what we had—how that would translate financially for me was still a hard thing to grasp. Cus told me I was training a future champion, and I trusted him. But I was naive when it came to money. I believed that if I moved through life with purpose, commitment, and direction, money would take care of itself.

A lot of people have talked and written about Cus's disregard for money, and how he was interested only in reclaiming young lives. He certainly helped many troubled kids, myself included. But a couple of things happened that made me begin to look at Cus in a different light. Ironically, it's Cus's own words—"You never know about people until they're tested"—that come to mind when I think about these things.

Cus had a number of people in local government whom he relied upon for favors. One friend had managed to help procure a twenty-five-thousand-dollar government grant for Cus through a political connection he had in Washington. The proposal for the grant stated that part of the funds were needed to pay one full-time trainer for the gym—namely, me.

Even though I never saw a dime of the twenty-five thousand dollars, at the end of the year Don Shanager asked me if I could sign the proper tax papers, to show that I had received a salary. Shanager assured me that I wouldn't be liable for any taxes, and I wound up signing the thing, though it made me uncomfortable.

What Cus actually did with the money, I can't say. He might have spent a couple of thousand on equipment for the gym, but the rest is anybody's guess. What I heard was that he used the money to reward the people in Catskill who were helping him keep quiet Tyson's run-ins with the authorities; in other words, it was hush money. I also know that one night Camille opened Cus's door unannounced (I've already mentioned how paranoid he was about anyone going into his room) and found Cus in there with one of his local cronies and ten thousand dollars spread out on the bed. He went crazy, scooping up the money frantically while screaming at her for entering his lair.

The other thing that occurred that really disturbed me had to do with a kid named Russell D'Amico, whom Cus basically ran out of the house. Russell was a fifteen-year-old who was terribly screwed up and had gotten into trouble with the law a number of times. Cus had no use for him because he didn't have any talent as a boxer. We had other kids who were never going to amount to anything as fighters, but Cus didn't run them off. It was just that Russell had the double whammy of being untalented *and* rubbing Cus the wrong way.

I didn't care. The kid needed us. He was desperate. I told Cus, I pleaded with him, not to forsake this kid. I said, "Tyson pulls the same crap, but you let him slide because he's Tyson. If this kid could box, you'd let him slide." It didn't matter what I said, Cus wouldn't listen. He kept calling Russell a liar to his face, giving him a terrible time, and Russell couldn't take it. He left the house, and not long after that he got arrested again. While he was in jail, he hanged himself with the drawstring from his hooded sweatshirt. I was extremely upset by it at the time, and even now, all this time later, I still think about it.

It was strange. I had been able to get from Cus the kind of encouragement and support that I had always wanted from my father, that my father had always had difficulty expressing. But my father never had to tell me who he was. He expressed his character in his actions and deeds. Now, here was Cus, telling me one thing, but in his actions beginning to show me he was something else.

His handling of Tyson was what ultimately led to the biggest problems between us. Tyson had begun to grasp that his growing power inside a boxing ring gave him increasing power outside it. When we went to Denver the first year to fight for the National Junior Olympic title, the contrast between him and his peers was striking. During the weigh-in for a bout, we had to get on a line with all the other kids, all these fourteen- and fifteen-year-old heavyweights who looked their age, had acne, and had no real definition to their muscles. Suddenly we came in, and it was like Clint Eastwood coming down the freakin' walkway. The only thing missing was the music. Tyson was up to 210 pounds by then, and he knew the moves. He didn't smile, he didn't talk to anybody, he just walked in, knowing he was intimidating the shit out of these kids. You'd hear them whispering. "Did you see that guy?" "I'm not fighting him, am I? If I am, I'm getting the fuck out of here."

Cus always liked to talk about imagination. How, if you let your mind run amok, it would destroy you. Here were these kids falling right into that trap. I remember a rumor that got started about Tyson that first year, that he was twenty years old and was Sonny Liston's nephew. Sonny Liston's nephew! It was remarkable. He was winning fights before he even stepped in the ring.

Something else was happening, too: attention and adulation. The first year in Colorado, we were taking buses to get to the arena; by the second year, with Tyson knocking everybody dead, it was, "Can we give you a ride?" It wasn't lost on him. For somebody who wasn't emotionally mature or grounded, acquiring that kind of power was dangerous.

In Catskill, more and more, he began to push the boundaries. There were incidents at school. He was assaulting kids, grabbing girls, disobeying and disrespecting teachers. Cus made deals with the school principal to keep Tyson out of trouble. "Listen," he'd tell the principal, "this is a different kind of kid. This kid could make this school and this town famous. We've got to keep this quiet."

At the gym and in the house, we had always instilled an atmosphere of discipline. It meant something to have a set of rules in place that was consistent for everybody. It made for harmony and balance. After Tyson showed up, two sets of rules developed, one for him and one for everybody else. I didn't think that was healthy for Tyson or the rest of the kids. I think that Tyson, like all kids, wanted boundaries, wanted discipline. But Cus was cutting corners with him. He was in a race against the clock. To discipline Tyson, the only punishment that would have had a real impact would have been to deprive him of time in the ring, the way Bobby Stewart had at Tryon. Cus couldn't afford to lose that time, though. Not if Tyson was going to become the youngest heavyweight champion ever. If Tyson didn't become the youngest heavyweight champ ever, Cus might not be alive to see it. So he indulged Tyson—he forgave and covered up his indiscretions—even though it was really himself he was indulging.

The more Cus let Tyson get away with, the further Tyson pushed, and the more out of control he got. If Cus had been younger, maybe he would have done things differently. Old age can make people fearful. Cus was afraid that he would lose Tyson, either by dying or by having him taken away. If the authorities in Albany found out about Tyson's troubles, the jig was up. So Cus worked the locals, and made sure they kept their mouths shut. The only information that made its way upstate came from Cus: Tyson was doing great in school and knocking guys out. All these years of Cus talking about discipline and purity and honesty, and the importance of being a professional, and all of a sudden it was, "Oh, wait, I didn't mean that." Or, "I only mean it when it's convenient."

I had become dangerous to Cus because I had actually bought into what he had been preaching. When Tyson got in trouble for throwing containers of milk at the wall in the school cafeteria, it was just the latest in a string of incidents. I'm not saying I'm a saint. I stood by and watched him get away with stuff. At a certain point, though, I reached my limit. I decided to suspend Tyson from the gym until he shaped up and improved his behavior. Maybe it was too late, and I was just trying to make myself feel better. Maybe it wouldn't have done any good anyway. Tyson certainly didn't submit to it. He went straight to Cus, who not only didn't back me up but brought Tyson to the gym himself, the next morning, and let Rooney train him.

For the four years I had been Tyson's trainer, I had given him a mixture of support, guidance, and discipline. Now, Cus—whether I was right or wrong—was undermining me. A six-year partnership between the two of us based on loyalty and trust and the dream of developing a gym and championship fighters was going out the window. Rooney, my childhood friend, took Cus's side. He thought I was the one being disloyal.

However you looked at it, it was obviously an untenable situation. Cus and Rooney were working with Tyson in the morning, and I was working with the other kids later on. Something had to give. Or someone. You'd think there would have been some other way to resolve things. You wouldn't think it all had to blow up. But that's what happened. And Tyson was at the center of it.

After a couple of weeks of living with this tension, I came home one night, and Elaine and her sisters were sitting in the kitchen, crying. Elaine said, "Don't say nothing to Teddy." Of course, I heard her. There was no way they were going to keep it from me after that.

"Don't say nothing about what?"

Elaine was more than six months pregnant. She didn't want to see me get upset. She was worried about the baby.

"Say nothing about what?" I looked from her to her sisters.

Nobody would say anything at first, but then one of Elaine's sisters reluctantly revealed that Tyson had done something to their eleven-year-old sister, Susie. I didn't go crazy right away, which for someone who knew me might have been scarier than if I had. Very calmly, I pushed for details. Tyson had grabbed Susie. Put his hands on her. Told her what he wanted to do to her.

I knew it wasn't a random thing. Tyson with his street instincts knew exactly what he was doing and what would happen. It was a game and he was playing it hard and mean. He understood power and weakness as only someone who had spent part of his childhood hiding between walls could. I had been the only one at the gym demanding that he abide by the rules of society. Now he was throwing that back in my face, saying, "Fuck you, we'll see who wins that battle."

I looked around the kitchen at Elaine and her sisters. They were all crying, except for Elaine, who was furious. The idea that one of my kids had done this was nearly unfathomable. Without saying anything, I headed for the door. Elaine ran after me. "Teddy, don't." I shrugged her off and kept going.

This was what had come of Cus taking Tyson's side. This was the ultimate move on Tyson's part to show that he had no respect for boundaries, authority, anything. He was finishing it off because of where Cus had let him go. At that moment, I hated Cus every bit as much as I hated Tyson. I had trusted Cus. We were partners. I felt very emotional, but in an ice-cold way. I knew that if I allowed this, next time Tyson would take it further. He would rape her. Or someone else.

I drove into town, to a place called Asti's, a disco owned by a friend of mine named Bobby Cargioli. He had an apartment upstairs, where I knew he kept a gun. I parked in the lot and went up the wooden stairs by the side of the building. Bobby was standing in the door of the club. He saw me. He walked a few steps closer. "Teddy? What's going on?"

"I came to get your gun. Are you giving it to me or am I taking it?"

"Whoa, whoa, slow down. What are you talking about?"

I ignored him and kept going. The door to his apartment was open. I went straight for the bedroom. That's where he kept the gun, under his mattress. It was a .38 revolver. I flipped the chamber open, saw it was loaded, flipped it back, and stuck the barrel in my pants. Bobby appeared in the doorway.

"I don't want nothing to happen, you understand. . . ."

"It's too late for that."

"Where are you going to go with that?"

"Nothing's gonna come back to you," I said. "If that's what you're worried about." I walked past him and out the door.

I drove to the gym, but Tyson wasn't there. The kids were starting to loosen up, skipping rope, shadowboxing, working the bags. I went up to Kevin Young.

"You seen Tyson?"

"He's probably home." Kevin picked up on the edge in my voice. "There a problem?"

"No."

"You want me to call and ask him to come out? He's always looking to get out. I'll call and ask him." Kevin was a tough kid, as loyal as they come. He was like Joe the Blade that way.

"No, Kev," I said. "You just stay here and loosen up and run things for me tonight."

I walked down the stairs and outside and saw a cab pulling up. I stepped back into the shadow of the building. It was Tyson. I crouched down and waited. He walked up to the door of the building. I sprang out of the darkness and grabbed him by the neck of his shirt. I put the gun to his head.

"You piece of fucking shit!" I pulled him into an alcove between the gym and the next building. "You think you're gonna do that to my family? After the way I've treated you? I will fucking kill you! That's my family! My family! You understand, you fucking piece of shit?" I was looking at him, staring straight into his eyes. If he didn't show me that he knew how serious I was, then I was going to kill him. "Make no mistake. If you ever put your hands on my family again, you'll be dead. There'll be no talking. No warning. You'll never know. You'll just be dead."

I was looking for a sign of understanding and I wasn't getting it. There was still a smugness about him. I stuck the gun in his ear and cocked the trigger. I said, "Are we clear? Do you see the reality of this?" He gave me a nod. Jerking the gun barrel up in the air at the last moment, I pulled the trigger. He fell to the ground, holding his ear. "Are we absolutely clear now? I will not let you do this to my family. I will not live this way, and I will not let you do this." He got to his feet. When I looked in his eyes this time, the understanding was there. I watched him stagger away. "You better not forget," I said.

From what I heard later, Tyson vowed he was going to kill me after that, but Cus hustled him out of Catskill for a few weeks, up to Bobby Stewart's in Johnstown, and either he was talked out of his vow or he lost his nerve.

The way things had been going, even before this happened, it's quite possible that Cus had been plotting his next move regarding me for a while. A couple of days after the incident, the doorbell rang. It was Don Shanager.

"What do you want?" I said. I suppose on some level I was still hoping that Cus would be the person I wanted him to be, that he pretended to be. I held out some vain hope that when push came to shove he would actually be the stand-up guy a lot of people thought he was.

"Can you come out and talk?" Shanager said.

Elaine was standing behind me. She was nervous. The baby was due soon. She wanted to be sure the baby's father would still be around. "He wants me to go out and talk," I said.

"About what?"

"I don't know. He didn't tell me. But I'm going out."

She stood there, by the door, while I went outside. A chill November wind was blowing fallen leaves across the yard.

"Cus told me to give you an offer," Shanager said.

The confusion must have shown on my face.

"To leave," he said.

It hadn't even occurred to me. They were going to pay me off the way they paid everyone else off.

"Cus said he'll give you five percent for life of all Tyson's future earnings if you just go away."

"He authorized you to do this."

"Yes. He realizes that Tyson was wrong. He knows all the hard work you put in and that you brought him to this point, and he's sorry that things worked out this way. So he's willing to give you five percent for life."

"Five percent? That's very generous. It really is. You know what you can tell him? To go fuck himself. Tell him I don't want his money." I went back inside and slammed the door.

Elaine, if she heard any of it, never said a thing about my saying fuck you to an offer of money. I realized afterward what was really behind the offer. When I put a gun to Tyson's head, that was serious enough; when I pulled the trigger, forget about it. If word got out, the state authorities would come down to investigate, and the whole thing would spin out of control. "Why did Teddy put a gun to his head? Something must have happened." They would have found out everything and that would have been the end of the dream. Cus would have lost him. He was scared to death of that.

The interesting thing is, I didn't leave. At least not right away. I had seven kids that were in the finals of the Adirondack Golden Gloves in Schenectady, New York, and when everything fell apart they were still a week away from the finals. They had fought for two months to get there, besides the four or five years they'd been in training. This was important to them. But obviously it was a strange situation. I thought long and hard about what to do. In the end, I went to the gym and trained them.

It was a little nuts. Anyone could have walked through the door those next few days. Tyson could have walked in. That was the reality. I knew that, just like I knew I had a commitment to those kids I couldn't ignore. I was always telling them not to walk away, not to quit. It would have undermined everything I had taught them if I left. So I stayed for that week, and took them to Albany, and that was a very long week.

Six out of the seven kids won the Gloves. The day after the tournament was over, I went to the gym to say good-bye. They stood there quietly. Nobody cried or said anything. I had been their teacher for five years and they knew that I was doing what I had to do. They knew everything without my having told them. They knew what had happened with Tyson, they knew about the gun, they knew about my sister-in-law, they knew everything. Nobody could lie to those kids, nobody could bullshit them, they knew everything.

A few of them said, "We'll come with you." They wanted me to open another gym in Catskill. I said, "No, you can't do that." I thought I was leaving Catskill, to be honest, so I told them no and I said good-bye to them. Suddenly, they handed me a plaque. I don't know when they had it made up. It said, "To Teddy Atlas, our trainer and guide, who has treated us like men. And one who has been like a father to us. We will miss you."

We all walked out of the gym together. I'd had these kids since they were eleven, twelve years old. It was funny—sometimes you didn't realize how much time had passed in your life until something marked it for you.

I'd said my good-byes to them and was walking back to my apartment when a pickup truck pulled up and someone yelled, "Teddy, you want a ride?" It was my kids. They were driving this truck. I hadn't even realized they were old enough to drive. I hadn't been paying attention. I said to myself, "Shit, it really has been a long time." For a moment, just a moment, I allowed myself to reflect that in a way I had done my job, that they were driving this truck, and that they were men, and they didn't need me anymore.

ELAINE AND I DECIDED TO STAY IN CATSKILL UNTIL WE HAD the baby. We had already started paying the hospital a little bit of money, and it seemed to make sense. Since I wasn't going to the gym and training fighters, I started taking Jeff Amen to therapy every day. His parents couldn't take him. They were both working. I volunteered to do it. They had bought him a van that was equipped for the wheelchair, and every day I would load him in and take him to the Catskill rehabilitation facility. In a way it was like he was my new fighter; I was training him.

In the beginning, there was a physical therapist from the rehab facility involved, but I wound up doing so much of the work with Jeff myself that after a few days the therapist just threw up her hands and left us alone.

We used the different kinds of equipment, the weights and pulleys and straps, and he continued to improve. I learned that swimming was probably the best kind of therapy for someone like him, particularly since it turned out that he had been a very good swimmer. I found out about this indoor pool over in Hudson, New York, across the bridge. I arranged to bring him there, though I never actually told them that he was in a wheelchair. I didn't lie outright; I told them that he had been in an accident, but I didn't use the word "paraplegic" because I felt they might not let us use the pool if they knew.

The first night we went there, I wheeled Jeff in, and the pool was full of old people. It was like in that movie *Cocoon,* all these geriatrics in bathing caps, treading around this overchlorinated pool water, and this young, very pretty blonde lifeguard sitting in a high chair watching over them. The blonde lifeguard came over and said, "Are you Teddy Atlas?"

I said I was.

"They didn't tell me he was in a wheelchair."

"Well, we don't use it all the time. It's not like he actually *needs* it." Which was true in a way: Jeff occasionally used crutches and could sometimes walk a few steps without them, but it wasn't often and definitely not around the wet tiles by a swimming pool.

Jeff watched me to see what I would say next. He was always saying to his mother, "You never know with Teddy what's going to come out of his mouth."

The lifeguard seemed satisfied by my answer and went back to her perch. Jeff said, "So what are we going to do?"

"You used to be a good swimmer, right?"

"Yeah."

"So you're going to swim."

"But how am I going to get in? Are you going to carry me?"

"If I carry you the lifeguard might get nervous and say you shouldn't go in."

"So what, then?"

"You're going to have to get in a different way."

"How? How am I going to get in?"

Our voices, which started out as whispers, were getting louder. The lifeguard was looking down at us. I flashed a smile, like everything was okay, and she smiled back at me, buying it, at least for the moment. "You just gotta get in," I hissed at Jeff.

"How am I gonna do that? I can't do that."

"Sure you can." All the old people had stopped splashing around. They had noticed the tense energy emanating from our direction. "C'mon," I said. "They're all looking at us."

"You're going to have to take me over to the shallow end and carry me."

We were standing by the deep end. "How good a swimmer were you?" I said.

"Good."

"Real good?"

"Real good."

"Okay." I rolled his wheelchair quickly toward the edge of the pool, then jammed on the brakes. The chair tilted forward and flipped him in. It was sudden and shocking. He splashed into the pool and sank. I'm sure, under normal circumstances, that the lifeguard would have gone right in after him. But she didn't budge. She must have figured that I knew what I was doing. Everybody was just looking at the pool, at the spot where he'd gone in. There were air bubbles coming up to the surface, and I was standing there, thinking, *What if he doesn't come up?*

He finally surfaced, screaming, spitting out water. "Teddy, you fuck, what the fuck is wrong with you?"

"Sshh, come on," I said, holding up my hand. "You're floating. Look."

And he was. I climbed into the pool and tread water next to him. He was flapping his arms, staying afloat. I helped position him to swim, and almost immediately he was swimming. It came back to him right away. Before he tired out, he did two laps.

The swimming became a regular part of his rehab routine. Over the next couple of months, he continued making progress. It was getting to where he could actually walk with a cane pretty well, and I'd take walks with him on the street. But then he hit a plateau, and got lazy, and I had to push him. I said, "You don't think I noticed, but for the last two weeks you didn't move without that cane because you're afraid. You think you might not be good enough or strong enough, so you're playing it safe, and that's holding you back." I took the cane away from him and said, "Let's find out what happens if you don't have this." We were on this long country road near his home. I started walking away.

"Hey, you bastard, don't leave me here! I can't walk!"

I turned around. "Yes, you can. Today is the day you're not going to be lazy."

"You son of a bitch!"

I walked just slowly enough that his anger propelled him after me.

"You see," I said. "You're doing it."

Man, he got mad, but it worked. It got him through the wall. He was never going to be a hundred percent, but he got to the point where he was functioning. He was able to walk a little. He could drive. He had this specially outfitted van that he could drive. It wasn't perfect, but it was night and day from where he'd been following the accident.

The mental part was harder. Years later, after I left Catskill and was no longer involved in Jeff's day-to-day life, his mother called me. Jeff was feeling suicidal and she didn't know where else to turn. Jeff and I still talked, but not every day. It was a bad time for me because Michael Moorer and I were leaving for Germany to fight for the IBF heavyweight title against Axel Schulz.

Jeff's mother was crying. "Teddy, you're the only one who can help. He won't come out of the basement. I don't know what he's going to do. He said good-bye to everyone, gave away his things. He said he's failed because he'll never be normal."

I called him up. I said, "Jeff, listen, I'm leaving for Germany tomorrow. I can't come up there. But I want to say something—" I had never talked this way to him before and he knew that. I said, "You owe me something. You owe me a little something, wouldn't you say that?"

He acknowledged that he did.

"So I'm going to demand that you don't do anything while I'm gone." He knew exactly what I was talking about, even if I didn't come out and say it. "You better give me your fucking word that you won't do nothing until I get home and we can figure this out."

"Teddy, I'm tired," he said. "It's not your fault."

"Jeff, remember the pool? Remember they said you were never gonna walk again?"

"Yeah."

"Were they right? I put in too much fuckin' time for you to talk like this."

I wound up staying on the phone with him for a couple of hours before I felt comfortable enough to hang up. When Moorer and I got to Germany, we found a place that embroidered Jeff's name on Michael's trunks. Michael was a good guy and he went along with it. ABC broadcast the fight, and they told the story on the air. "That 'Jeff' on the trunks is the name of a friend of Michael's and Teddy's. He wasn't doing too well. He was having a bit of a hard time, and they thought it might pick him up a little. So hopefully, Jeff, this picks you up."

After the fight, I got the trunks framed and gave them to Jeff. On the bottom of the frame there was a little plaque that read, "Trunks worn to win the Heavyweight Championship of the World."

NICOLE WAS BORN ON APRIL 3, 1983. SO MANY PEOPLE CAME to visit that the hospital was overwhelmed. They put up signs on the second day, "No visitors for the Atlas baby." I had friends who drove up from the city walking around the halls smoking cigars and drinking beer. They had never seen anything like it in that hospital.

So Nicole was born, and a lot of things were different in my life, and it was time to go. Jeff's family took it hard when I went to say good-bye. They said, "Now who's going to take him to rehab and keep his spirits up?" I know it sounds a little selfish on their part, but they were good people. I said, "He can do it himself now. He's all right. He's got a pretty good life."

It had been six years in Catskill. Now it was over. A lot of things were different. I was a husband and a father, and certain things had come to an end. We packed up and moved to Staten Island—me, Elaine, and the baby—into the basement of my parents' house. And I started looking for a way to make a living training fighters in New York.

THE LAST DANCE

AS SOON AS WE GOT UNPACKED AND SETTLED IN MY parents' basement apartment, I went to a gym in Brooklyn above the Walker Theater, where my friend Nick Baffi was working. Nick was an old friend of Cus's who I'd met in Catskill during my time there. When he heard I was moving back to the city, he told me to come by.

Pretty quickly I found a couple of guys to train there—or, to be more exact, they found me. One of them was Johnnie Verderosa, who was trying to launch a comeback. I knew Johnnie from when we were kids in Staten Island. I'd sparred with him and helped him get into shape when he was training for the New York Golden Gloves. He'd always been appreciative of the fact that I made some sacrifices to do that.

Johnnie was a little guy, 130 pounds soaking wet, but a hell of an athlete. His father was an alcoholic. I remember that there was always a garbage pail full of beer in the kitchen of their house. Johnnie had these older brothers, Guy-Guy and Tom-Boy, who became drug addicts and were in and out of Rikers. As a result of growing up with them, and seeing what they were, Johnnie stayed away from drugs and alcohol. He was very hard-line about it; he wasn't going to be like them. He wouldn't hang out on the corner or go to bars. We always understood why, that he had his head on straight.

"I'm taking care of my body," he'd say. His addiction was sports. Football. Baseball. Boxing. Especially boxing. He was tough and had a lot of heart. He won the New York City Golden Gloves two times, and then turned pro and became the USBA super featherweight champ. He got written up in *Ring* magazine along with Boom Boom Mancini. A lot of people, his mother in particular, were proud of him.

Then, just like that, just when he was in that position, and it seemed like his discipline and hard work were paying off, he began doing cocaine, and doing it openly, doing all the things he said he was never going to do. It was baffling. On the verge of real success, he took this 180-degree turn. I don't know if it was guilt that he was leaving his brothers behind or if all that discipline was finally too exhausting. I just know you can drive yourself crazy trying to figure out stuff like that.

When his manager approached me, it was after drugs had already dragged down his career, and he was trying to revive things. He asked me if I would help him. I agreed, provided he stayed clean. I knew it wasn't an easy thing for him, so I had him stay with us, with me, Elaine, and the baby, at the house, so he could have that support. I gave him a curfew and stayed on top of him. It worked. He got into shape, and won a couple of fights.

Then, right before his third fight, he came home one night while I was out training another fighter. He told Elaine not to tell me, but he was going back out. When I got home, I asked her where he went, and she didn't know. I knew something was up. I went driving around the neighborhood to all his old haunts, trying to track him down. I walked into this one bar where I heard he sometimes used to go to cop cocaine. I went up to the bartender and asked him if Johnnie Verderosa was around. He said, "No," but I knew it was a lie because he was nervous. I saw his eyes dart over to a corner of the room. In the reflection of the mirror behind the bar, I saw Johnnie cowering on the floor behind a pinball machine. As mad as I was, I didn't say anything. I just walked out as if I hadn't seen him.

About midnight that night, he came home. I was up, waiting. I didn't waste any time; I got right to the point.

"I saw you," I said. "I know what's going on." I didn't have to say anything else. He knew why I hadn't said anything earlier, that I hadn't wanted to embarrass him.

"You don't have the discipline it takes to be a fighter anymore," I said.

He didn't argue. He didn't fight with me. His head was down. He was ashamed. He said, "I'm sorry. You took me in and I let you down. I betrayed you."

"No, you betrayed yourself," I said.

This was a kid I'd had living under the same roof with me and my family. A kid who'd told me how much it meant to him not to have to sleep with cotton in his ears, which he'd had to do where he'd been staying before so the cockroaches wouldn't go in his ears. I'd been training him and feeding him and really trying to straighten him out. It tore me up to see him slip back. Even though it was something I thought I understood a little from my own life, maybe I didn't understand it as well as I wanted.

Johnnie went and fought his next fight without me and got knocked out. He called me a few times after that and asked me for money. I gave him a twenty here and there. I had real feeling for him, but it was just weakness on my part to give him money. He'd tell me it was for food, but I knew it was for drugs. So the next time he asked, I said, "I ain't giving you a cent. If you want something to eat, if you're hungry, I'll sit with you. I'll take you to a diner and buy you dinner. But I ain't givin' you no money. I'll take you to a drug rehab. I'll help get you in, and when you're allowed a visit, I'll come visit. Or if you're not allowed a visit, I'll write. Whatever it takes to make you feel a connection."

The thing is, even with the drug problem, Johnnie was a good kid. There was something about him that I liked. With all his problems, he never hurt anyone else or blamed anyone but himself. I appreciated that. He had character even though he had a weakness. His boxing career ended after the knockout; he retired after that, but eventually, after drifting for a few years, he straightened himself out. He found a girl, he started working construction, and from what I understand, at least the last I heard a few years ago, he was in a decent place.

After the break with Johnnie, I started going to the old Gleason's Gym, over on Thirty-first Street between Seventh and Eighth. I'd take the ferry and the subway, and go in there every day. I was still at a point in my career where I was doing spade work, digging up holes, planting seeds, hoping things would grow. I got a few amateurs, and I was working with them. It was just like Catskill, working all day, making no money, trying to turn these guys into fighters. They weren't the right guys yet. I was just putting in the time, working my trade, improving as a trainer.

Ira Becker, who ran Gleason's, knew what I was; he knew my background, that I had worked with Cus. He thought I had some talent. This was in the early 1980s, when the whole white-collar boxing craze was beginning. These Wall Street guys were showing up at Gleason's, paying good money to learn how to box. A lot of them wanted to work with me, but I always rejected them.

Truthfully, it wasn't smart on my part. It didn't make financial sense to say no. But I was coming from a place, having worked with Cus, that I was a professional trainer who would make world champions, and that there was a purity to what I was doing. You grow up, you get over that kind of thinking. You realize that you don't have to compromise yourself to make money along other avenues, that it's okay and can even be another level of your trade, teaching and developing guys who would normally never have a clue or a chance in that world. But that's the way I thought then. I was the Young Master, and I was fulfilling my destiny. It didn't include these white-collar guys. Ira Becker used to come up to me and say, "Teddy, do me a favor. Can I talk to you? Why don't you take some of these guys?" I understood where he was coming from. These guys were asking for me, and I was rejecting them, and he wanted their membership, he didn't want to lose them. He said, "Listen, there's this Spanish guy that trains ten guys in a class each morning and makes a hundred and fifty dollars. You could get three hundred dollars easy." I should have done it. I was living in my parents' basement. I had an infant daughter. There were plenty of good reasons. But I kept saying no. It was just a way of thinking that I was stuck in.

One day this guy I knew there, Rudy Greco, an attorney who was involved in the boxing business, came up to me and said, "I have an interesting proposition for you. Do you know who Twyla Tharp is?"

"No."

"She's the Muhammad Ali of dance. I just got a call from somebody that she needs to get back in shape to dance. She's decided she wants a boxing trainer, and your name came up. I think you should do it."

"I ain't training no ballet dancer," I said.

"Teddy, do me a favor, just talk to her."

He started telling me more about her, that she was this famous dancer and choreographer who had done the musical *Hair* on Broadway and a bunch of other things. Being a lawyer, he made a good case. The truth is, Rudy knew my situation financially, and he was looking out for me. His persuasiveness plus the thirty-five dollars an hour I stood to make got me to agree to talk to her.

Tharp called a couple of days later. I made an appointment to meet her.

I still had the keys to the Walker Theater in Brooklyn, Nick Baffi's gym, and I met her there. She was both grateful and apologetic. She kept saying, "I know this all must seem a bit silly to you. I'm a dancer, and you're a boxing trainer." At the same time, she told me how sincere she was about undertaking this. She was very gracious and humble. It was smart of her. She won me over.

Right off the bat, she asked me lots of questions about the philosophy of boxing, and I told her about dealing with fear, controlling emotions, and how those were things that could be transferred to other disciplines. It appealed to her. She was forty-four, which was old for a dancer, and she was getting ready to perform for the first time in a while. She had a lot of pride, ego, and professionalism, and she wanted to be in better shape than she had been when she was in her twenties, if that was possible.

I told her it was. "I'm willing to teach you boxing for two reasons," I said. "One, so you can have the ability to undertake a physical regimen with it, which entails learning enough technique so that you can get the benefits of this workout. Two, so that you can learn how to go into dark places and not get broken down. I think that would help you. If you can learn a bit of the discipline that fighters learn, you can take that onto the stage with you."

She loved that kind of thinking, that kind of philosophy. She was into yoga and all that stuff. This was yoga with a punch. I created a training program for her. I made her run up and down the steps in the Walker Theater—and there were a lot of steps. I had her skip rope, shadowbox, do push-ups, kick-outs, sit-ups, everything I'd have my fighters do. I ran her ragged, and she dealt with all of it and never complained. You could see why she was successful. She had a capacity to work extremely hard.

The first time I had her slip a punch, I said, "Listen, I'm going to throw a punch at you. Now athletically I know how talented you are, and the move you need to make is obviously something you can do, but there are other elements involved." As I explained the mechanics of moving her upper torso, and how she might instinctively want to turn away but would have to resist doing so, she began to smile.

"Why are you smiling?" I asked.

"Because it's so simple. I'm a dancer. I make moves like that all the time."

"Yeah? You think it'll be easy? I'll make you a bet right now," I said. "That when I throw a punch you can't do it."

"Okay."

I told her to put her hands up, and when I threw the punch, she jerked back from it.

"Wait a minute," she said. "Let's try that again."

Now I was smiling. I threw another punch. Again, she turned away from it.

"What happened, Twyla?" I said. "I thought it was a simple move."

She pretended to get all huffy and said, "You're not treating me like a lady, Teddy."

"It's interesting, isn't it? You know I'm not really going to hurt you, but just the idea of my punch, the danger it represents, is enough to screw you up. That shows you where we're going. Learning to contain that emotion. Not to pull back. Not to close your eyes. But to face what you have to face and slip the punch. This isn't about anything but the physical action. You're not thinking about avoiding getting hit, or worrying about being hurt, you're just focused on the action of the move. This isn't so you can become a prizefighter, but so you can become a better pro. So you're better equipped to deal with anxiety and fatigue and fear onstage."

She understood and she learned. Pretty soon, I had her slipping punches. She got good. Then I had her on the hand pads, and I was throwing punches at her more freely. One time, though, she didn't move, and I hit her. She got a black eye. She wouldn't put makeup on or anything. I felt a little bad. She said, "Are you kidding me? I'm gonna make sure everyone sees this." I heard later that her dancers began calling her "Boom Boom" Tharp.

At the other end of the spectrum, when I wrapped her hands for her, she said, "Remember, I am a lady and I like these nails. It's important for my hands not to look like a fighter's. Anything else, fine, but make sure my hands are protected."

"Don't worry," I'd say. "Your nails will still be beautiful when I take the gloves off."

"You sure?"

"I'm sure."

We worked five days a week for nearly a year, and she got into great shape. At a certain point we moved out of the gym and I began training her at the American Ballet Theatre. Right on the polished wooden floors. When her dancers started arriving at the studio, toward the end of our session, she introduced me to them. She was both sweet and self-deprecating. "This is Teddy Atlas, who has allowed me to take up a little space in his world, even though I embarrass him." Afterward, she asked me to stay and watch her rehearse her company, in part, I think, because she wanted me to see what she was like when she was giving orders, not taking them.

Twyla took some of the moves she learned from me and put them into one of her dance pieces. I don't know if she had that in mind before the training, but she made this piece called "Fait Accompli," using boxing movement. When it premiered in November 1983, she flew me and Elaine down to Washington. We got all dressed up and went to opening night at the Kennedy Center. We were sitting in the front row, and you know the kind of people who go to these things—not the fight crowd—and right behind us, when Twyla came onstage for the first time, this guy exclaimed, "My God, she looks like a champion fighter!"

Elaine hit me in the side with her elbow. "You hear that?"

"Yeah, but is that a good thing?"

"What do you mean? Of course it's good!"

"Not if she dances like Sylvester Stallone."

"Stop it."

The truth is that Twyla really did look sensational. Her muscle tone, her whole aura—I hadn't realized how different she looked until that moment. Under the lights, she glowed.

When the performance was over, she got a standing ovation. People were cheering and throwing roses up onstage. I had come prepared, having learned beforehand that it was a tradition to throw flowers up onstage. While Twyla was taking her bows, and the crowd was applauding, and she was looking out at me with this big smile, I walked up, took a pair of boxing gloves out of a bag I had brought with me, and threw them up onstage. People were saying, "Look at that!" I guess you don't see boxing gloves thrown up on dance stages too often.

A couple of years later, I was training Simon Brown, who was the welterweight champ, and he was getting ready to make a defense of his title. We were in the locker room before the fight and flowers came. Which was unusual. Don Elbaum, the fight promoter, said, "Teddy, you got flowers. Someone sent you flowers."

Of course, it was Twyla.

I HAD BEGUN MAKING A LITTLE MONEY AT LAST. NOT MUCH, but enough to get by. Enough so that eventually Elaine and I were able to move out of my parents' basement into an old brick building up on Grymes Hill, above my parents' street, where we paid three hundred dollars a month for a one-bedroom with dark wood floors. It was while we were in that apartment that Elaine got pregnant and gave birth to our second child, Teddy III, in May of 1985.

Gradually, my career began to pick up. I started training guys like Tyrone Jackson and Chris Reid, guys who had talent and a future. I hooked up with Reid, the Shamrock Express, through Mickey Duff, a British boxing guy, who was managing him. Duff and his three partners, Jarvis Astaire, Mike Barret, and Terry Lawless, basically ran boxing in London. I considered Mickey one of the five smartest guys in the sport. A wily and successful promoter, he looked like a jovial Irishman and had an Irish name, but in fact he was Jewish. His real name was Monek Prager, his father was a rabbi, and he had been born in Kraków, Poland, in 1929 and owned a kibbutz in Israel.

Mickey was a lovable rogue who could swim with the piranhas, but he was also a pretty straight shooter—which is to say, he wouldn't steal you blind. I'd first met him in Catskill when he'd brought a young Frank Bruno to spar with a young Mike Tyson. He was complimentary of my work as a trainer, which was very flattering coming from a guy like him, who'd done everything you could do in boxing, from being in the ring as a fighter and a cornerman to matchmaking and promoting.

Reid was the first American fighter Mickey had ever managed. He was a quiet, serious kid, with dirty blond hair, blue eyes, and a mustache. You didn't realize how decent a kid he was until you met him and spent some time with him; his sullenness could be a little off-putting, but it was just protective, it wasn't who he really was. In fact, he was caring and loyal and had the ability to recognize and appreciate those traits in others; his standoffishness mostly came from being a white kid in a primarily black sport.

You'd never have guessed Chris was an explosive puncher. Certainly not to look at him. He had those long Irish arms (a shamrock tattooed on the upper part of one), with absolutely no muscle tone. It was a misleading physique. He was a little like a human missile silo: explosive power inside an innocent-looking façade.

In our years working together at Gleason's, Chris used to just destroy other fighters in the gym. He was legendary. All the best fighters who came through there, guys from Puerto Rico, guys who had never lost a fight, boom, he knocked them all dead. People walked around saying, "Oh, he's a monster." And he was. He could punch like a bastard, and he wasn't afraid to let loose at the right time. He was a hard worker, too. He listened well. Just to give you an idea of his commitment, every day he would travel in from Little Silver, New Jersey, which is on the Garden State Parkway. He would take the train, four or five hours a day back and forth, and he was never late. Not once in four years. If he hadn't had a drinking problem, there's no telling how far he could have gone in boxing.

I trained Chris to 18–0, with seventeen knockouts, and we thought he was going to get a title shot against Marvin Johnson, who was this great old warrior, a southpaw and a tough son of a bitch, but who was pretty much over the hill by then. We thought we were in line for that, and there was no question in my mind that if we had gotten the fight, Chris would have knocked him out and become champion. He was young and strong and confident. At the last second, though, we didn't get the fight. Leslie Stewart got it, and Stewart knocked Johnson out in the ninth round.

Sometimes that's just the way it goes. A month later we landed Chris a nontitle fight against Fulgencio Obelmejias, who had twice fought Marvin Hagler for the title. We thought it was the right fight for Chris, but we were wrong. The fight was at the Garden. Chris got dropped six times, but the crazy bastard kept getting up, until he got stopped for good in the tenth. Strangely, he was ahead on all the scorecards even after all the knockdowns (that fight actually changed the rules of scoring in New York from a rounds system to a points system, precisely to prevent such a situation).

In the aftermath of losing out on the title shot and then losing to Obelmejias, Chris started drinking more heavily. Sometimes he'd leave the gym and never even make it home. He'd go to Times Square and wind up drinking in some dive Irish bar all night. A couple of times he came straight to the gym afterward without going home, and when he sweat I could smell the booze. He couldn't understand how I knew what he'd been doing, but I knew because his sweat stank of booze.

Part of the problem with him was the Irish thing. He was the Shamrock Express and he had this big Irish following, and they'd play the bagpipes when he came into the ring. It was nice, but it had created a kind of expectation. It taught me something about human psychology: that no matter how you're perceived, no matter what people see on the outside, what's inside you can be completely different and probably is. Inside, Chris was unsure of himself; he was afraid that he wasn't living up to his potential. He drank to hide from that and to have an excuse to lose.

The sad part is that we got through some of those issues. I helped him get sober. He got control of his life. When an opportunity came up to fight Graciano Rocchigiani, who was the IBF super middleweight champion, we took it. Chris deserved the shot and we gave it to him.

The fight was in Berlin, and Mickey sent the two of us over to Europe three weeks early so that we could train there and get acclimated to the time change. Now, Mickey wasn't known for being a lavish spender, and this wasn't a fight with a big purse for us, so to save money, even though the fight was in Germany, we went to England to train in the Thomas à Becket gym. It was a famous gym, on the second floor over a bar. On the floor above that there were these tiny rooms with no heat that were basically like the rooms in a flophouse. You had to go downstairs to shower or use the bathroom. So that's where we stayed. Me and Chris in adjoining cells.

When I talked to Mickey on the phone, he said, "It's not the Ritz, is it, Teddy?"

"It's not even the Itz," I said.

"Ha-ha, that's good, Teddy." That was the kind of relationship Mickey and I had. He said, "It'll toughen you up for the fight."

The thing was that Mickey and I both felt that, even though there wasn't the money to do things first-class, going over early still gave Chris his best shot to win. Chris appreciated that. He thanked me. He said, "I know you're making no money and you have to be away from your family for three weeks in a place that's not even nice. I know that."

"You just concentrate on what we came here to do," I said.

We found some space heaters to warm up the rooms a little bit. The only problem was they emitted these fumes, so one of us would have to remind the other to turn them off before we fell asleep or else we'd get asphyxiated. We'd also use the heaters to dry out the wet workout clothes that we'd washed in the sink downstairs.

Chris and I were together all the time during those three weeks. We ate together, slept in adjoining rooms, did roadwork together, went to the gym together. All the Brits admired the diligence of our training regimen. At night, we would go out to eat, maybe take a walk around the neighborhood, then head back home. We were in the North End, which was supposed to be a rough area. People warned us about walking at night, but we didn't care. We walked everywhere, through the parks, down dark streets, everywhere. Sometimes we'd treat ourselves to a movie. We were inseparable for those three weeks. We were on a mission together. We talked about what it meant. I'm not sure we ever said it in so many words, but we both knew it was Chris's last real chance to salvage his career.

The bar downstairs from the gym was owned by this guy Gary Davidson, an ex-fighter, who'd turned it into something of a museum. There was all this great boxing memorabilia: Henry Cooper's trunks from when he fought Ali; a pair of the heavyweight Joe Bugner's gloves; a facsimile copy of the Marquess of Queensbury's Rules; all this great stuff. On Fridays and Saturdays, the bar would turn into a discotheque. It got packed and rowdy.

One Friday night, I walked Chris back after our dinner and I dropped him off at our quarters. I said, "I'm going to take a bit more of a walk."

"Okay, Ted. I'll be upstairs."

"Make sure you turn off the heater," I said. "Don't want you to suffocate to death a week before the fight."

When I got back from my walk, the side door that we usually used to get into the residence part was locked, so I had to go through the bar. The bouncers stopped me. They wanted me to pay the cover charge. I tried to explain the situation, that I was staying upstairs and the side door was locked. The lead bouncer shook his head. He said in a British accent that wasn't nearly as friendly as Mickey Duff's, "You're not getting in without paying, mate." I tried patiently to make my case, but he wasn't listening, and one thing led to another and pretty soon we were scuffling.

The fight moved from the doorway out into the street, and by the time his fellow bouncers joined in, I had given him a pretty good beating. I was still tussling with the other bouncers when the bobbies showed up in a paddy wagon, wearing their funny hats and wielding their nightsticks. I immediately stopped throwing punches, and, truthfully, in part that was because I was looking at this paddy wagon. I had never seen one before and I was thinking, *It's a real paddy wagon, with a little barred window in the back just like in the movies.*

It was clear right away that I was in trouble, that the bobbies assumed that I was the instigator of the fight, and that on top of that I was a Yank. They started trying to maneuver me into the back of the paddy wagon. As much as I was entranced by it, I knew I didn't want to see it from the inside. I was saying, "I ain't going in there. I ain't fucking going in there," and they were saying, "Yes, you are, you blooming Yank!" Just when it was getting really bad and they were starting to muscle me into the back, the manager from the bar came out. He said, "Leave him alone! He's in the right!" He explained who I was and what had happened, and he basically told the bobbies that the whole situation was the bouncers' fault. They let me go.

It turned out that the manager had no great fondness for the lead bouncer and his crew; nor did any of the bar's patrons, who had been abused and hassled regularly. They all tried to buy me a drink, but I wasn't drinking because of Chris.

"You sure gave him a good shellacking, Teddy," the manager said.

The next day, word got around. Chris heard about it, but he didn't say much more than "You all right?," which was his way. That night we went out for dinner as usual, and when we got back, around eight o'clock, the bar was starting to get busy. Gary Davidson, the owner, was there, as was the manager. Right away, the manager said, "Teddy, can we talk to you for a minute?"

Chris's loyalty kicked in immediately. "Are they back?" He was ready to get into it.

"Oh, no," the manager said. "They're never coming back. They want no part of him, believe me. That's the thing—it's not your fault, Teddy, but as a result of what happened we've got nobody to work the door tonight."

"Gee, I'm sorry," I said. "I didn't intend to create any headaches for you."

"No, no. You did us a favor, got rid of that arsehole. It's just that we were wondering if you could stand in tonight."

"Stand in?"

"Work the door and be our protection."

Chris had a big smile on his face. He was shaking his head.

"We'll pay you," the manager said.

I couldn't believe my ears. "I'm training for a world title," I said. "I didn't come here to England to be a bouncer."

"We know, Teddy. We know."

"So, no, you can't pay me." We were standing there by the door and it wasn't busy yet, but people were starting to show up. The manager was looking at me, this sheepish expression on his face. "Christ. You really can't get anyone, huh?" I said.

He shook his head.

I sighed. "All right. I'll take the job. But not for any money. Just as a favor."

Chris was dying. "Hey, Ted? I'm available. If you need backup."

I worked the door that night until two in the morning. It was hilarious. People had heard, and they stopped to chat with me and give me advice. A few guys I had to turn away, but I was friendly with them, and nobody gave me a problem. In fact, some of the tougher-looking guys, who I thought might be a problem, actually stayed outside with me and became my assistants. "Yeah, Teddy, he can't come in here. You can't come in here. Don't you know who this is? This is the Yank boxing trainer who beat the bejesus out of his predecessor."

The manager said, "Christ, Teddy, you're good at this. Can we use you again?"

The next day, I got a phone call from Mickey Duff. "I understand you're picking up a few extra shillings. I know you're underpaid, but I never knew you had to fight people to get their jobs."

"Screw you, Mickey."

"Maybe I can put you on the undercard against that bouncer."

I got a call from Joey Fariello, who had worked as a trainer for Cus before me and was a good buddy. "I thought you were training a guy for a world title," he said. "Now I hear that you're working the door at a bar?"

"How the hell did you hear about it?" I asked.

Everyone in Gleason's knew. The boxing community was like that. Word traveled fast. They all wanted to give me crap about it.

It was good to have that bit of comic relief. In the end, though, it rang hollow, because Chris lost the fight. Chris might have been able to give Graciano a tough time a couple of years earlier, but not now. He had done too much damage to himself with the drinking. Not physically, but psychologically. He was a sensitive kid, and when he got in that ring, he didn't feel the warrior mentality the way he should have. Instead, he felt like the drunken, no-good guy who had lied to his trainer. He felt like the guy who was throwing up in the subway at four in the morning. Graciano was too good a fighter for Chris to go in against him that way. When Chris lost—I threw in the towel in the eleventh round with his face getting all cut up—it hurt doubly because he felt he'd let me down.

If he'd won he was going to get $300,000 for a fight against Chris Tiozzo in France. It was all set to go. When he lost, I refused to take my cut of the $15,000. I knew it wasn't the end for me, but it was for him. That's why I refused. Back in the States, we met up a few days afterward in the basement of his house. He wanted to talk to me privately, and he wanted to apologize. He was very somber and he was very serious. In the end, he would always take responsibility for his failings.

"I want to thank you," he said, "for everything you gave me. You went all out, and you stayed away from your family for all that time, and I appreciate it. I don't feel like I owe an apology to anyone else. I don't owe one to Mickey Duff. But you lived it with me. I wasted your effort, and I'm sorry for that."

I wanted to give him something, to make him feel better. "The thing that really destroyed you," I said, "is that you have a conscience. You knew what was right and what was wrong, unlike some other guys, guys you beat in the gym. But having a conscience isn't necessarily the best thing for a prizefighter. Where it will serve you, long after these other guys have lost their titles, is as a human being and a father."

I was looking at him. His face was still puffy and bruised from the fight. "The only thing I ask is that you don't fight again. Will you make me that promise?"

"Yeah, if that's what you think."

"If you were supposed to fight, I'd tell you. But I'm telling you you're not supposed to fight no more."

He trusted me. Which says a lot about him, about his loyalty and allegiance. He never fought again. When he had his last kid, Philip, he asked me to be Philip's godfather. It meant a lot to me because I knew how much thought and care Chris put into a decision like that.

After boxing, he got a job with the electrical union. Chris knew guys in the Local 3 who loved him, and they got him a job in the union. He stayed with it for a few years, but he never liked it, and he wound up starting a demolition business in Little Silver, New Jersey. He just jumped in, the way he did with everything. He would tell me about it whenever we talked. He told me how he nearly electrocuted himself knocking down a wall. I got mad at him. "Yeah, that would have been a shame," he said, typically low-key and offhand about it.

"You got a family," I said. But he learned, he started getting blueprints, he became a pro and grew a little business.

One day he got a lump in his throat. He let it go. I hadn't seen him for a while, and he came over and he had this big bulge on the side of his throat.

"Jesus," I said. "How long have you had that?"

"Nine months."

Everyone had been telling him to have it checked, but he kept putting it off. That was Chris. He finally went in, and found out it was cancer. It was too late. He'd waited too long. If they'd caught it earlier, he might have had a chance.

He survived a bone-marrow transplant operation, but it took too much out of him; four days later he died of a heart attack at the age of thirty-eight. His heart—his big, loyal heart—just gave out.

At the wake, little Philip, my godson, came up and said to his mother, "Did you ask him?"

"No. Not yet, but I will."

"Ask me what?" I said.

"Philip wants to know that you'll train him when he turns twelve," she said. "His father was supposed to train him, and he said if he couldn't, then you would."

I promised that I would. As I write this now, Philip is ten years old. Two years to go.

More immediately, I put together a tribute on my show on ESPN, cutting together film clips of Chris's old fights, the bagpipes in the ring, him knocking guys silly, crooked, everything, and then we faded to black, with his name up there and the dates of his birth and death. I didn't do as good a job talking about him as I wanted. I just got too emotional. I thought I would be able to go right through it. But I got too choked up.

THE MURDER IN
MY HEART

DURING THE TIME I WAS TRAINING CHRIS IN THE mid-1980s, Donnie LaLonde called me up. He was a Canadian fighter, who was managing himself and promoting his own fights with the help of Top Rank. He could punch a little with the right hand, but he wasn't much of a fighter. He had tried to turn himself into the next "Golden Boy" by bleaching his hair blond; in fact, he even called himself "the Golden Boy," but other than that he didn't have a lot to recommend him.

He called me one day and said, "I'm Donnie LaLonde, would you train me?"

I said, "I'm Teddy Atlas and, no, I won't."

He called me again a few days later. He said, "I'm here in New York. I flew here at my own expense. Would you at least see me?"

I was at Gleason's. It was about five-thirty in the afternoon. I was getting ready to leave. It was the end of a long day and I was tired. I said, "If you can be here in half an hour, I'll see you."

He must have taken a cab. He showed up fifteen minutes later. I was still of the mind-set to say no because I didn't think he was serious or for real. But it meant something that he was coming to me—that he had flown to New York. I decided to suspend judgment until I heard what he had to say. We went downstairs to the basement of Gleason's, where I had an office, so we could talk privately.

LaLonde was slight of build. He had that bottle-blond hair, which went along with what I knew about him, that he was a bit of a con man and a self-promoter, and that he was more proficient at that than he was at fighting. Lou Duva, among others, had told me he'd never amount to much. But I always trusted my own instincts and wanted to see for myself.

"I want a chance to be a real fighter, and I know that you're a teacher," he said. "I've heard a lot of things about you, that you're a pro and you do things right, and you force people to face things and accomplish things, and I've never had that."

I kept listening. He was saying the right things to keep me listening.

"I don't want to be a sideshow, a circus, anymore. I want to be the real thing, and I'm willing to put myself in your hands and let myself be taken where you tell me to go. You can manage me, you can do everything, and I'm willing to risk finding out that I'm not good enough, but if that's the case at least I'll know that."

He had a bad left arm from a hockey injury when he was a kid. He had a pin in the shoulder. The handicap was mostly psychological at this point, but favoring the left for years meant there was physical and technical ground to make up, as well. I decided to take him on anyway.

At first, he wanted me to manage him, too, but I said, "No, I don't think that'll work. I'll get you a guy. I need to concentrate on training you. I'll get you a guy who's the right guy for you, who'll be able to market your personality, and who's a good fit." I was thinking of Dave Wolfe, who managed Boom Boom Mancini. I knew him from training another one of his fighters, Donnie Poole, a tough little Canadian welterweight. When I approached Wolfe about LaLonde, he said, "This guy's nothin', what are you wasting your time for?"

"I already told him I'd take him on," I said. "I'm training him."

"If you're training him, you must see something," he said.

"Michael Spinks is about to give up the light heavyweight title, and that's gonna open up three titles. It's gonna be a free-for-all, and after I train this kid for a while, I think he can figure in the picture. He can punch and he can be marketed, and if he's managed the right way he can be moved into one of those spots because it won't be a great guy in there."

Put that way, Wolfe saw the possibilities. He was a guy who could maneuver and market fighters, like he had done with Mancini. He knew how to put a guy in the right spot to make the most of his talent. He said, "Okay, I'll manage him."

I set up a meeting for the three of us, and an arrangement was made and we shook on it. Not long after that, a manager who I won't identify, except to say that he was supposedly Meyer Lansky's first cousin, tried to lure LaLonde away from Wolfe. This manager was around a lot of wiseguys, including Sonny Francese, and when he saw me training LaLonde at Gleason's, he approached him. No matter what's said now, LaLonde was going to sign with him. The guy made a bunch of promises and LaLonde was swayed.

When I found out, I was furious. "You son of a bitch," I said to LaLonde.

"Well, it's not like I've signed a contract with Wolfe yet or anything."

"Has he been putting you up in his apartment? Has he been buying you meals, taking care of you?"

"Yeah."

"Why do you think he was doing that, because he likes you? Because it's adopt-a-Canadian week? You have an agreement. I don't give a fuck if you didn't sign the paper. You have an agreement. Now you sign a fuckin' agreement with him tomorrow or you get another fuckin' trainer and get the fuck out of my life."

He signed an agreement the next day. It was ironic because I never signed a contract myself, and two years later, Wolfe, the guy I'd stood up for, fucked me. But before that happened, and all the subsequent things I'm going to tell about, I spent two years working with Wolfe, building up LaLonde's confidence. I did a lot of technical stuff with him, hours and hours a day working on his left hand, teaching him not to pull straight back to get away from punches, turning him into a more complete fighter. We brought him along slowly, taking him to small arenas in nothing places and getting him the right kinds of fights.

We got him a fight in Enid, Oklahoma, right after Thanksgiving one year. I wasn't making a dime on the fight but I went into the gym on Thanksgiving Day to train LaLonde. This was one of the things, later on, when I thought about sacrifices that I had made for these two guys, that bothered me the most. My son, Teddy Atlas III, was three years old then, the cutest little kid in the world. He had never been to the Thanksgiving Day Parade, and I had promised him that we'd go.

Thursday, Thanksgiving Day, I got my father, as old as he was, to come into the city with me and little Teddy. I didn't have the money to drive in, because I couldn't afford to park the car. I didn't tell my father that. I just told him that we'd take the subway because I did it all the time and it was easier. We went in to the city, up to Gleason's. Then I said good-bye and sent them off to the parade while I stayed to open up the gym.

I still remember the way my son looked, with his little green wool cap and his cheeks red and shiny from the cold. My father was in his shabby white raincoat, an old man who was a good man to be tromping around the city on a cold day. I should have said, "Fuck Donnie LaLonde," and gone to the parade with them, but I was being a pro the same way my father had been a pro. I opened up the gym, which was freezing—the heat was off because of the holiday—and I waited for LaLonde to show up. I trained him until they came back.

Two days later LaLonde and I went to Enid, Oklahoma, and he knocked out this Mexican fighter who came up to about his belly button. I felt so sorry for the poor guy—because I knew what he had gotten paid—that I went back to the locker room after Wolfe and LaLonde packed up and we were leaving, and I gave him twenty dollars. I never told them what I was doing because they would have looked at it as weakness. I think I just said, "I forgot something," and I went back to the locker room, and the guy was sitting there, still bleeding from a cut over his eye. I handed him a twenty-dollar bill. He looked at me like I'd lost my mind. But I knew why the guy was taking the fight. He had kids at home. I saw the kids at the weigh-in. He'd even had to borrow another guy's cup. It was sad. Twenty dollars wasn't much, but it was all I had.

We fought a bunch of fights like that, bringing LaLonde along slowly against guys who we used to build up his confidence. He was so full of doubts and insecurities. I took him to doctors to confirm that what I was trying to tell him about using his shoulder was true, that he wouldn't hurt it. I also spent a lot of time in the ground-floor apartment at 50 Barrow Street in the West Village that Dave Wolfe was lending him, trying to convince LaLonde that leaving Canada and coming here was going to pay off. He'd call me in the middle of the night sometimes, and I'd have to talk him off the ledge. It wasn't just working with this guy in a gym. It was a round-the-clock job. He constantly wanted reassurance from me that this was going to work out. So I'd talk to him about being a pro. I'd tell him all the reasons I thought he was going to make it.

The defining moment in his development came one day while he was sparring with Johnnie Walker Banks, and Banks hit him in the balls. I'd been working with LaLonde for months and months by then. Although he'd come quite a ways, I wasn't sure if we would get further, or if we'd ever get him to where he needed to go. Johnnie Walker Banks was a great gym fighter and a regular sparring partner for Marvin Hagler. He was a monster when he had the safety of headgear and big gloves, but he fell apart in an arena under the lights. I put LaLonde in with him as a test. I knew Banks was tough, but I thought we had an edge because LaLonde was a light heavyweight and Banks was only a middleweight.

Sure enough, LaLonde was using his strength to his advantage, leaning on Banks and clubbing him with right hands. Banks, old gym rat that he was, knew exactly what he was doing when he hit LaLonde in the balls. It was no accident. LaLonde started to slow down, though he didn't stop entirely.

Now, the old Gleason's was quite a place. There were two rings and a balcony up above, paint peeling off the walls. The floors were seasoned with spit and blood and sweat. It was a gym with atmosphere and character to spare. Characters, too: all these old-timers hanging around, ready to share their stories and knowledge. On this day, the whole place was watching LaLonde and Banks in the main ring, including Freddie Brown, a great cut man and one of Roberto Duran's trainers, who was about eighty years old. (He used to tell me, "Don't let the managers and fighters fuck you—'cause they will. They're all pimps and whores.")

When Banks hit LaLonde with a second low blow, LaLonde stopped fighting entirely. I got right up on the ring apron and climbed through the ropes.

"What are ya doin'?"

"I'm in pain."

"You're in pain? Come here!"

"That's why I stopped."

"Come here!" He walked toward me, everyone watching. "This is it," I said. "You listen to me right now, or you go across the street to Penn

Station and get the fuck back to Canada and let me forget all the time you've wasted in my life."

He looked at me and he started to talk. I cut him off. "You turn around, and you go hit him in the balls right now," I said. "You go over there and you hit him in the fuckin' balls and become a fighter or you get on the next train and you get the fuck out of my life!"

The whole gym stopped cold. All the old-timers, all the kids, Freddie Brown, everyone. It was one of those moments, those moments of frozen time, where you actually see someone having to make a decision about what kind of man they want to be. The next time I would be part of a moment like that came in the Moorer-Holyfield fight. This moment was almost like a prelude to that one. I had no hesitation making my demand of LaLonde. I had given up my Thanksgiving for him. I had disappointed my son for him.

He took in my words, then turned around, walked back toward Banks, and hit him square in the balls. Freddie Brown let out a little "Whoa." It shocked everyone. LaLonde and Banks continued fighting through two more rounds, LaLonde punching the shit out of Banks the whole time. There was no more hitting in the balls—Banks never threw a low punch again. That was the day LaLonde became a fighter.

Of course, you don't really know about someone until they've been tested. Cus had drilled the concept into me over and over—and I believed it even though Cus himself had come up short when he was tested. In the case of LaLonde and Wolfe, their relationship and loyalty to me was tested by a situation that involved Wolfe and another one of his fighters, Donnie Poole, who was taking Wolfe to court to break his contract.

Poole claimed that Wolfe had screwed him on a few things and that's why he wanted to get out of his contract. With the case coming up, Wolfe asked me if I would be a witness at the hearing. I thought Wolfe was a good manager, but I didn't want to get involved in the dispute and I told him so.

"The guy is smearing my reputation," Wolfe said. "I just want the truth to come out."

"Okay, I'll tell the truth, if that's what you want. But don't ask me to do anything beyond that."

"That's fine," he said. "That's all I want."

The morning of the hearing, I showed up at the Boxing Commission's office, down on lower Broadway. Wolfe was out in the hall with his lawyer, who was wearing an expensive suit and had the smooth voice of a radio deejay. Meanwhile, Poole showed up with his lawyer, who was actually a veterinarian—the guy had graduated from law school and had a law degree, but had gone on to became a vet instead. He was also one of the white-collar crew at Gleason's, which is the way Poole had met him, and he was a bit of a nut, too, always looking to fight tough guys who would punch him around. As a result, his nose was all bent and busted up. It was like a badge of honor or something. One time he got in the ring with Roberto Duran, who was there training, and Duran didn't give a shit that he wasn't a real fighter and knocked him out.

So here he was, Poole's veterinarian/lawyer, smelling of animals from being in his vet's office all the time, a guy I wouldn't bring my dog to, much less try to get legal help from (and all the punches he'd taken at Gleason's certainly weren't improving his memory of case law). Meanwhile, on the other side of the aisle, there was Wolfe's freakin' four-hundred-dollar-an-hour lawyer with his salon tan and Paco Rabanne aftershave. When Wolfe saw me, he came over, foaming at the mouth, saying, "I'm gonna fuck this Canuck against the fuckin' wall. I'm gonna tear his liver out!"

It was crazy. He was talking like a madman, like a guy who was way too vengeful for his own or anyone else's good. My instincts told me, just by the way he was talking, that this went way beyond anything normal or rational. I said, "Don't try screwin' this kid, Dave. I'm telling you. I don't even want to be here, so don't try anything funny. Don't lie about him, and do not put me in a position where you're trying to get me to support some lie."

We went into a hearing room that was like a mini-courtroom, with an elevated platform, a witness box, and uncomfortable wooden chairs. I got sworn in, and Wolfe's lawyer started asking me questions, basically leading me down a road.

"Did Dave Wolfe do a good job as manager?"

"Yes."

"What constitutes doing a good job?"

"Well, when Poole got with him, he wasn't rated, and under Wolfe's guidance he moved up to number five in the USBA. Wolfe got him a Canadian title shot."

"So did he do a good job, in your expert opinion, as a trainer?"

"Yes."

Suddenly, he dumped it on me. "Okay, Teddy, let's cut to the chase. You've said that Dave Wolfe's a good manager. Why are we here today?"

"I don't know. Why are we here?"

"Aren't we here because Donnie Poole asked Dave Wolfe to do something that was impossible for Dave Wolfe to do?"

"What are you talking about?" I knew that he was taking me to some bullshit place. I didn't know where, but I knew it was bullshit.

"Isn't it true," he said, "that the real issue here and the real problem, the reason we're here, is that Donnie Poole asked Dave Wolfe to get him drugs and Wolfe refused?"

This is how treacherous Wolfe was. Poole was a messed-up kid, no doubt about it. He had fractured his kneecap when he was younger— another Canadian with a scar from an ice hockey mishap—and he'd gotten addicted to Percocet, a powerful painkiller. Wolfe knew about it because the kid had been honest with him.

Now Wolfe's lawyer was using that information. "Didn't Donnie Poole tell you," he said to me, "that he asked Dave Wolfe to get him drugs and Dave Wolfe refused?"

"No." I wasn't going to be a part of it. I wasn't going to help him take this kid down in this way.

The lawyer was momentarily thrown by my refusal to cooperate. He gathered himself, pointing a finger in the air as if gauging the direction of the wind. "All right," he said. "Let me rephrase that."

"No," I said again, before he could continue.

"I'm just going to put it in different terminology—"

"No!" I said.

"Well—"

"*Hey!* What part of 'no' do you not understand? *No!* I don't care how many freakin' ways you want to ask me—"

"Could you please instruct the witness to answer only what he's asked?"

"Maybe someone will instruct you to stop lying," I said. The whole room was murmuring now.

"Mr. Atlas, please," the arbitrator said.

"This guy's trying to get me to say something untrue," I said. I looked at the lawyer with contempt. "I know what you're doing. You can phrase it any way you wanna phrase it and the answer will still be no!"

By the time I was excused, the room was in a complete uproar. I walked out of there, and nobody on Wolfe's side would look at me. I understood what it meant, that they were going to take LaLonde from me. I had no contract. I knew.

The next day, I went into Gleason's. I was scheduled to work with LaLonde, only he never showed up. I didn't bother calling him. I wasn't going to beg or crawl. Fuck him and fuck them. I knew what was right and wrong. I had warned Wolfe not to try to make me lie on the witness stand, and he hadn't listened. It wasn't complicated to me. There were no subtleties to the situation.

LaLonde was getting two hundred dollars a week from Wolfe, plus the apartment at 50 Barrow Street. When forced to choose, it was easier for him to go with Wolfe. He had gotten what he wanted from me. At least he thought he had. I'd built up his confidence, taught him to use his left hand, brought him to the next level.

Less than a week after the hearing, I found out that Wolfe had hired LaLonde a new trainer, Tommy Gallagher, a former cop. I'm not going to lie and say it didn't affect me. It did. What made it worse was that during the time I was still LaLonde's trainer, I had been offered a job with boxing manager Josephine Abercrombie that would have given me security and peace of mind. Abercrombie was one of the richest women in the country. She was new to boxing, but she brought a lot of money to the table. One weekend, she flew me down to Houston on her private jet to see the situation there. She had a nice stable of fighters, state-of-the-art facilities, a very impressive setup. By the end of the weekend, she wound up offering me a job, a house, and all kinds of perks. It was an offer that would have alleviated all my financial worries. But accepting would have required me to leave LaLonde, so I said no.

I don't want to blow it up into something that it wasn't, but I wouldn't have been able to bring LaLonde with me to Houston because Wolfe had a problem with one of the people in Abercrombie's organization, Jeff Levine. So I said no. I felt obligated to my commitment. Not long after, and for the same reason, I turned down an offer from the

Duvas to train some of their stable, which included Vinnie Pazienza, Meldrick Taylor, and Pernell Whitaker.

Months went by after that day at the Boxing Commission with Wolfe and Poole. I was barely making it. Elaine and I and the kids were living month to month, never able to get ahead, always just scraping by. Meanwhile, in 1987, LaLonde fought Eddie Davis for the vacant WBC light heavyweight title.

I watched the fight with the sportswriter Wallace Matthews, Nick Baffi, and some other guys at the Sporting Club on Hudson Street. Just as I had predicted the day I approached Wolfe about him being LaLonde's manager, LaLonde won the title. He knocked out Davis, who was forty years old and shot, in two rounds. I probably shouldn't have watched. It was just fuel for my anger. But I guess that's partly why I watched.

LaLonde had a second good payday a few months later, defending the title against another shot fighter, Leslie Stewart. I actually ran into LaLonde around that time. I was in the city, on my way to the Felt Forum, and he was walking across the street with somebody. He saw me and I saw him. He was in a white suit. I began walking in his direction, right toward him. He didn't know how to react. He started to say something, trying to gauge my intent, but I didn't say a word. I just kept walking toward him. When I got about fifteen feet away, he turned and jogged away. I didn't chase him or anything. But he was right to run.

Dave Wolfe was smart. He managed LaLonde beautifully, matching him against the right guys. He orchestrated his career like a maestro. The pot of gold at the end of the rainbow was the Sugar Ray Leonard fight. Leonard, who was no dummy himself, saw in LaLonde a guy that would allow him to move up in weight so that he could add another championship belt to his legacy. LaLonde got six million for the fight, which he lost on a ninth-round TKO. My share would have been six hundred thousand.

It's funny, with Tyson I never really thought about the money. For one thing, it wasn't real to me when I left Catskill; I was young, I couldn't envision that kind of payoff. It had the same reality as a lottery ticket. Then, when it did happen, when Tyson became the youngest heavyweight champion in history, Cus was already dead. So that changed how I felt. I could have dwelled on the millions that Tyson made, that Rooney made, but as much as possible I didn't let myself go there.

LaLonde was different. When he got the six million for the Leonard fight it tore me up. It made me want to kill him. I had sacrificed for him, and in return he had betrayed me. The idea that he should be *rewarded* for that? It made me murderous.

I'm not proud to say that. I understand that we live in a society of laws. I understand all that. But at the time I simply felt he no longer had a right to live.

It's hard for me to remember the exact moment I decided I was going to kill Donnie LaLonde. My anger just kept festering and growing. It didn't go away. I realized it wouldn't until I did something. I got a gun.

On a cold, rainy night in December of 1988, I drove into the city with a friend, who I'll call Tony. He came with me because he wanted to be with me. He felt the same way I felt, that there were dues to be paid. He was my friend and he was angry for me.

We parked the car blocks away from LaLonde's apartment. We were very careful not to open the car doors until we could get out without being seen. We both wore hooded sweatshirts. I had the gun hidden in my waistband.

We walked through the rain to 50 Barrow Street. There was a gate out front. I told Tony to wait. I went through the gate, and there was a door with a row of mailboxes and buzzers on the wall next to it. I rang one of the buzzers. No answer. I tried another.

"Who is it?" It was an elderly woman's voice.

"I'm a friend of Donnie's."

"Are you one of the ones that was making all that noise the other night?" Despite the admonishment, there was a pleasant quality to her voice. I could tell there was something I could work with in that voice.

"No, ma'am," I said. "Ma'am" wasn't a form of address I used ordinarily, but I just knew to use it.

"Oh, well, you sound like a nice fella. Do you wanna go in?"

"Yes, ma'am."

The buzzer sounded, and I pushed open the door. LaLonde's apartment was on the first floor. I walked down the short hallway, which was dimly lit and had dingy green flowered wallpaper. I got to the familiar door of his apartment. I thought of all the nights I had come over to talk him through his doubts and fears. I pulled out the gun and knocked.

If he had opened the door, he was dead. Nobody had seen me. The old lady upstairs had heard a disembodied voice, nothing more. I had gloves on, so there were no fingerprints. It would have been easy and clean. I would have pulled the trigger, turned around, and walked away.

Only he wasn't home. Thank God.

Of course, I wasn't thinking that at the time, and I didn't give up that easily. I went back out, but first I jammed up the door bolt with a matchbook cover so it wouldn't lock. Tony was waiting in the rain, across the street. I crossed over.

"You take care of it?"

"He's not there."

"What do you want to do?"

"We'll wait."

"Okay."

There was a phone booth a couple of blocks away near a deli. We stood under the awning of the deli, out of the rain. Every twenty minutes I walked over to the phone, dropped a dime in, and tried calling. Even though it had been nearly two years since I called that number regularly, I remembered it. Eleven o'clock came and went. Then twelve. Then one. I kept calling.

At two a.m., his girlfriend answered.

I put the neck of my sweatshirt over the mouthpiece to mask my voice. "Donnie there?"

"Yeah, hold on a minute."

There was a rustling sound as the phone was handed over. "Hello?" It was LaLonde.

I hung up.

Tony looked at me as I ducked back under the awning. I guess my expression told everything.

"Let's go."

We started walking. My heart was thumping hard. I heard this rushing sound in my ears. It was so loud it distorted everything else, as if I were underwater or in a plane taking off. Behind it was just the usual sounds of the city. Cars' tires on the wet asphalt. People's voices. A horn. But I couldn't seem to hear them right. I wasn't hearing things the normal way.

When we got to LaLonde's block, I saw the gate outside number fifty, and I started to get cold. I began shivering. I was thinking about the girl who had answered the phone. LaLonde's girl. I was thinking that I was probably going to have to kill her, too, because I couldn't be seen. If I got lucky and LaLonde came to the door, I could shoot him, and maybe I could get away without her seeing me. It was a small apartment. I didn't know how it would go. There was a chance I wouldn't have to kill her.

The more I thought about it, the more it bothered me. Thinking about LaLonde's blonde girlfriend, I flashed on Nicole. I thought about my daughter. My beautiful five-year-old daughter. Then I thought about my son.

As I thought about them, I remembered what had happened on Christmas Eve, after I put them to bed.

It was strange the ways the anger came out. LaLonde fought Leonard in November, and I stopped being able to sleep. Every night, lying there in the dark, I could feel my jaw clenched and my teeth grinding. Then one night, a few days before Christmas, I was in a bar. This big skinhead was shooting his mouth off. He was a Hitler Youth guy. I didn't even know what that was at the time, but I knew what he was saying. He was drunk, and he was saying, "All the Jews should have been killed."

And I said, "My father is Jewish."

The odd thing is that although I had never exactly hidden the fact that I was half Jewish, I had never been open about it either. Because I was raised Catholic, everyone assumed I was Irish, and I never made a point of correcting that assumption. Now here I was, after all the problems I'd had with my father growing up, turning to this guy and saying, "My father's Jewish."

Not surprisingly, it set him off. He came after me, which I guess is what I wanted. I smashed him in the face and messed him up pretty bad. A few days later, on Christmas Eve, right after I put my kids to bed, there was a knock on the door. It was a New York police detective. He wanted me to go down to the station with him and answer some questions. It wasn't as bad as it could have been. I was processed and fingerprinted and given a desk appearance ticket, which meant I had to return for the arraignment, but I got to go back home that night. Eventually the problem went away entirely. My lawyer paid the skinhead's lawyer off on the steps of the courthouse with seventy-five hundred dollars that I had borrowed from a friend. In return, the guy didn't press charges. But before that, what I remember is sitting with my kids on Christmas, not knowing what was going to happen, this thing hanging over me, and they were so happy and they loved me so much, and Elaine said to me, "You're throwing this all away because some jerkoff said something stupid. You're throwing this all away?"

HALFWAY DOWN THE BLOCK, ALL PHYSICAL SENSATION LEFT me. The cold. The noise. The ringing in my ears. The rushing of my blood. It all left me, and there was nothing. Hollowness. Detachment. Like I was dead and the world had ceased to exist. All my reservations were gone; I was going to do what I had come there to do.

I got to the gate. I opened it. And then I could hear Elaine again, crying the way she'd been crying on Christmas Day, saying, "You might not be able to do this with us no more."

I wanted to kill him so badly. So badly. And the faces of my kids kept flashing in front of me.

I turned to Tony.

He looked at me expectantly.

I shook my head and started walking away.

"Teddy, what? That's it?" he said.

"That's it."

I wish I could say the rage went away. But it wasn't that easy. I had to keep reminding myself of my responsibilities, thinking of the people who loved me and counted on me. I had to keep thinking about what would happen to them. Otherwise I was lost.

I WON'T TELL ANYBODY
YOU TOOK A DIVE

WILLEM DAFOE CAME TO ME IN THE FALL OF 1987 because he needed a boxing trainer to help him get prepared to play the role of a Jewish boxer in a movie called *Triumph of the Spirit*. The film's producer, Arnold Kopelson (who's big film before that was the Academy Award–winning *Platoon*), had contacted Mickey Duff, and Mickey had recommended me. After meeting and talking to Willem, I wound up being hired for a thousand dollars a week.

The movie was based on the true story of Salamo Arouch, a Greek Jew from the Balkans who got sent to Auschwitz during World War II and literally had to fight for his life in boxing matches with other concentration camp inmates. Though I wasn't aware of it, among the many atrocities committed by the Nazis during the war was the practice of taking camp inmates and pitting them against one another in Friday-night fights while SS officers sat around with their girlfriends and drank cognac and gambled on the outcomes. The winner of the bout might get an extra piece of bread so that he could live a bit longer, while the unfortunate loser got sent to the ovens.

The challenge I faced in the job was to bring an actor, in a period of a few months, to a point of proficiency where a movie audience would believe that he was a real fighter. Dafoe was a tremendous actor, very thorough and committed, and his primary concern was that he be authentic. He had never done any boxing before, so we started with the basics. I taught him how to hold his hands, how to throw the various punches, and how to move. It was important that he be believable as a fighter from that era, so I looked at old fight films to prepare myself. I didn't want him to be too slick or fancy or use his feet too much. A fighter from the Balkans in that era wouldn't fight like fighters of today.

Willem worked very hard, and he absorbed things quickly. Even though he had no background as a fighter, he was a real professional. You can recognize that quality in anybody if they have it. I had already seen it with Twyla. It was interesting—I never would have guessed that I'd see a parallel between the kind of toughness and discipline that my world required and what was needed to be a professional actor or dancer. But Willem and Twyla both opened up my eyes in that way.

Willem was a guy who believed in the spiritual side of life; he was intelligent, thoughtful, and took pride in his profession. He was a purist, who did all this stuff outside of Hollywood for the Wooster Group, which was an avant-garde theater company. His work with them reminded me of my work in the gym with the amateurs, where it was just a matter of being committed and not with hopes of money or glory. Willem was almost embarrassed about his big Hollywood movies. "I just do them so I can afford to do the stuff I really love," he told me.

He was constantly on a quest for knowledge, going off on retreats to meditate. He was trying to find a higher place, and he thought I knew some things. During the time I was training him, we had dinner frequently and talked about big questions. One time he said, "I'm having trouble with the truth."

"The truth is just an exercise," I said.

He loved that. He loved the sound of it. "Tell me exactly."

"Like how much truth can you stand?" I said. "How much can you lift? How many reps can you do?"

"Yeah. I've never thought about it that way before," he said. "But that makes a lot of sense to me."

Though Willem was not actually going to fight in the movie (the boxing scenes would be choreographed), I felt it was important that he get in the ring and experience what it felt like to hit and be hit. He agreed.

I put a mask on him so he wouldn't get marked up (it was a mask I had gotten custom-made for Chris Reid because Chris used to get cut a lot), and we did some sparring. There's no doubt that it gave him a feel for what it was really like to be in a ring with another fighter in actual combat.

We were training three hours a day in the middle of the day, and by the time Willem arrived each afternoon at Gleason's, he had already been up since four in the morning, because he was also rehearsing a play that he was doing with the Wooster Group at the Performing Garage. I guess he started to get a bit run-down from it all. I noticed at a certain point that he was looking a little ragged.

He was such a pro that he never said anything. Willem didn't know if what he was feeling was sickness or mental fatigue, and because he wasn't sure, he refused to capitulate. That pretty much defines a pro, for me: someone who will not allow himself the *out* of thinking that there is something wrong, because then there is a tendency to give in or formulate an excuse. It was up to me, as a professional trainer and teacher, to recognize if something was really wrong.

At a certain point, I decided that something was wrong, and I took him to the best doctor I knew: my father. It turned out that Willem had pneumonia. He had been training for days with it. My father put him on penicillin; he also gave him vials of liquid penicillin to inject as additional treatment while he was off in the Philippines shooting the movie *Born on the Fourth of July* with Tom Cruise. If Willem hadn't been such a pro, he would have been stopped by a lot less.

When he finished the Cruise movie, Willem got ready to go to Poland to begin working on *Triumph of the Spirit.* He told me he wanted me to go with him. I hadn't been expecting to go, and we had never discussed it, but he had decided it was important to him that I continue training him. He also thought that I should choreograph the fight scenes in the movie. At that point the producers hadn't hired anyone.

I had no idea what I should ask for, in terms of money. I had been getting a thousand a week to train him in New York, but this was going to be full-time and much more responsibility; I was going to have to be away from my family for more than a month. Willem and I discussed it. He'd asked around, and we came up with four thousand a week as a fair number, albeit on the high end. He said, "Call Arnold and work it out with him."

"You don't think it'll be a problem?"

"No. You're going to get that because I'm going to back you up. To be honest, you could ask for whatever you want and you would get it." Willem, who had just made a breakthrough in his career with *Platoon*, was getting a million dollars to star in this one (which was good money at the time), so he had real clout.

I went to Kopelson. I didn't have an agent or a lawyer. I told him what I wanted. He said, "Why would you ask for that much? I guess you figure, 'Why not?'" Kopelson had worked in the garment industry before Hollywood, and he had that rag-trade mentality that everybody was a hustler.

It hit me the wrong way, him saying that. It offended me. I said, "I don't fuckin' do that. I don't make a price just to make a price. I gotta be away from my family and my work for a month, and that's a fair price for what the job is, and if you don't think so you can go get someone else." He got very quiet at that point, and that was pretty much the end of the conversation.

Willem, meanwhile, had already gone over to Poland. When I talked to him, I told him what had happened. He went to see Kopelson, who told him that he had decided to use the stunt coordinator to choreograph the fight scenes instead of me.

"Teddy's asking for too much money," Kopelson explained.

Willem got very upset with him. He threatened to go home if Arnold didn't change his mind. I think it even got to the point of him making plane reservations.

Kopelson got in touch with me at that point. He said, "Teddy, I think that we had some kind of misunderstanding." He told me that he had always wanted me to work on the movie, and of course he'd pay me what I was asking for.

When I arrived in Poland, everyone there seemed to know that there had been some drama involved. I was a little bit naive and didn't realize stuff like this took place on movie sets all the time.

Poland was still an Iron Curtain country at that point. It was a bleak place, very poor. You had people working on conveyor belts in factories for thirty dollars a month. There was a lot of drinking, a lot of vodka, and people passed out on the sidewalks. They didn't use much oil heat, so people made coal fires to stay warm and the sky was dark with smoke and soot.

The production was giving us these Polish *złoty* for our per diems, handing it out like it was Monopoly money, which in a way it was, because they had gotten a black-market rate of exchange of something like three thousand *złoty* to a dollar. The waiters in the hotel where we were staying were making nothing, and I was giving them huge tips. Edward James Olmos, one of the actors in the movie, gave me a hard time about it. He said I was throwing off the whole economy. He was serious, too, he wasn't kidding around. I said, "What the heck are you talking about, Eddie? There is no economy here."

"You're tipping them three months' salary in a day," he said.

"Yeah? So? What's your point?"

"When we leave there's gonna be a big crash."

"A crash? They crashed here a long time ago. This country is in ruins."

"But it'll make them feel bad when we leave."

"Hey, at least while we're here they'll feel good."

Anyway, we disagreed about it, and that was that. I kept leaving big tips. It was the funniest thing, though. One day, we were in the hotel restaurant, me, Willem, and Costas Mandylor, and where were all the waiters? At our table. Meanwhile, Eddie was at another table, looking for a waiter, going, "Waiter! *Waiter!*"

Even at the best hotel in the city, some amenities were hard to get. Like toilet paper. So when the maid came by my room, I gave her a twenty-dollar bill, American, which was unheard of. Well, forget it. You remember that old Frank Sinatra commercial with the towels? That's how it was with me and toilet paper. It was like a freaking toilet paper store in my room. Nobody else in the whole hotel had toilet paper. I had it all. People were coming up to me saying, "Teddy, I hear you have toilet paper. I was wondering if I could get a roll?," and I was saying, "No, I'm sorry, I can't help you." "Teddy, come on, just a few sheets. . . ."

WILLEM AND I TRAINED VERY HARD DURING THE MONTH I was over there. My job was twofold. One, to make Willem look, feel, and respond like a fighter; two, to choreograph all the fight scenes in the movie.

As far as getting Willem to where he needed to be, we hit a spot where he wasn't responding very well. He was getting a little funny with me. We were close and he was always respectful of me, but he started to get a bit nervous, and that made him resistant to some of the things I was telling him. It was like a fighter looking for an excuse not to fight. He wanted to look like a fighter, but wasn't sure he was looking like one.

Frequently, when you're doing a thing, you're only aware of the way you feel. You connect the way you feel with the way you must look. If you feel inhibited, which people often do when they're performing difficult and demanding tasks, especially physical ones, then you feel that must be the way you look. You don't realize that you look *fine*.

Willem was starting to fall into a bad way of thinking in that regard. It was making him trust me a bit less, because he was worried I wasn't telling him the truth. One day, when his mood was particularly negative, I grabbed hold of him. I looked him in the face. I could smell something coming out of his pores.

Smoke. He had been smoking cigarettes. He was so nervous and stressed that he didn't realize what that meant, that he was actually undermining himself, contributing to his worries about his credibility. Would his character smoke cigarettes, knowing that he was going into the ring and if he lost he would die? He would put a shotgun into his mouth before he would do that. He would eat razor blades. Yet here was Dafoe, doing something his character would never do.

"You've been smoking," I said.

"How did you know that?"

"Never mind how I know. I know." I looked him right in the eyes. I didn't care that he was a movie star and that you're not supposed to act in certain ways with movie stars if you want to stay employed. "Now starting right fucking now, you ain't gonna smoke no more. You're gonna act like Salamo would act, and you're gonna act like a pro."

You know what he did? He looked at me and said, "Okay," and he never smoked another cigarette. From that moment on, we never had another day that came close to not being a great day.

The choreography was a different sort of challenge for me. I had never done anything like that before. I had to sort of make it up as I went along.

There was a scene where Willem gets into a fight with one of the Jewish trustees, who were in their own way almost worse than the German guards. The fight takes place while the inmates are laying train rail up on this elevated mound. In the script there was no description of the fight whatsoever. It was just left blank. So before shooting this scene, we went to the location to see how to do it. I was there with Willem and Robert Young, the director, and the director of photography and the other actors. It was clear that the fight couldn't take place up by the tracks, because there wasn't enough room. I decided that they could roll down the embankment and fight on the flatter ground. That was how we would solve the problem.

After we had gone over the actual physical specifics of the fight, I realized I had to have a way of making sure that it would be consistent, that it would be the same every time we shot it. All of a sudden it hit me. I had to write out every step of it, every punch, every move. I wound up staying up all night to do it. I showed Willem what I had done. He said, "This is great. Now I know exactly what I'm going to do and I'll be able to prepare for it."

"Yeah, it's gonna be just like a dance," I said. It was funny that I said that. Maybe unconsciously it came from Twyla, I'm not sure. But it was clear to me that was how it had to be done. Writing it out that way also made me more comfortable and confident. In a situation like that, if the people you're working with think you know what you're doing, then it's actually like you do know what you're doing.

We rehearsed the fights in the movie every day, getting ready to shoot them. We got to the point where each fight was memorized down to the last punch. There was one particular fight that took place between Willem and this Polish actor. The Polish actor was a nice guy, but he was a big actor in Poland, and on this film he had just this small part, so he had a bit of a chip on his shoulder. Physically, he was bigger than Willem, and he kept getting a little rough with him. It bothered me because Willem was my guy.

I took Willem aside and said, "Listen, this time when you step to the side, you hit him on the jaw."

"You mean the shoulder, right? I thought I'm supposed to hit him in the shoulder." That's what was in the script and was the way we had been doing it.

"No, you hit him in the jaw."

"You sure?"

"Yeah. You're not that big a puncher. You're not gonna knock him out."

He smiled. "All right. You sure?"

"Yeah."

They started shooting the scene. The Polish guy was moving forward with this little smirk because he'd been pushing Willem around. This time, Willem stepped to the side and *bang,* hit the guy, and the guy went down.

I was watching through the monitor with the director, Bob Young. All of a sudden I heard him asking me, "What's that in his mouth?"

I leaned in for a closer look. "That? It's nothing. Just a little blood."

"Blood!"

"Yeah, Bob, c'mon, it's not serious. Every once in a while, you're gonna miss a little. But he's fine."

Willem helped the Polish guy up, and it was a little bit like what had happened with Donnie LaLonde and Johnnie Walker Banks. The Polish guy kind of tapped Willem, and it was understood, he wasn't going to be rough no more. At that moment, Willem looked over at me and winked. I clenched my fist and gave him a little fist shake down low.

As the weeks went by in Poland, Arnold Kopelson and I actually wound up getting close. We'd eat lunch together on the set, him, Robert Young, Willem, and some of the other actors and me. Arnold and Bob Young loved to hear my boxing stories, especially the stuff about the smokers in the Bronx. In fact, Arnold was interested in doing a TV series about the smokers, but the negotiations fell apart, mainly because he was such a cheap bastard.

The funny part is that on the movie he came to recognize my worth. He saw that I was actually valuable and earning my keep. He even said to me one day, "You should have asked me for more money, Teddy." That was his sense of humor.

The biggest fight scene in the movie was one between Willem and this German prisoner, Klaus Silber. We were using fighters from the Polish Olympic team in the movie, and we still hadn't picked one to play Silber. Arnold and I were discussing it one day, and he said, "What about you, Teddy? You want to be in the movie?"

"Me?"

"Who could play it better than you? Just so long as you realize I'm not paying you anything extra."

I smiled. "Yeah, all right, I'll do it," I said. "Free of charge."

"The only other thing is, you're gonna have to shave your head."

"Shave my head? Uh-uh. That I won't do."

"Teddy, you gotta."

"No fuckin' way, Arnold. I'm not shaving my head."

The thing about Arnold, once he made up his mind that he wanted something, he wouldn't let go. He really wanted me to play Silber and he was very upset that I wouldn't shave my head. He called up Mickey Duff and asked him to talk to me. So Mickey called me. He said, "Teddy, I hear you're doing great on this movie."

"Yeah, Mick, things are going pretty good."

"Arnold tells me he asked you to be in the movie."

"Yeah, that's true."

"He said he asked you to shave your head, but you wouldn't do it."

"That's right."

"Teddy, what are they paying you to work on that movie?"

"Mick, you know what they're paying me. Four thousand a week."

"You want to know what I think? For four thousand a week, I'd shave my balls if they asked me."

Eventually, I relented. I agreed to get the haircut. When it came time, the girl who was going to cut my hair was very cautious. The truth is she was a little afraid of me. She used a pair of scissors instead of the clippers. She cut it short but like a real haircut. With everyone else, she had just used the clippers and buzzed off all their hair. Not with me. When she was finished, she held up a mirror and asked me, "How's that, Teddy?" I still had a pretty full head of hair. I said, "Yeah, that's good."

Arnold came into the room at that point. His jaw dropped. He said, "What is this, a barbershop? This is Auschwitz!"

I had to hand it to him. He knew how to make me laugh, he knew how to deal with me.

"Teddy, they didn't get the option in Auschwitz to say, 'Just a little off the top.'"

"All right, all right," I said. I looked at the hair cutter. She was in a tough spot, caught between me and Arnold. "Go ahead," I said. "Take it all off. Don't worry about it."

She buzzed it clean. When she was done, Arnold said, "Shit, no wonder you didn't want it all taken off. Wow. I thought you were scary before." You could see all the scars on my head, where I was hit by a tire iron, and all kinds of other nicks and dings.

The night before the big fight scene, I wrote out the sequence of moves, the way I had done with the others. This was the biggest fight, the most dramatic, the most hateful—a German and a Jew. I wrote it up so that I beat the crap out of Willem for most of the fight, and then in the end Willem won. I showed it to Arnold the next morning, and he started reading it. Halfway through, he put it down and said, "Teddy, I love you, and I'd do anything for you, and I know you're underpaid, but at this point in the film, I cannot afford to throw out Willem and make you the star of the picture. Willem needs to win this fight."

"Arnold, Arnold, just keep reading a little longer."

"You sure?"

"Yeah, yeah. Just keep reading."

He kept reading, and finally breathed a sigh of relief. "You had me worried," he said.

"So you like it?"

"Yeah, I like it."

We began rehearsing a while later. Everything went well, but at the end of the fight, instead of going down, I had it so that my guy, Klaus, gets hung up on the ropes and keeps getting punched. He never goes down.

Robert Young, the director, said, "It's very good, Ted. I like it a lot. There's only one thing. . . ."

"Go ahead, Bob. Say whatever you want to say."

"No, it's good," he said. "It's just the end. . . ."

"What about the end?"

"I'm just wondering why you don't wind up on the canvas."

"It's a character thing. See, this guy knows that if he loses, he's going to the chimney."

"Right. But he's been hit with so many punches, how does he stay up on the ropes like that?"

"Unconsciously, it's so entrenched . . . ," and I started going through this beautiful explanation that was detailed and deep and I talked about this guy's humanity and his stubborn will to live, and Bob went, "Uh-huh."

Arnold was in the background, and he hadn't said anything to that point. Suddenly he cleared his throat. "Teddy, could I say something?"

"Sure."

"Do you think it's possible that you just don't want to go down?"

"No! It's the guy. He thinks he's gonna go to the chimneys."

"Yeah, but he takes all those shots. Have you ever seen a guy take that many shots and not go down?"

"Sure. Absolutely."

Nobody wanted to say anything. I guess I was pretty intimidating, especially the way I looked with my head shaved. Finally, Willem said, "Don't you think it's just a little to do with you not wanting a schmuck like me standing over you forever on film?"

"No, no. I swear to God that's not it."

Arnold said, "What if we pay you more to take the dive?"

"Fuck you, Arnold. I ain't taking a dive for no one."

"So you admit it!"

"No, no . . . all right, maybe a little." I mean, suddenly I realized that they were right. I wasn't being honest with myself. I hadn't realized it, but it was true. "All right, let's do it again," I said. So we went through the scene again, and we got to the point where I was supposed to go down, and again, I wouldn't go down. I couldn't.

Arnold was shouting, "Just fall! Fall! Come on!"

But I couldn't. I couldn't fall down. Arnold was beside himself. Willem was grinning, shaking his head. "Teddy, I promise I won't tell anybody you took a dive."

"I don't know what it is. It's a crazy thing."

It took all my willpower, but the next time we tried it, I made myself fall down. The whole place erupted. I got a standing ovation. For falling down.

The funny postscript is that at one of the premieres, my young son, Teddy, said to Willem afterward, "You didn't knock out my dad. He let you win because you're the star."

Willem smiled, and I looked over at him and shrugged, like, "What can I say? He's my son."

FIRE, NOT FEAR

NOT LONG AFTER I GOT BACK FROM POLAND, IN THE beginning of 1988, I met Sammy "the Bull" Gravano. He was a rising star in the mob, the underboss to John Gotti, and he had a reputation for being a ruthless, stone-cold killer. Playing off the tough-guy image, he started going to Gleason's and training with Edwin Viruet, an ex–professional fighter who in his prime had once gone fifteen rounds with Roberto Duran, but was now broken down, overweight, and desperate to make whatever money he could make.

I think Sammy was paying Viruet a couple of hundred a week. Every morning Sammy would come in with his driver, Louie Saccenti, and work out and spar with Viruet. Sammy and Louie were an odd pair. Sammy was short and stocky and wore plain gray sweatpants and a hooded sweatshirt, and Louie was tall and elegant and wore a double-breasted suit and shoes that shined like mirrors.

I was training Chris Reid at the time, and Sammy, who was a real boxing fan, knew who I was. He followed the sport closely and knew the personalities. We would nod hello at each other, but I never really talked to him. Then one time, Viruet was away or didn't show up, and Sammy came over to me. He introduced himself and said, "My name's Sammy," though obviously I already knew who he was.

"You're the kind of person," he said, "from what I understand about you, that you stand up for things. I follow boxing pretty closely and I like the way you handle yourself. I know the stories about you and I respect you. Would you consider training me?"

"No, I couldn't do that. Edwin trains you and it wouldn't be right."

"How about just for today, since he's not here?"

"Yeah, okay, I guess I could fill in for him just for the day."

"Good. What'll I pay you?"

"Nothing. It's just a favor."

I wound up training Sammy for the day. It wasn't a serious training session; I kept it fairly casual. But he liked what we were doing. He was extremely short. Maybe five feet five, and muscular. He had weight lifter's muscles. Viruet had been teaching him to box from the outside, which was crazy. Gravano had very short arms. In a way it was the perfect con: Viruet made Sammy box like Ali, dancing and staying on the outside, because that way Viruet could stay out of range, and it was easier and less stressful for him. He didn't have to worry about accidentally getting hit by Sammy, who was pretty strong.

Still, it didn't make sense, so I spent the session showing Sammy how to slip and get inside. When we were done, he said, "This is the way I should be fighting. This is the right way for me." He wanted to pay me. I wouldn't let him. I said, "It was just a favor for one day."

After that, even though Viruet was still training him, Sammy and I got friendly. He would corner me and ask all sorts of questions.

"What's the most important thing for a fighter?"

"The most important thing? Discipline."

"What about hand speed? What about power?"

"Nah. Those things don't mean nothing if you can't control yourself."

"What do you mean?"

"Control yourself. Make the right decisions."

I knew we were talking about boxing, and that was certainly how I intended it, but I also realized that he was applying what I was telling him to what he did outside the gym. I can't pretend I didn't know that. There was a parallel between boxing and what he did, as far as facing the moment. At the same time, when someone asked me something, I wasn't going to duck it or avoid it.

"What do you mean by making a choice?" he asked.

"Making a choice whether or not you're going to quit and make an excuse to get out. Fighters sometimes lie to themselves." I had no idea how important and relevant this conversation would seem a couple of years later when he flipped. It's pretty interesting to look back at it in light of what happened.

"What do you mean, 'lie to themselves'?"

"They sometimes make excuses to get out and not face what they should face."

He was looking for the same thing that a fighter is looking for: how to deal with pressure and fear.

"Are you saying that the most important thing is for a guy to be tough?" he asked.

"No. Not to be tough. Tough is just a word. To understand what you're facing, to be in control of yourself, to have the confidence to face what you have to face and not break down under pressure."

So that was it. That was the real connection between us. He needed advice and counsel, because he was under a lot of pressure, and on some level he thought maybe I could give it to him.

One day not too long after this, my friend Nick Baffi called me up and said, "Teddy, I need to talk to you."

He came over to the gym and we went and sat at one of the tables by the coffee machine. I knew before he said anything that it was about Gravano. Nick had this friend, Philly, who was with Sammy, and I realized Philly must have said something to him about me and Sammy.

"Be careful with this guy," Nick said to me. "He's getting very friendly with you."

"Nah. We see each other in the gym, that's all."

"He's been talking about you a lot. Asking questions. He's checked you out."

"What do you mean, he's checked me out?"

"He's made inquiries. He found out about some of your history, that you got in trouble when you were a kid, and a few other things. He knows a little bit about you. He says he likes you, but be careful."

"All right. But I really don't think there's anything to worry about." I knew that Nick loved me, and that he was just trying to look out for me.

Sammy kept coming to the gym and working with Viruet, and we continued our conversations and got friendlier. One day, he asked me if

I worked out. It just so happened that I was looking for a gym where I could do some weight work.

"There's a place I train," he said. "I'd be honored if you'd allow me to give you the small gift of a membership."

"That's very generous of you, Sammy, but—"

"Why don't you try it?" he said.

I shrugged.

"It's called the Narrows Fitness Club. It's right off the Bay Ridge exit on the Belt Parkway in Brooklyn. You can see it from the highway. Meet me there tomorrow at ten o'clock and I'll hook you up with a membership. It's up to you. If you don't want to go, don't go."

I met him there the next morning. The gym is actually a New York Sports Club now, but back then it was the Narrows Fitness Club. Sammy arranged for me to get a free Gold Membership. It didn't cost him anything. I guess that's part of why I let myself accept it. I knew he wasn't paying.

He had a personal trainer, a guy named John, who began training both of us every morning at ten o'clock. It became a routine. I would go there before going to Gleason's. This went on for more than a year. We were working with this trainer, and it got very competitive between us. One time, we were doing curls, and Sammy made it a contest of who could do more. I was hurting, but I just kept going. He looked over at me, and he kept going, too. Finally, he had to stop. He said, "Fucking son of a bitch," and got up and threw the weight at the wall. Then he took the whole freakin' rack of weights and threw them against the wall, one after the other. There were signs up, saying, "Please replace weights carefully." Other guys in the gym looked around when they heard the weights crash against the wall, but they saw who it was and quickly went back to what they were doing. They didn't want him to see them looking at him. Even the owner didn't dare say anything.

Sammy looked at me as I continued to do curls, and he said to whoever might hear, "This kid's got some balls, some heart, this little son of a bitch."

Occasionally, after the workout, we'd get lunch together, and he'd want to continue our discussions.

"This thing about control and discipline, what is it they're disciplining?"

"What do you mean, what are they disciplining?"

"All right, controlling. What are they controlling?"

"Fear."

"You're saying fighters are afraid?"

"Everyone's afraid."

He didn't like hearing that. He said, "Not me. I ain't afraid of nothin'."

"Everybody's afraid of something."

Someone else would have been in trouble disagreeing with him that way, but I guess he made more allowances for me.

"Fighters are afraid because there's a reason to be afraid," I said. "They can be hurt. They can be killed. So if they're not going to be defeated by their fear, they have to learn to control it, and use it to help them. It's like controlling fire."

"Fire. I like that word," he said. "Let's use that word instead of fear."

"It doesn't matter. It's the same thing."

"Yeah, I like 'fire' better, though. Let's use that. We all got fire. So how do we control it?"

"The first thing is to understand it."

"Understand it how?"

"Understand not to ignore it. Not to deny it. Not to hide from it. You need to make yourself aware of it and realize that it doesn't have to be a weakness. If you're denying it, you're doomed to be controlled by it."

"What is that supposed to mean?"

"If you're running around saying, 'I don't got fear—'"

"Fire!"

"All right, 'fire.' If you deny having it, then it can't help you, and you have to be victim to it. But if you understand that it doesn't have to be an enemy, that it's not necessarily a weakness, that it doesn't necessarily make you yellow, then you're in a place where you can use it, you can harness it. That's the difference between champions and the guys that don't get there. The champions understand that and are truthful with themselves, even when it's uncomfortable. That enables them to make choices, instead of just having knee-jerk responses."

Sammy had a hard time digesting a lot of what I was saying to him. It shook him up. He was almost like a kid in a way. Asking big questions, and then, when he heard the answer, going "But why?" He kept needing to hear the answer expanded upon and repeated—and still he didn't

really understand. We had a lot of conversations about the idea of fear—
or fire, as he needed to call it. It was funny how the whole essence of
what I was talking about was encapsulated by his inability to even utter
the word.

For a year, we saw each other nearly every day at the Narrows Club.
Besides the weights, Sammy also played handball and racquetball. He
was a workout fanatic. I found out he was taking steroids because one
day he asked me if I wanted to try them. He said, "Do you want a pop,
Bo?" He called everybody Bo. He got that from Gotti, who had picked it
up in prison. It was like a derivative of Bro.

"What do you mean, 'pop'?"

"You know, do some juice."

"No, I don't do that."

"It's not bad," he said. "The only bad thing is sometimes you get pimples on your back." He was wearing a tank top and I noticed that there
were pimples all over his back.

"No thanks," I said.

"All right, Bo."

He also tried to get me interested in racquetball. He bought me a
brand-new racket. I didn't want it, but he insisted. I said, "I don't play."

"You'll learn how to play," he said.

I'd watch him occasionally, through the glass wall. A lot of people
would watch. Every once in a while, an FBI agent would try to infiltrate
the club. They were following him and keeping him under observation
all the time. If Sammy or any of his guys thought that a new member of
the club was a cop, they'd refer to him as being "British." That was the
code word. One of them would say to Sammy, "That guy's British."
And Sammy would go, "He's British? That motherfucker."

I saw Sammy play racquetball with one of these guys one time.
Whenever he got the chance, he'd whack the ball at the guy's back.
Every once in a while, you'd hear this guy yell "Ahhh!" and you knew
he'd gotten slammed in the back. In a normal racquetball game, that
might happen on rare occasions, but when Sammy played this guy, it
happened three or four times in a game. Sammy kept apologizing. "Oh,
sorry, you gotta move a little quicker there, Bo." But by the time the
game was over, the guy was all bruised up.

I took Sammy to a few fights at the Garden. We sat in front with his crew of guys. His driver, Louie Saccenti, was always with him. Louie had a job on the docks in the local union. He was a shop steward, then he became a delegate, but he didn't have to show up too much, I guess because of Sammy. When we were weight training, Louie would just stand there in an expensive overcoat and suit, watching.

I remember Edwin Viruet said to me one day about Sammy and Louie, "You know, this is the opposite of what it looks like." Viruet was a guy who looked at things purely for what they were.

"What do you mean?" I said.

"It's a little guy and a big guy," he said, because Louie was a lot bigger than Sammy. "But the reality is that the little guy is actually the big guy and the big guy is the little guy."

"Yeah, that's true," I agreed, laughing.

"You ever notice, when it comes time for me to be paid? The little guy tells the big guy to pay me, and the big guy pays me."

He was right. Louie carried around the money. That was the way it worked with them.

SAMMY TREATED HIS SPARRING SESSIONS AT GLEASON'S LIKE they were a big deal. He even asked me to work his corner for him a few times. These weren't real fights. The guys he sparred knew they had to work easy with him, and he knew that would be the case. He sparred with Renaldo Snipes one time, a guy who had once fought for the heavyweight title, and Sammy acted like it was for real, even though it was all bullshit. While I was putting the gloves on him, tying them up, he said, "I always had more balls than brains." Which was just the kind of thing that he was expected to say, being a tough guy, but was in fact the opposite of the truth because it wasn't a real fight and balls had nothing to do with it. I mean, what was there for him to be afraid of?

The funny thing is, he actually was afraid. Even though Snipes would never in a million years let loose and bang with him, Sammy was still afraid. And having to deal with that fear for one round wiped him out. Exhausted him. All Snipes did was put pressure on Sammy. He never hit him. He just pursued him. But the pressure, the idea that he might get hit, even though he knew he wouldn't, wore Sammy down. He got wild, threw all these haymakers to keep Snipes from advancing, but he couldn't connect, he wasn't in control, and it physically wore him out.

There came a day when Sammy took me to lunch at this little café across the street from Gleason's and proposed we go into business together. He just said, "Listen, me and my partner are thinking about going into boxing." He never mentioned Gotti's name. He just said "me and my partner."

"This isn't something I would even consider," he said, "unless I could get into it with a person who knows the business and is somebody I could trust. We'd give you whatever you'd need. I was thinking about seventy-five thousand dollars seed money, two thousand dollars a week in salary to start. Plus, there's a building I'm looking at in Brooklyn. . . . What do you think? Would you be interested?"

Once I got over my initial surprise, I said, "Sammy, this isn't a business you just go into. There's a lot to it, and if you plunge in and spend a lot of money, you're just going to lose it. You can't start at an elite level—"

"Nah, we'll go right up to that level. Don King would be tickled pink to help me and my partner. To help me and John." He had finally said the name.

"Fine. I understand you have resources. But I'm telling you, it's a very fragile business, very shaky in lots of ways. You don't get into it and just make money. Shows cost money. It costs money to keep fighters and develop them. It doesn't happen overnight. It's a much longer process than you think."

"Not for us it won't be."

"People don't keep their word."

"Well, you won't have that problem no more. I know you've had problems before and walked away from things."

"I've made choices. It wasn't like I couldn't handle things."

"I understand that," he said. "I'm just saying you won't be walking away from nothing this time. They lie this time, I put them in the trunk."

"I like to take care of my own problems."

"That's why I want someone like you. You're your own guy. You know the business and I can trust you."

"I don't think I'd be interested."

"Do me a favor," he said. "Would you at least have dinner with me? I've got some friends who all want me to go into the business. I'm not stupid. They want me to go into the business so I can give them jobs, but I ain't going in unless you go in. Would you at least have dinner with us?"

"I'm telling you right now, I'm not gonna do it."

"Meet with them. Let them speak. If you still don't want to do it, say it in front of them. That's all I ask. It'll be a nice dinner, and I would appreciate it."

I agreed to the meeting. It was a big deal, very secret. Sammy said, "Louie will call you an hour before and tell you where it is."

On the appointed day, Louie called me at seven p.m. and said, "It's at La Tavola."

It was a place out in Brooklyn. In Bay Ridge. I drove there, and Sammy pulled up in his tan-colored Lincoln right after I arrived. The valet hustled up to take his car. When we walked in, I looked around the bar and I could see that he had guys placed in different spots at the bar. I could tell they were his guys just by the way they looked.

The owner came running up. The rest of the restaurant fell into a respectful hush. The owner was gushing, "Mr. Gravano, so nice to see you again." I couldn't help thinking, *Here's a guy who's never done anything except kill people, yet he's being treated like he's Frank Sinatra.*

We walked toward a big table in the back. There were nine guys, and Sammy introduced me to them all. Everybody was there for a reason, each person. There was a guy, Jimmy this, another guy, Al that, another guy, Danny whatever, and they all had a purpose. One guy was going to do the promotion, another guy was going to do ticket sales, another guy was going to do a thing with the hotels.

The chef came out from the kitchen, fawning all over Sammy. "What do you want tonight, the veal? I'll make it a special way. It'll be beautiful. You'll see." The waiter brought over bottles of wine, the best wine they had, and asked, "Is this good for you?" Sammy enjoyed every moment of it.

When we were all sitting, Sammy got up to do something, leaving me alone with the others. They all looked at me.

"Teddy, you know he's only going to do this if you say, 'Yeah.'"

"I'm gonna do what feels right for me."

"No, no, we know, but it would be nice. There's a lot of money. He's got a lot of money behind him. It would be a good opportunity for you." They kept looking at me, letting that sink in.

Sammy came back, and we got down to it, he broke it all down. He said, "You know, I've gotten really good in the construction business, but I didn't know nothing about the construction business when I started. I brought people in that knew. I'd never get involved in a business that I didn't know unless I had someone that did know and that I could trust. I'm smart enough to know that."

Everyone nodded enthusiastically. You got the feeling he could have been saying anything and they would have been just as intent and focused on him. "I'm not going to get involved in the boxing business," he continued, "unless Teddy Atlas gets involved with me, because he knows the business and you can trust Teddy Atlas. His track record shows he's a man and he's been tested." He turned in my direction and our eyes met.

"The key to running a successful business," he went on, "is having the right people putting things together and getting the whole thing . . . what do you call it? Getting it . . ." He was struggling for the right word, and they were all looking at him, but no one would say it. They all knew the word he was searching for, but they were afraid to say it.

"What's the word I'm looking for?" Sammy said.

"Organized," I said.

"Yeah, that's it. Organized."

Now they were all laughing.

"That's the word," Sammy said. "You could say it, Ted. I can't say it."

They all thought it was hysterical, the funniest thing they'd ever heard.

When Sammy had finished talking, they again turned toward me, and I felt compelled to launch into a whole explanation of the mechanics of the boxing business, making clear that it wasn't what they thought it was. I was wasting my time. They wanted to get into it. Their minds were made up. Sammy said, "Teddy, everything will be in your name," and I was thinking, *Does that mean the indictments, too?*

I told them I appreciated that they thought so much of what I did, but that I was committed to the guys I was training and didn't feel like being tied down and getting involved in the business end of boxing.

A couple of Sammy's guys tried to reassure me that it wouldn't work that way with them.

"You won't have to do that stuff. We'll do all that. You won't be burdened with the promotional and business side of things, we will."

"Yeah, but I just—"

Sammy cut it off. He said, "You want to stay free is what you're saying. You wanna be your own man."

"Yeah, I guess that's what I'm saying. I've turned other things down for the same reason."

"Yeah, I know. I know I'm not the only one you've said no to."

In fact, he knew I'd turned down Josephine Abercrombie; I'd turned down the Duvas.

"Well, that's good enough for me," he said. "If that's your final word, that's your final word. Like I said at the beginning, it doesn't work out, we'll just enjoy a good dinner together."

So that was that. When I told Nick Baffi about the meeting later, I mentioned how Sammy had said everything would be in my name, and Nick said, "The indictments, too?"

I laughed. "Jesus, Nick, that's exactly what I was thinking when he said that."

Nick said he had been worried that I'd wind up saying yes to Sammy, but the fact that I'd said no also worried him.

"This guy is dangerous. You don't know how he's gonna react. I know he says he likes you, but he also told Philly that you know a lot of stuff, all the discussions you've been having with him about boxing and fear. He wanted to know from Philly whether you've ever said anything to me about him. He might think you're talking about him and be worried you know his weaknesses. He's the kind of guy who kills people for that."

But Sammy never brought it up again, and there were no repercussions. We kept training together at the gym and everything was okay. Then one morning he showed up and said, "There's indictments coming down."

"Yeah?"

"I might have to . . . You might not see me around for a while."

We went into our regular routine with the weights. I spotted for him, he spotted for me. He didn't tell me exactly what he was going to do, but it was clear that he might go into hiding or something.

"It's the fuckin' U.S. government coming after me, Bo. They invade countries and they're coming after me. What the fuck are they coming after me for? They want me to do bad things to my friend John. They want me to hurt my friend. They want me to forsake him."

I was stunned that he was telling me this. He wrestled the weight back on its rest and got up off the bench.

"They want to take my manhood. They want to take it, but they can't take it. The only way they can get it is if I give it."

"That's right," I said.

"Take a walk with me," he said. We left the weight room and went outside. We stepped outside into the cool, late fall air. The street was empty. We started walking. Halfway down the block, he said, "Listen, I hate to even ask you this. . . ."

"What?"

"Could you do me a favor? Would you train my son in boxing while I'm gone?"

I looked at him.

"I just want him to be all right," he said. "If he's with you I know you'll make him strong and you'll make him all right."

"Yeah, I'll do you that favor," I said.

"Thank you."

He never showed up at the gym the next day. It was strange, after all that time, to be there alone. I was training and he was gone. Louie was gone. They went on the lam. Pennsylvania, Florida, all over the place. One night, they even snuck back into town and showed up at one of Snipes's fights in the Garden wearing fake beards. But eventually they came back for real because Gotti ordered them to come back. Sammy didn't want to, but Gotti did a lot of things that got people screwed.

A few days later, December 11, 1990, the feds went to the Ravenite Social Club on Mulberry Street and arrested Sammy and John and Frankie Locascio and Tommy Gambino and Jimmy Fiello, a.k.a. Jimmy Brown. They brought them out single file. It was on all the news channels. Everyone in the world saw them parading out in handcuffs five of the heaviest wiseguys around.

Not long after that, Louie got in touch with me. He said, "Sammy said you promised to train his son while he's in the can." At that point, Sammy was still being a stand-up guy, and I felt something for his kid,

Gerard, what he must have been going through, so I made good on my promise. Four or five days a week, Louie would pick up the kid, then he would pick me up, and we'd drive over to Gleason's.

I trained him like I trained any other fighter. He was only fifteen, but he was strong, and he learned. When he progressed to a certain point, I let him spar with Tyrone Jackson, my old fighter. It was good. Louie videotaped it with these small video cartridges, and he was able to get them to Sammy's lawyer. Louie was funny. He would make everybody get in on it. Sammy's father-in-law, who was there, me, Tyrone, everybody. Louie would say, "Okay, this is Howard Cosell here with Gerard 'the Bull' Gravano, getting ready for the Golden Gloves. . . ." And he would do this whole shtick. "I got his trainer, Teddy Atlas, here. Teddy, you got anything to say?"

"Yeah, the kid's doin' all right. He's looking okay. . . ." It was funny, the stuff Louie would put together. The lawyers would sneak the tapes in when they were conferring with Sammy in a meeting room. They had monitors and VCRs set up there, because sometimes they needed to go over footage of stuff for the trial. But instead of or in addition to doing that, they'd watch tapes of the kid training and sparring. Sammy would ask Louie while he was watching them, "Is Teddy gonna put him in the Gloves? Does he think he's ready?"

The thing was, Gerard didn't want to fight in the Gloves. "Are you gonna make me go in the Gloves?" he'd ask me.

"I'm not gonna make you do nothing."

"My father wants me to do it."

"The only thing I'm doing is training you. Your father felt it would help give you confidence and some direction. But something like the Gloves is up to you to decide, if you want to take boxing that seriously."

Gerard was very quiet and careful, and he was a little beaten down by having a larger-than-life father. He was afraid of saying how he really felt. One day we were driving to Gleason's. Louie was driving, and we were crossing the Verrazano Bridge. I could see that Gerard didn't want to train, that he was lacking enthusiasm. I said, "You don't wanna train today, do you?"

"Oh, no, I—"

"Tell the truth if you don't wanna train. You don't feel good, take a day off."

"No, my father will go crazy."

"You can take one day off."

"No, I mean I like doing it, it's just sometimes I don't feel like it."

"Louie, turn the car around."

"What!" Gerard said.

"It's better to take the day off today. That's what I think," I said. "I don't want you to be faking it. It's not healthy."

We turned back. At first Gerard didn't say anything more. He wasn't much of a talker anyway. But then he turned to me and said, "I don't know what I want. I don't know what I wanna be."

"That's okay. You're young," I said.

"Sometimes I think about being a fireman. What do you think about that?"

"I think that's good."

"Really?"

"A fireman's good."

"Yeah, I think of that sometimes. But I don't know. . . ."

"A lot of people don't know what they wanna be," I said. "Especially at your age."

"You really think I could be a fireman?"

I felt for Gerard because I understood what he was wrestling with. He was afraid to tell his father what he was feeling. Like every son, he just wanted his father's approval, and he was afraid to tell him. Even though he was hesitant with me, I could tell that he was talking more freely than he ever had with his father. It made me feel bad for him. I knew how much Sammy was a prisoner of his need to be a tough guy, and how his son was really just an extension of that need. Gerard was paying a big price for something that had more to do with his father than it did with him.

Near the end of October, a woman named Louise Rizzuto, who was friends with Louie and Sammy and me, called up. She was crying.

"What's the matter?" I said.

"Louie will tell you," she said. "He's on his way over to see you."

"Did something happen to Sammy?"

"Yeah."

"What happened?"

"He'll tell you."

As soon as I hung up, I got a call from Louie. "Meet me downstairs," he said.

I walked downstairs, I didn't take the elevator. As I was going, it hit me, it just clicked. The fucking guy flipped. I tried not to think that's what it was, because it was as if the fact that I thought it made it true. When I got downstairs, Louie was there, dressed in a suit, as always. "Let's take a walk," he said.

We went up near the park. It was raining lightly. He was shaking his head slowly and I could see there were tears coming from his eyes. I put my hand on his shoulder and said, "Lou," and he kept walking and looking ahead, not at me.

"This fucking guy. I can't believe he did this."

Louie had gone to see Sammy that morning at the Manhattan Metropolitan Correctional Center, like he did every day. The MCC was where they kept all the high-profile guys. But Sammy wasn't there. They had taken him out. Before long, every news station had the story. Sammy "the Bull" had turned state's evidence. He was going to be a government witness and testify against his old boss, John Gotti. The headline of the *New York Post* called him "King Rat." I had seen too much by that point to be surprised by anything. I wasn't alone in that. A New York police detective named Joe Coffey had said about Sammy even before they arrested him, "You see that guy? When we get him he's going to roll like a tumbleweed. 'Cause he's got no balls. Cowards make the best informants."

The first thing I thought about, though, wasn't that; it was Gerard. I knew he was going to be devastated. It was like he was one of my fighters and I had an obligation and a responsibility to him. Somebody even told me that he was asking for me, and that added to it, knowing that.

It was strange because once his father did what he did, once he flipped, it changed everything. Sammy was no longer perceived as a tough guy and criminal but as something much, much worse. People I talked to were like, "Fuck his kid." People actually said that. "Fuck the fucking kid, his father's a fucking rat." I heard that Gerard was afraid that I would abandon him, that I wouldn't be his friend anymore.

I went over to his house that night. I was so naive that I thought I would just be able to go over and see the kid. But when I got off the Staten Island Expressway, the place was surrounded by every news truck in New York. As soon as they saw my car, even though they didn't know who I was, they started running toward me. I had made the mistake of slowing down, but I recognized what was going on and hit the gas. It was crazy. This mob of TV and print reporters chased after me, running down the street after my car.

I thought about giving up at that point and leaving. A lot of people had been telling me not to continue training Gerard. But I thought, *No, I can't leave. I want the kid to know that I don't hate him. That I haven't abandoned him just because his father is a rat. That would be too easy.* Instead, I ditched my car around the corner and made a mad dash for the house. The news reporters had already backtracked from where they had chased me, but when they saw me sprinting for the house, they tried to cut me off. It was like a freaking hundred-yard dash to the front door.

I got there ahead of them and started banging on the door. The camera guys and reporters were rushing up the walk toward me. Just before they got to me, the door opened and I squeezed in, slamming it shut behind me. Though the outside of the house was fairly ordinary, the inside had a few touches that you might expect to see in a Hollywood movie about a high-profile mob underboss, including a giant saltwater fish tank and a small pool with a waterfall. Sammy's wife, Debra, said, "Teddy, they almost got you, huh?"

"Yeah," I said. "That was close."

"It's crazy," she said. We tried to joke about the situation, but what was going on was no joke. It was real. I could see the pain in her face. There were a bunch of people there, mostly family. The house had the mood of a wake. Debra yelled out, "Gerard! Teddy's here."

He didn't hear her, or at least he didn't respond.

"He's in the basement," she said. "Why don't you just go down?"

I went down the stairs. There were weight machines and a Jacuzzi. I remembered that Louie had told me that Sammy had built a big vault into the wall down there, and that sometimes there was so much money in there that it literally went higher than Sammy's head. I wondered where all that money was now.

I found Gerard sitting on a black leather couch, reading a comic book. He looked up. There were tears in his eyes. "Why did he do it, Teddy? Why?" Gerard had always hidden his emotions and had been careful about what he said, but now he looked open and vulnerable and terribly young. "Why did he do that?"

I tried to think of something that would help him. I was thinking about the kid, not the father, even though I had to talk about the father. "You know, sometimes a person is under pressure and he wants to do the right thing but he's just not strong enough to do it. You just never know until you're in that position."

Gerard was almost sobbing at that point. "I guess what I'm trying to tell you," I said, "is that the feeling I'm talking about can overwhelm everything else. A guy comes in a room wanting to be a fighter, wanting to go out there and hear the crowd cheer for him and have his hand raised and feel good, but then something happens and suddenly all he can think about is his fear. It becomes too much for him." When I said "fear," I thought, *Here I am talking to Sammy's kid about fear when Sammy couldn't even say the word.* I had to push aside what I had been thinking about Sammy. "What I'm trying to tell you," I went on, "is that what your father did doesn't mean he don't love you. It's just that he couldn't face the fight. Do you understand?"

"Sort of," Gerard said. "I guess so."

"It's your father, it's not you. It's his weakness, not yours. But you don't have to hate him for that. He wasn't trying to hurt you. He just wasn't thinking about anything but this fight that he couldn't face."

I didn't know if Gerard understood what I was trying to tell him or not, or if it helped. I think it might have a little. I told him I'd still train him if he wanted to. I thought it was important to offer him that. He was surprised. "You will?" he said. So we kept training for a couple of weeks after that. But then we stopped. He didn't want to do it anymore. His father wasn't around. His whole reason for training with me in the first place had been to get his father's approval. Now, not only was his father not around, he wasn't the guy he pretended to be, so the kid didn't want to train anymore. I felt bad about it, but there wasn't much I could do.

Sammy went into the Witness Protection Program in 1992. His family didn't, but they did leave New York shortly afterward. The city was too dangerous. Gerard got beaten up and Sammy's daughter, Karen, was running around, drinking, drugging, staying out all night. It was sad.

Less than a year later, Sammy left the Witness Protection Program, and his family joined him in Arizona. Sammy had always told me he would try to steer Gerard away from the criminal life. But in February of 2000, Sammy, his wife, Debra, his daughter, Karen, and her husband—along with the twenty-four-year-old Gerard—were charged with running a massive drug ring, trafficking in the club drug ecstasy. Sammy was sentenced to nineteen years. Gerard got nine years.

WHAT IT MEANS
TO BE A PRO

J OHN DAVIMOS APPROACHED ME IN THE FALL OF 1993 and asked me if I'd be interested in training his fighter Michael Moorer. At the time, Moorer was undefeated and the number-one contender in the heavyweight division. He was a guy with enough physical ability to win a title, but he was something of a problem child who'd gone through a number of trainers over the course of his career, driving them crazy with his moodiness and bad training habits. Guys with terrific reputations, like Emanuel Steward, Lou Duva, and Georgie Benton, ultimately found Moorer unmanageable and threw up their hands in despair.

I had a reputation at that point as a psychology guy, as someone who would stand up to difficult fighters and discipline them and not take any prisoners along the way. So Davimos came to me. After Tyson's shocking loss to Buster Douglas in 1990, the heavyweight division had opened up. Riddick Bowe, the current world champ, was about to fight a rematch with Evander Holyfield, but with Mike Tyson at least temporarily out of the heavyweight picture because he was serving time in an Indiana penitentiary for the rape of Desiree Washington, Michael Moorer was next in line.

Everyone thought Bowe would knock out Holyfield, and then we would fight Bowe after that. At that point Bowe was a young, popular champion who a lot of people thought would be around for a long time. But Holyfield shocked everyone by beating Bowe and reclaiming the title. My assessment was that it was probably a good thing for us. Bowe was bigger and stronger, and I thought he'd give us more problems. Moorer matched up well against Holyfield. He was a southpaw (there had never been a left-handed heavyweight champion) and a counterpuncher with a good jab. The question was his character and mental toughness. He had a history of walking out of training camps, refusing to spar, and drinking too much. I didn't consider him a nut. I knew he had problems, but most of his problems stemmed from the same thing: He was scared and he was constantly testing people to see whether they were going to be there for him when he needed them.

I had heard about some of the things he did. Before one fight, he called up Davimos at two in the morning and said, "I'm sitting here in my room drinking a bottle of vodka and I've got a gun that I'm pointing at my head. Tell me why I shouldn't pull the trigger." Another time, he took a giant bowie knife and cut his legs up. The scars are still there.

The point is, he was a troubled and tortured soul, and now he was going to be asked to fight for the heavyweight championship of the world against a true warrior. When Davimos came to me, I told him that I would meet with Moorer and we'd see how it went.

Michael flew in to Jersey a few days later. He brought his four-year-old son with him—basically he was using his kid as a security blanket. At least that's how it struck me. We met at a House of Pancakes in West Orange. We sat in a booth. I didn't waste any time with preliminaries or bullshit. I had done my homework on him and found out some of the things I've just mentioned, so I was prepared, I was armed. I'd formed a preliminary diagnosis of him, the same way that my father would have with one of his patients. I'd noted the symptoms; now I was ready to conduct a more thorough examination.

One thing that struck me right away with Michael was that he had difficulty meeting my eyes. He kept looking down. This was a guy known as a badass and a troublemaker. To me, though, it couldn't have been more obvious what he really was: a scared, insecure guy with an inferiority complex and a fear of what he had to do and had to face.

I used the same tactics with him that I had used years earlier with

Mane Moore: I told him a story. Just like with Mane and his bully, I knew things about Michael that he didn't necessarily know I knew. I incorporated them into a story so that I could grab his attention in a way that would make an impact but not be too direct.

"There was one fighter I knew who reminds me a little of you. I'm not going to use his name, but he was an undefeated middleweight, who a lot of people thought had a shot to be world champ. . . ." Michael was only half listening to me, and I thought, *I'm going to test him out.* I said, "Now, this guy had a reputation for being a real badass kind of guy, and when he got closer to a fight, he would go out and start drinking. . . ."

All of a sudden, Michael looked up. I said to myself, "I got him. I'm on the right track." As I continued the story, I noticed that every time I touched on something that reminded him of himself, he would get very interested and curious. It showed me that I might actually be able to help him. He wouldn't perk up like that or get curious if he didn't care.

"So this guy would go out and drink and do all these things, but he always made sure everybody saw him." Again, Michael looked up. "Whether it was him walking out of a sparring session, or getting drunk in a nightclub, he made sure everybody was watching."

"Why would he do that?" Michael asked.

"Because he wanted an excuse to lose. He didn't have the guts to lose on his own. If people saw him out drinking, then they could say that he lost because he didn't care. But the strange part is that later on, he'd sneak into the gym to make up for what he did wrong."

"He'd sneak in?"

"There was a part of him that actually wanted to win. It was kind of like hedging his bet. You know, he might actually have to fight, so maybe that would give him a chance, if he actually was in shape."

"Well, what happened to him?" Michael asked.

"One day, he met somebody who understood what he was doing. This guy told him he knew and he said, 'Now you can't hide no more. I know what you're doing. I know you're sneaking into the gym. Now if you lose it's not because you're not in shape. Which means either you better quit entirely or start giving yourself reasons to win instead of reasons to lose.'"

"Did he quit?" Michael asked.

"He became middleweight champion of the world."

Michael took that in. "That's for real? Who is he?"

"That's not the point. You know that's not the point."

"Okay. So where we gonna train, Teddy?"

"Right here."

"It's cold here. I like to train somewhere warm. I don't—"

"I don't care what you like. We're training here. What else you want to know?"

He looked at me and I stared right back at him. He looked away and started talking to his son, whispering in his ear and hugging him, and again I knew I was right about him, that he was very, very weak but wished he could be strong.

Cus always used to tell me that when fighters came to the Gramercy Gym on Fourteenth Street in Manhattan that he knew the minute they walked in the door if they had a chance to become a fighter. There were three flights of steps to get to that place. Three long flights. Cus said that as you walked up those steps you would hear different things at each level. "When you got to the first level you could just start to hear the speed bag. By the second level you could hear the heavy bag. At the third level you began to hear people sparring, gloves hitting flesh, grunting. Each level forced you to consider anew whether you wanted to keep going. . . ." By the time someone finally came through the door of the gym, Cus was in a position where he could see them. He said, "If they walked in alone, they had a shot. If they walked in with a friend or their father, I didn't want them. To me, if they made that journey up those three flights of steps by themselves, they had already exhibited a certain amount of ability to be a fighter. They had shown discipline and control. If they needed someone with them, either I didn't want them or I said, 'I got a hell of a job on my hands.'"

I thought about what Cus had said the moment I saw Michael show up with his son. And then again when he focused on his son to avoid dealing with me. As we continued to discuss the possibility and mechanics of my becoming his trainer, the final thing he said to me was, "What time am I gonna run?"

"Five in the morning."

"I always run in the afternoon."

"You *used* to run in the afternoon."

"Why is it so important that I run at five in the morning?"

"Because you don't want to."

Michael grunted, shook his head a little, and let the smallest of smiles form on his lips. That was it, basically. That was the way our initial meeting wrapped up.

Our first fight together was one that Davimos had already contracted, an HBO bout against Mike Evans. If Michael won that, he would get his shot at the title against Holyfield. So it was a tricky fight, and a dangerous one. If he tripped up, his opportunity would be lost. Given his psyche there were compelling reasons to think that he might mess up for precisely that reason—so he wouldn't have to face Holyfield.

We trained in West Orange, New Jersey, for seven weeks, and there were days when he would start to get out of the ring right in the middle of a sparring session. When he tried, I put my leg in front of his head, blocking him, and said, "What are you doing?"

"Your leg's in my way."

"No, your head's in my way. Get your freakin' head back in the ring."

He backed down and got back in the ring. That was on an easy day. On a tough day, he might refuse to even get in the ring. One time, he took off his headgear in the middle of a sparring session and started to climb out between the ropes. I tried to stop him.

"Where do you think you're goin'?"

"I don't feel good."

"Yeah? What's wrong?"

"My wrist is sore." He climbed out and tried to move past me.

I grabbed his headgear out of his hand and threw it across the room. "If you don't want to be a fighter, then get out and get out for good!"

It was a very fine line you had to walk as a trainer. The guy could really be hurting, and if that was the case, it was your responsibility not to get him injured further. But I had good instincts. I usually knew what I was looking at. My father had been the same way. I remember this time when I was a kid, telling him that I was sick and couldn't go to school.

"Your stomach hurts?" he said, putting his fingers on my stomach.

"Yeah."

"What else do you feel?"

I laid it on thick, a real Academy Award performance, groaning and grimacing as I described my symptoms. When I was finished, he looked at me and said, "All right, now get dressed and go to school."

That's how it was with me and Michael. I knew when it was real and when it was a lie. I knew he was trying to escape. I wouldn't let him. He had been getting away with crap his whole life. I knew if I let him slide even one time, I'd lose my authority. I knew, no matter what his actions showed, that in the end he did want to face his fears. He just needed some help.

Still, there were times when we'd leave a training session barely speaking to each other, or with me having nearly threatened him. Then, later that night, ten or eleven o'clock, he'd call me and say, "Are we okay?," because he was afraid that he might have lost me, that maybe I wasn't coming into the gym the next day. He didn't understand how I was built. That my not coming in would have been like my father not showing up at his office or not going out on a house call when he was needed. For my part, I couldn't comprehend him feeling that way at first, but then I remembered something that Davimos had told me, that all the other guys—Benton, Steward, Duva—had left him. Every one of them had left. Just like his father had left him when he was a kid. Then it made sense.

Anyway, I managed to get him through the training camp, and he won the Evans fight, though he didn't look good doing it. I was still learning about him. There were things I didn't have a good handle on. In the dressing room, before the fight, he suddenly wanted everything quiet, no music or anything. He even lay down and tried to sleep. He was going into his shell, trying to avoid thinking about the fight, but I didn't fully realize it. I indulged him. Coming out of the dressing room, I tried to pep him up a bit, but I didn't do enough. He was lethargic and it showed in the ring. The lesson wasn't lost on me.

It has also occurred to me that I was less focused at the time than I should have been. Looking back now, that seems entirely possible. My father had died two weeks before the day of the fight.

What had happened was that three months earlier, at the age of eighty-eight, he had decided to get a hip replacement. What a tough son of a bitch he was! His heart had been skipping for years, and he was taking medication for it, but he didn't care about the risks of undergoing a major surgery at his age and in his condition. He felt the pain in his hip was bad enough that it was worth any risk. The doctors he consulted told him surgery was a lousy idea, but he was a different kind of man, my father. He insisted, and nobody could tell him otherwise.

He had the surgery done on Friday the thirteenth, 1993. Everybody busted his chops for that. "What are you getting an operation on Friday the freaking thirteenth for?" He said, "What difference does it make?" We all said, "Do it some other day." But my father looked everything right in the face. "No, it's a good day, as good as any day."

The surgery went well. It was a success. The next day an intern stopped by his room—the main doctors were gone for the weekend—and my father very calmly told him, "Give me one hundred cc's of heparin." Or whatever it was.

The intern said, "I can't do that. You just had an operation."

"I'm having a heart attack," my father said. "So you're going to have to give it to me."

"But you can't take that," the intern said. The drug my father was asking for was an anticoagulant that was used to combat heart attacks, but it would also have thinned the blood and quite possibly have led to a hemorrhage in his hip.

"Listen," my father said, "if you don't give me what I'm asking for, I'll have a massive heart attack and die in two or three hours."

"Dr. Atlas," the intern said, "I really think what you're feeling is just anxiety from the operation."

"I don't have anxiety," my father said. "I have never had anxiety." The intern stood there uncertainly. "Let me put it another way," my father said. "If you were fixing a car and you were going to do something that would destroy the brakes, but if you didn't do it the engine would be ruined, you'd give up the brakes. Now you're right to worry about hemorrhaging. I might die from hemorrhaging. But I will definitely die from a heart attack if you don't do what I say."

"I'm sorry," the intern said, "but I disagree with your diagnosis." He refused to administer the heparin.

Three hours later, as he had predicted, my father had a massive heart attack. I got there late that night. My mother called me and I went straight to the hospital. I was upset, obviously, but I didn't let anyone see. My father had never wanted any of us to show emotion.

I walked into the hospital room and he was on a ventilator. Like I said, he was a tough bastard. The heart attack hadn't killed him. With the help of the ventilator, he hung on for months. I was there with him every day for hours, half-asleep, walking the halls. He was a medical marvel. I'd hear doctors going, "Boy, that guy's incredible. Can you believe he's still alive?" At first I didn't even realize it was him they were talking about. It was like the scene in *The Godfather* with Brando. "He took eight shots and he's still alive, the son of a bitch!"

Eventually, I put things together, as far as what had happened to him. My mother and sister had been in the room at the time, so I got the information from them. No one else in my family really wanted to deal with it. This was the hospital my father had founded and loved. But what had happened made me furious. I went right to the director of the hospital and said, "Your doctors killed him!"

He said, "Teddy, I think you're overreacting."

"Don't tell me I'm fucking overreacting. Your incompetence is going to cost this doctor, my father, his life."

They were afraid I was going to sue the hospital. But in the end I couldn't do it. It was his hospital, and I couldn't do it.

He stayed alive for three months. He couldn't talk, but he understood everything, and he could write things down in this scribble on a pad. One day, he indicated to me that he wanted all the medicines that were on the intravenous—and there must have been twenty of them—turned around so that he could see what they were. He pointed a finger toward his eyes, and I got his glasses and put them on him. Then he motioned that he wanted the IV rolled closer. I rolled it closer. He pointed at one of the medicines and nodded at me.

I called in a nurse and said to her, "One of his medicines is wrong."

"Honey, your father is under a lot of medication."

"No, no, no, I'm telling you, one of the medicines is wrong. Please! Please call the pharmacist downstairs and have him check it."

So she called the pharmacist and he looked it up in his book, and he told her, "He's right. Get him off of it right away. He's right!"

My father nodded at me, a slight smile, and it was like I was transported back to being a kid again, going out on house calls with him. I was so proud to be connected to him. It was equal to being in the dugout watching Mickey Mantle hit home runs, or on the court as Michael Jordan drove the baseline. I was right there. I was a part of it. It was just me and him, my childhood hero, on the field together. Only here he was doing it on his deathbed.

It was an excruciating few months, but awe-inspiring, too, watching him die, seeing his strong, clear mind refuse to capitulate. A week or so before his kidneys shut down, I was in his room discussing his treatment with his doctors. My father was listening, and he shook his head. "Ted," Dr. Caractor said to him, "you've got to stop being a doctor. You're a terrible patient. We're the doctors."

But my father shook his head again. I brought him the pad, and he wrote something down. I showed it to Caractor.

"Ted, that's only if you have kidney problems," he told my father, "and you don't have any kidney problems."

Five days later, my father's kidneys failed.

I guess he knew even he couldn't come back from that. When nobody was in the room, he pulled out all his tubes. Shortly after he did that, he went into a coma.

After hearing about it, Jerry Izenberg, a writer for the *Newark Star-Ledger*, did a story about my father's life called "The Real Root of Toughness." I took it with me the next time I went to the hospital and read it to him. My father always hated to hear things about himself. He'd never allow it, but now, lying there, all the machines and tubes hooked back up to him, he couldn't stop me or say shut up. The thrust of the story was that the guys you think of when you think of tough, guys like Mike Tyson, weren't really that tough. If you wanted really tough, you had to hear about this doctor in Staten Island.

The story ended with Izenberg quoting me. It was strange when I reached that part, because I was reading about myself aloud in the third person. "'You want to know about tough?' Atlas asked," I read. "'Do you realize how many times he could have quit? He's the toughest man I ever met. He's my father and I love him.'"

I lowered the newspaper and looked at the body on the hospital bed. My father's eyes were shut. You could barely see his breath moving his chest. The monitors pulsed, indicating he was still alive, but there were no other obvious signs of life. Yet the only way I could tell him I loved him was to read it to him out loud from a story in a newspaper. Only then could I say the words—when he wasn't awake or aware that I was saying them.

He was so much a part of me. That's why I continued training through this whole period—because that's what he would have done. I was working with Michael Moorer and another fighter I had, Shannon

Briggs, a young heavyweight. Briggs had a fight down in Atlantic City. A few days before we went down there, he caught a cold and decided he wanted to back out of the fight. I made him go through with it anyway. I knew Briggs was just looking for an excuse, and I didn't want to give it to him. The day of the fight, a Wednesday, I spent the morning with my father in his hospital room, then drove down to Atlantic City. I knew there was a good chance Dad wouldn't make it through the night, but I felt I needed to honor my commitment.

During the first couple of rounds of the fight, Briggs was drifting and unfocused, but I stayed on him. He wound up knocking the guy out in the third round. I talked to my mother afterward. My father was still hanging in. Just after I fell asleep, about three in the morning, the phone rang. I knew before I answered what it meant. It was weird. Thursday had always been the one day a week my father didn't have office hours. It was just like him to wait until his day off to die.

After the call, I showered and got dressed. Then I got in the car with Elaine and the kids—they had all come with me—and we drove back to Staten Island at four in the morning. My whole family was there. My brother Terryl and my sister and my mother. I helped with the arrangements, and later that same morning—the wake wasn't until the next day—I went to the gym to train Moorer.

Michael came into the gym. He said he didn't feel like training.

"You go get dressed and put your shoes on and get ready to work," I said.

"I'm tired and sore. I need a day off, Teddy."

This was after I'd already been through all kinds of this bullshit with him, so he was a little bit less forceful than he would have been a few weeks earlier, when I practically smacked his head into a wall.

"It's just a day," he said. "What's the big deal?"

"Just a day! Just a fuckin' day!" I was livid, which probably wasn't fair. He had no idea what had happened. "You're supposed to be a professional," I said. "If you win this fight, you're gonna fight for the heavyweight championship of the world. 'Just a day!' Don't you understand anything about commitment, about being a pro, about sticking with what you say you wanna be? You don't do it just when you feel good. You don't do it just when you're not tired. You don't do it just when it's sunny. You do it every day of your life. You do it when it hurts to do it, when it's the last thing in the world you wanna do, when there are a million reasons not to do it. You do it because you're a professional." I didn't scream. I just said these things quietly and firmly, and when I was finished, Michael looked at me and said, "I'll go get dressed."

That night, John Davimos called Michael and told him that my father had died. Michael immediately called me at home.

"Why didn't you tell me your father died?" he said.

"I don't know. There was no reason to tell you."

"You shouldn't have come to the gym. We didn't have to train."

"You got a fight in two weeks."

"But your father died."

"It's two separate things."

"I'm sorry," he said.

"There's nothing to be sorry about. When you're doing something you believe in, when you're committed to something, you do what you need to do. I'll see you tomorrow, Michael."

"You sure there's nothing I can do?"

"Besides showing up on time? No."

AGAIN, TEDDY?

I N THE WEEKS AFTER THE EVANS FIGHT, MICHAEL started running amok, eating too much and drinking heavily, falling back on old bad habits. It was the holidays, so it was a tough season for that kind of stuff anyway, but having the Holyfield fight looming on the horizon didn't encourage Michael toward discipline. Once a date was set for the fight, a weeklong publicity tour was arranged by TVKO and HBO. I decided that rather than wait until we headed to Palm Springs to set up training camp, which was still a ways off (it was January now and the fight wasn't until April), I would run a minicamp for Michael in West Orange, New Jersey. I knew he wouldn't like it, but my instinct was to draw a line in the sand. I could already see that he was heading in the wrong direction. I wanted to cut him off before things really got out of hand. The easiest thing would have been to just wait and run one camp starting at the end of February. Something told me not to.

Michael wasn't happy when I told him what I had in mind, but he came in because I didn't give him a choice. He flew into Newark with one of his guys, Flem, a near-fifty-year-old semiretired cop from Detroit. (Michael loved cops and guns. In fact, he got very friendly with the cops in Detroit, to the point where they let him ride around with them and go out on raids, which was how he hooked up with Flem and some of the other guys who made up his entourage and security team. People made all sorts of assumptions about why Michael was drawn to cops and guns, but I always knew his real affinity was the brotherhood of it, the sense of family.)

Originally, I planned for Michael to stay five days at the minicamp, but after two days he told me he was leaving. Wednesday morning I was in the gym, waiting for him to come in, and he called and said, "I'm leaving. I'm going."

"What are you freakin' talkin' about? I'm here in the gym waiting for you."

"I'm leaving. I'm goin' home."

"No, you're not. You're comin' in."

"I got a plane to catch. I'll talk to you later," he said, and hung up. I was stunned for a moment, although when I actually gathered my thoughts, I realized it was almost predictable. I got in my car and drove straight over to his hotel, which wasn't as easy as it might sound. I didn't even know where he was staying. I wound up having to call Davimos to find out.

When I arrived at Michael's room, Flem opened the door. Michael had his clothes laid out on the bed. He was packing his bag.

"Michael, you think I'm joking about this? You think this is a fuckin' joke?"

"You ain't gonna tell me what to do, Teddy. I'm leavin'."

"Yeah? Then you're gonna have to find yourself a new trainer."

I looked over at Flem, but he was no help. I liked Flem, but in most instances he was just Michael's yes-man. He was there to protect him and support him in whatever he wanted to do. Unfortunately, like a lot of guys who are captured by the glamour of professional athletes, Flem had sold himself out a little, compromised his own dignity to be in that world.

Michael kept folding shirts and laying them into his travel bag.

"You think I'm fuckin' kidding?" I said. "I'm going back to the gym now. You don't follow me, you won't be the only one packing your bag."

I turned around and walked out. I drove back to the gym. When twenty minutes had passed and Michael hadn't shown up, I called Davimos. I told him what was going on, that Michael was skipping out. He wasn't surprised.

My father, Dr. Theodore
Atlas, Sr., recently graduated
from NYU Medical School.

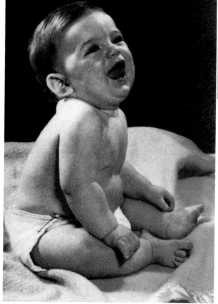

Here I am, shortly after I was born
in July 1956.

My mother and father, Mary Atlas
and Dr. Ted Atlas, 1992.

Here I am at around the
age of twelve.

In the locker
room of the old
Felt Forum at
Madison Square
Garden before a
fight in the
Spanish Gloves
Finals in 1979.
From left to right:
Bob Jackson, Cus
D'Amato, Kevin
Rooney, me, and
Salinas. I was
training Rooney.

A group shot of my fighters in the Catskill Boxing Club, before an amateur show in Hudson, New York, circa 1980–1981. *From left to right:* Frankie Minicelli, Kevin Young, Rodney Young, Jigger, Pat Shanagher, Mike Tyson, Gary Young, Mane Moore, Billy Ham (ten years old), Greg Young, Bobby Owen, John Chetti, and me.

Me and my wife, Elaine, on our wedding day, September 25, 1982.

Me and my three-month-old daughter, Nicole, 1983.

I'm illustrating a punch to Canadian welterweight champion Donny Poole in 1987 in Rochester, New York, where I also trained Simon Brown, then welterweight champion of the world. Poole is the fighter Dave Wolfe asked me to lie about in his legal case over managerial control. It led to his taking LaLonde away from me.

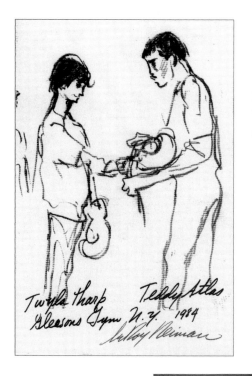

LeRoy Neiman sketch of me and Twyla putting on gloves before training at Gleason's, 1984.

Me and Twyla Tharp training in the basement of Gleason's Gym on West Thirtieth Street in Manhattan, 1984.

Wrapping Michael's hands before a workout, in training for the
Michael Moorer–George Foreman fight in Palm Springs,
California, in 1995.

Me and Michael
Moorer at the
weigh-in, two days
before the 1994
Holyfield world title
fight at Caesars
Palace, in Las Vegas.

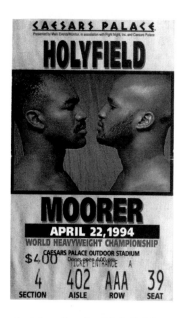

A ticket for the Holyfield–Moorer fight in 1994. Ringside seats went for $1,000.

In the ring at Caesars Palace as Michael Moorer has his hand raised by the referee after beating Evander Holyfield and winning the world heavyweight title in 1994.

Twenty thousand people came out for the victory parade in Michael Moorer's hometown of Monessa, Pennsylvania, in 1994. Manager John Davimos and I hold the two world title belts won in the fight against Holyfield, while Michael sits between us.

Me and Willem Dafoe training in Gleason's Gym in 1988 for his role as a concentration camp boxer during World War II in the film *Triumph of the Spirit*. We later trained in Auschwitz and Birkenau.

My family. Me, Nicole, Teddy III, and Elaine, in Manhattan, for the ceremony for my Trainer of the Year Award from the Boxing Writers of America in 1998.

"He's done this before, Teddy. There's nothing you can do about it. You're right about him. He's scared."

Listening to someone else express it, I got worked up all over again. "What flight is he on?" I said.

"American flight one-forty-two," he said.

I was stubborn. I couldn't just let him go without trying one more time to make him understand what he was doing. I got in my car and sped over to Newark Airport. It probably took me twenty minutes. I arrived at the terminal and found Flem doing all the grunt work, checking the bags, doing the tickets, while Michael sat there like a spoiled athlete.

I walked up to him, angry but trying to contain it. "You think I don't know what you're doing. I know exactly what you're doing, and you're not gonna get me to go along with it. You think I'm gonna let you freakin' dictate what we do? That we're not gonna train here now, and then you think I'm gonna go train you somewhere later on, and get you ready to fight Holyfield and watch you make more excuses not to win?"

Flem wandered back over to where we were. Michael got to his feet. "There'll be plenty of time to train later on," he said.

"Bullshit," I said. "Will you listen to yourself? You're afraid of fighting this fight. What do you want? Somebody who'll lie to you and let you lie? Is that what you want? Fine. Get somebody else. 'Cause it ain't gonna be me. I'm telling you, Michael. I'd have to let you take my manhood away for that to happen. For me to let you do what you wanna do, I'd have to give up my manhood, and I'm not doing that. I ain't givin' it away."

He didn't know how to respond to that, so he nodded to Flem and they began walking away, heading off toward the gate.

"You walk," I yelled after him. "You're gonna keep walkin'."

He kept walking. A while later I called Davimos and told him I was quitting. The hard part came later, at home.

Elaine was in the kitchen of our tiny apartment making lunch for the kids when I got back.

"You're home early," she said.

A lot of times in the past, I hadn't said anything. I hadn't talked much. With Tyson, with LaLonde, I'd done what I'd done and that was that. But this time I owed her more consideration. I knew she was depending on the Holyfield fight, counting on it, because the fight was already made, and it was going to be a $200,000 payday for me, the first time we were ever going to have any real money.

"I had to walk away," I said.

"What?" She nearly dropped the plate she was holding.

"Michael wasn't listening to me," I said. "He wouldn't do what I wanted. So I quit."

"Again, Teddy?"

The look on Elaine's face in that moment, the way she said "again," really got to me. In that moment, I questioned whether it was a matter of principle and honor that I was acting on, or whether it was just self-ishness and pride. Suddenly, I was unsure, and then almost instantly I felt myself getting angry with her. It was unnerving. My responsibility to her and to my family had clouded the truth and the purity of the de-cision I had made—a decision that had felt right at the time, but now, weighed against the disappointment in her face, seemed wrong. It was a nearly unbearable clash of opposing feelings. I couldn't allow myself to think that I had done the wrong thing, and yet at the same time I didn't want to be angry with her for being disappointed in me. I turned and walked out of the kitchen.

The next few days, not surprisingly, were tense with us. I was sure that I had done the right thing, but Elaine's disappointment was palpa-ble, and that made things very difficult. I was almost relieved when I had to leave home to take Shannon Briggs an undefeated heavyweight from Brooklyn whom I'd been training, to Biloxi, Mississippi, for a fight there.

The night before the fight, Shannon and Mark Roberts, his manager, and one of his guys, Troy, and I went to eat dinner at a joint in Biloxi called the Bombay Bicycle Club. It was close to our motel, along one of those stretches of highway made up of motels and fast-food restaurants. We parked the car in the lot off to the side, and Shannon, Troy, and Mark started walking toward the front entrance. I was about fifteen steps behind them, thinking my own thoughts, not really tuned in, except that suddenly I was aware of these voices and this harsh laughter, some-one saying in an ugly, drunken twang, "What the fuck is that on your head, boy? What kind of monkey are you?" Even then it took me a sec-ond to realize that it was directed at my guys, that it was a racial thing, because Shannon had these dyed orange dreadlocks that he sometimes tied up in a pile on top of his head.

The three of them, Shannon, Troy, and Mark, were by the door of the restaurant, up this set of steps. There were these other guys standing there, and words were being exchanged. I started up the steps. I could see Shannon trying to go past these guys into the restaurant. One of the guys, the biggest one, a muscular bruiser with long hair and a beard, in an oil-stained gimme cap, stepped in his way.

"Where do you think you're going?" he said. Then he shoved Shannon, who fell back into me.

"You better go back to where you came from, boy," the guy said. The rest of them laughed.

I stepped past Shannon and got right in the face of the guy who had pushed him.

"Who the fuck you talkin' to?" I said.

"Why? You gonna do something? They ain't gonna do nothin', you gonna do something?"

"Yeah, I sure am!" I said, and cracked him one on the jaw. One of his friends came at me and I turned and cracked him. Then the first guy grabbed hold of me, and he was big. He pulled me toward him. We started to fall backward toward the stairs. As we started to fall, I heard Shannon scream, "Teddy!," like he thought I was going to get hurt. But as I was falling, I twisted the big guy around and fell on top of him. We crashed down the stairs and his big body cushioned my fall. All my weight was on him and his head slammed against the ground and cracked wide open. I was able to get right up, but he was out, unconscious and bleeding.

Then these other guys came out of the restaurant. It turned into a brawl. Mark and Troy stayed off to the side, but Shannon joined in, and we busted up a bunch of them. We worked our way back to the parking lot. I said to Mark, "Get Shannon in the freaking car and get him out of here." He was my fighter and my instinct was to protect him and get him out of there. While I was holding these guys at bay, I told Mark and Shannon to take off. Shannon didn't want to, but Mark pushed him into the car. They drove away.

Troy and I made our way back to the road with a couple of these guys still following us. They were acting a little bit braver now that there was just me and Troy—plus it was clear Troy wasn't a fighter. We were walking toward this gas station down the road, and they were about fifty feet behind us. Troy was getting all nervous.

"Ted, they're following us."

"Slow down. Let 'em catch up."

"They're coming after us."

"I'm just leading them to where I want them. They got anything in their hands?"

Troy looked back. I didn't want to look back. "No," he said.

"Good."

I was very calm, which reassured him. We'd gotten them to where it was a little dark, just past the gas station, away from all their friends. We were out of sight of the roadhouse. They were right behind us now. I could hear them saying things. "Motherfucker this" and "nigger that."

Suddenly, I turned around. "Yeah, motherfucker? I'm a mother-fucker?" I walked right toward them. They weren't expecting it, they were taken off guard. I hit one of the guys so hard I thought I might have killed him. I dropped him with one shot. The other guy, when I started toward him, took off.

Troy said, "Oh, shit!"

"C'mon, let's get out of here," I said. We started across the street toward our hotel, which wasn't more than a couple of hundred yards away. All of a sudden I noticed that a car full of them had pulled in front of us. I could see one of the guys was on a radio. Then another car came. I realized they were talking to each other on their CBs. They were calling all their friends to come over.

I tried to stay calm. "Come on," I said to Troy, leading him across the street but away from our hotel.

"Where are we going?" he said. "The hotel's there."

"No, we can't let 'em see us go in there. We'll be cornered." We started jogging through people's yards, circling back around, until we could enter the hotel from the back. When we got there, the whole place was lit up with headlights and the spinning lights of cop cars.

We managed to sneak up to our room unseen, and we kept the lights inside off, peeking through the curtain. The whole place was cordoned off and surrounded by the police.

We looked down through the curtain and we could see them go into the main office. Then they brought out the manager. He had a ring of keys in his hand. We had rented four rooms, and we saw them heading toward the stairs leading to our rooms. The cops had their guns out. Troy was losing it, saying, "We better go out. Let's get out, Teddy."

"No, we can't. We can't go out." I looked out past the curtain. Down below was one of the guys I had beaten up at the restaurant. It was the one who'd cracked his head on the stairs. "Shit, they're friends with the cops," I said. "You go out now, who knows what they're gonna do."

A couple of the cops started up the stairs toward us. I heard them go in the room next door, their voices raised, things banging. A moment later, I saw them bring Shannon and Mark down the stairs.

"Oh my God," Troy said.

When I peeked out again, a few of the cops were standing down below with Shannon and Mark. Another group headed back upstairs toward our room. Troy was practically crying now. "Listen," I said, "lay down in the tub behind the shower curtain and don't make a sound. If they come in here, chances are that I'm the one they're lookin' for. I'm the one who did all the damage. I'll just let them take me. Then you can come out later."

He agreed and got into the tub. I could hear the cops approaching our room. Just before the footsteps reached our door, they stopped. Someone was yelling something. A minute went by and nothing happened. I peeked out through the curtains again. Now I saw an amazing thing: Les Bonano, the former police chief of New Orleans, who was one of the fight promoters, was down in the courtyard, talking to the head police officer.

It was like the cavalry had arrived. Les and the head cop kept talking, Les gesturing toward Shannon and Mark while the other cops stood next to them, holding shotguns. Finally, the talking was finished. All the cops started leaving, heading toward their cars. Only after they drove off did I go out. Mark and Shannon couldn't believe it when they saw me.

"We thought they'd got you for sure," Shannon said. "We didn't know what to think. Where's Troy?"

At that moment Troy came out of the room. It was almost comical the way he slunk out. The four of us were nearly giddy with relief. "We fucked those crackers up," Shannon said. We all congratulated each other and compared stories. Apparently, the guys we'd beat up had told the police that we had guns, and the cops would have gotten us for sure if Les hadn't shown up and explained the situation, that we were boxers, there for a prizefight. They hadn't believed that we could beat all those guys up with just our fists, but when he explained everything and how we didn't have guns, they left.

Overnight, the story turned into legend. When we went to the weigh-in the next day, the building was packed. Everyone knew about what had happened, all these old Southern guys who were the commissioners, they'd all heard. We were treated like celebrities. This one guy, Billy Lyons, a real character, about seventy years old and from a family of Confederates and slave owners, said to me, "We heard you tussled with some of our boys. Jes' wanted to let you know we're with you. We're behind you. If there are any problems, you let me know."

The details of the incident got exaggerated. We'd beaten up eight guys, ten guys. Tommy Morrison, who was fighting on the same card, came over to us and said, "Ten guys had you cornered? Man!" Shannon Briggs told everyone, all his friends, and the story made it all the way to Michael Moorer in Detroit. By then it was, "Hey, Teddy kicked the shit out of, like, twenty rednecks. He knocked out ten of them. Two of them died."

The day of Shannon's fight, I got a call from Michael. "Hey, Teddy, I heard about the crazy shit that happened. You say the word, I'll come down with the boys. We'll get on a plane."

You have to understand how Michael's mind worked. He heard what I'd done and he wished he'd been there. It was like all the stuff I'd been saying to him wasn't just talking. It meant something. He called me up and I could hear it in his voice. He wanted to be a part of it. "I'm coming down with my boys."

"For what?" I said.

"You got a problem, we'll be right there."

"The only problem," I said, "is if you come down and I have to see your face."

He didn't get it. He thought he could just call me up like everything was okay and nothing had ever happened between us. "You really kicked some ass," he said. "Oooh, if I were there, ooh boy! We would have been doing some business. Oh yeah!"

"Yeah, okay, whatever." I wanted to get off the phone. "I gotta go."

"I talked to Emanuel Steward."

"Good."

"I told him you wouldn't train me no more."

"That's right."

"So I start training with Emanuel in two weeks."

"Good. I gotta go now."

He wouldn't let the call end. "So, how's your son?"

"Good."

"How's your family? How's your wife? Everyone okay?"

"Michael, I don't want to talk. I have to go now. I don't want to talk no more."

"Teddy, I need you to train me."

"Michael, you already made your choice."

"Please," he said. "I need you. There's no one else who can do the job. You're the only one, Teddy."

"No," I said. "I'm not going to do it."

When I got back to Staten Island, he called me again, and we had, basically, the same conversation. It's hard to say exactly why I wound up changing my mind. Part of it was his vulnerability. His neediness. But it was more complicated than that. I had walked away from a big payday with him because I felt my authority as a trainer would have been compromised if I had stayed. Now he was trying to entice me back, and I wanted to be sure that the temptation to say yes was based on my belief that I would be able to accomplish as a trainer all the things I wanted to accomplish, not because of what the fight could do for my bank account. Did I really believe that Michael was capable of giving himself over to me—which was the only way we could be successful? Or was I simply letting his desperation and my own desires influence my better judgment?

There was really only one way to find out.

ONE SMART BASTARD

JOHN DAVIMOS MET ME AND MICHAEL AT THE AIR-port in Los Angeles and drove us all the way to Palm Springs. I remember this terrible, empty hole in my stomach during the drive, the same kind of feeling I'd had on that bus going to Rikers Island all those years ago. I can't say that I didn't know what I was getting myself into. Or that I thought dealing with Michael was going to be any easier than before. It wasn't as if he'd experienced an awakening, or any of the psychological barriers that he faced had been stripped away. He was still afraid, and though he desperately wanted my help to get past his fear, it continued to control his actions. Barreling down the dark highway, I kept thinking about my kids, how young they were, and how much I was going to miss them. The prospect of two months of isolation filled me with a powerful loneliness, especially because Michael was already acting morose and surly, not answering me when I talked to him, withdrawing into his shell.

The trick for me was to stay focused, to think about why I was there, which was to win the heavyweight championship. I had told my father before he died that I was going to win it, and then, after the crazy stuff in Mississippi and the way that affected Michael, it began to seem as if fate were taking a hand in things. Still, if we didn't win the fight, if there was no heavyweight title, then all the years my father paid for me to be in Catskill would feel like they had meant nothing.

The long drive in the darkness gave room to all these thoughts, so I was glad when we saw the exit for Palm Springs. Even then, it seemed like it took hours, driving around the little winding roads on the grounds of the Riviera Hotel in the moonless night, before we found the hotel's main office.

At the front desk, the manager greeted us with a big smile, telling us how proud they were to have the future heavyweight champion staying with them. He went over the room assignments with us, handing out keys. The hotel was set up like a compound, a series of stand-alone buildings surrounding a swimming pool and tennis courts. "I've put Mr. Atlas in the room next to Mr. Moorer," the manager said, because he thought I would want to be near my fighter.

Davimos, who understood the difficult nature of my relationship with Michael, immediately chimed in, and said, "No, Mr. Atlas wants to be in the building farthest away from Mr. Moorer's." Which was the beginning of the manager's realization that we might not be the most unified, harmonious group ever to challenge for the heavyweight title.

In turbulent seas it's particularly important to run a tight ship, so I meticulously planned every detail of the camp. One of the reasons we didn't train back east the way we had for the previous fight was that I wanted Michael to be in the same time zone as Las Vegas. I didn't want him to have to adjust later on. Also, I didn't want to worry about him getting sick. I wanted him to be able to sweat and not get chilled afterward. In that respect, the weather in Palm Springs at that time of the year was ideal; it wasn't that hundred-and-twenty-degree weather they sometimes get. The Riviera itself was like a safe, secluded island, free of distractions and temptations. About the only element I hadn't foreseen was the hotel booking a huge lesbian convention for one of the weekends we were there. I tried to get them to cancel it, but it was too late, they were committed. In fact, the lesbians tried to get them to kick us out—which of course they wouldn't do either.

Michael was thrilled. "A bunch of women? Coming here? Goddamn! You really screwed this one up, huh, Teddy?"

Training camp involves a huge amount of hard work and discipline. Anything that relieves the drudgery—even if it's just reading a book by the pool or playing basketball in the afternoon—is welcome. The day the lesbians began arriving, we'd finished training, and we were walking and looking out at the pool. Some of them were already lying in the chaises, soaking up sun. Michael could barely contain himself. He said, "Flem, think about it. This time tomorrow there's gonna be a thousand naked women out there!" As he said that, this big bull dyke with a pack of cigarettes rolled up in her sleeve came up behind us and growled, "Yeah, and not one of 'em will want a fucking thing to do with you!"

Michael went crazy. "What? What are you—" He was so angry he couldn't even get the words out.

"You got a problem with that, pal?" she said.

"Oh, shit," Davimos said. We looked at one another and started laughing so hard we had to hold on to each other.

"Get her name," I said. "We can use her when we run out of sparring partners."

"Maybe we better wait until Michael gets into better shape," Davimos said.

"Yeah, he may not be ready for her yet."

By that point in the camp, Michael was running a couple of miles a day. I had him on a strict schedule, beginning with a five a.m. daily run and ending with a nightly curfew of ten o'clock. In between, his real day would begin at one o'clock, when we would start our training sessions. The hotel put up a tent on two of the tennis courts, with a ring and seats for spectators, as well as heavy bags, double-end bags, speed bags, and other boxing equipment.

We had good, tough sparring partners, Adolpho Washington and Big-foot Martin among them, and we videotaped the sessions so that later on we could look at them and analyze what we needed to do, recognize certain tendencies, and refine technique. We also had videos of Holyfield's fights, although Michael resisted watching them. We banged heads over it. I knew that if he didn't want to watch a videotape of Evander Holy-field, it was because he didn't want to think about what he had to do on April 22. It was a real battle, but in the end I prevailed. It was the same way on days when he didn't want to spar. I'd make him spar. I didn't want to smother him, but I had to stay on top of him.

Michael's entourage came to the camp: Flem, another ex-cop named Wick, and a bunch of other guys from Detroit who protected him and kept him pumped up. Whenever he came to a training session without them, I knew it was going to be a good day. When he would arrive with them, I knew it was going to be rough. Cus had been right when he said a drowning man always wants company.

One day, Michael showed up with his guys, and he was wearing these dark glasses that he had never worn before, these wraparound Oakleys that had become very fashionable. I knew right away that I was going to have a real problem with him that day. Sure enough, he said, "I ain't training today." His guys had all come into the tent with him, and they were standing around, flanking him.

"I didn't hear you," I said.

"I said, I'm not training."

I turned to his guys and looked right at them. "Get out!" I said.

They hesitated, looking at Michael.

"Get out!"

They left.

I got right up in Michael's face and said, "You're trainin' today, do you understand?"

He was staring me down through his impenetrable mirrored sunglasses.

"Take those friggin' sunglasses off," I said. "You want to stare at me, take the glasses off."

He wouldn't take them off.

"What's the matter, you afraid to look at my eyes?"

"I ain't afraid." He took off the glasses, but he couldn't hold my gaze. He stared at me for a second then looked away.

"Listen," I said, "I told you from the beginning, when you called me up in Mississippi, begging me to train you for this fight, I'm only doing this for one reason—to win. I'm not here to get in the ring that night and say, 'We fought for the heavyweight title.' Do you understand me? I'm here to win. If you have any other ideas, then let's stop right now and go home. Because if you don't train today, it's not that this one day is gonna make you out of shape physically, it's gonna make you soft mentally. You duck what you're supposed to do today, the night of the fight you'll think it's okay not to face what you gotta face there. On the other hand, if you do what I tell you to, what you're supposed to do, on that night you'll know that you faced what you had to face every day— and you'll draw strength from that."

John Davimos heard about the encounter, and asked me about it over dinner that night.

"It's okay. I took care of it," I told him. "But you better tell him to get new fuckin' bodyguards because these guys are useless. When I told them to leave, they left. The whole idea of bodyguards is they're supposed to stay with the guy in case somebody's gonna do something to him. I told 'em to get out and they all left."

We had a good laugh about that. But each day, it seemed, Michael and I had to climb the same hill we'd climbed the day before. I knew there were limits. That you needed to give your guy a little leeway in certain areas. Some trainers demanded total abstinence. I told Michael he could have girls up until three weeks before the fight—but on the condition that he didn't bring them around during training sessions. Cus had always said that it wasn't the act of sex that was hurtful to a fighter, it was the chasing around and late-night socializing that was damaging. I agreed with that. I never believed all that crap about sex sapping your energy. Mentally, however, it could become an excuse in a tough fight.

Along those lines, Cus had two fighters back in the 1950s and 1960s, Mike Bulich and Jimmy Arness, who were both deaf mutes (they were the reason they instituted the red lights on the ring posts to signal the last ten seconds of a round). Bulich and Arness were tough bastards who broke all the rules about going out. They'd have sex all through training camp even up to the night before a fight, but they never got tired during a fight, and Cus said it was because they never heard all the bullshit from people about how it was *supposed* to hurt them.

The point is, I wasn't unreasonable, and I didn't believe in a bunch of fairy tales or superstitions, but I did want my fighter to be focused. One morning, I saw Michael walk out of his building with a girl. I could see them through these hedges outside the tent. It was before noon, but she was wearing evening wear, a shiny blue dress and high heels. They stopped walking for a minute. He turned and said something to her, then she began walking toward where I was standing while Michael stayed back. I kept out of sight and watched her enter the tent. About five minutes later, Michael approached. I stepped out of the shadows.

"Tell her to leave, and then let's get ready," I said.

He didn't even try to act innocent. He knew I had him. When we entered the tent, he walked right over to her and whispered something in her ear. She got up and left. We were there to work; it wasn't about show-ing off for a girl. It was about the business at hand and being prepared.

One night, I was in my room, lying in bed after a long day, and the phone on the nightstand rang. I used to look at that phone each night and pray for it not to ring. I knew if it rang, nine times out of ten it was going to make my life difficult. Sure enough, it was Michael. "I ain't runnin' tomorrow," he said, and hung up.

I got up, put my sneakers on, and hiked over to his building. I climbed the stairs to his floor and knocked on his door. He didn't an-swer. I kept knocking. Finally, I heard footsteps.

"What?"

"Open the door!"

He opened the door a crack, but the chain was on.

"You better let me in before I kick this fuckin' door open."

"You threatenin' me?"

"Open the freakin' door, Michael."

He took off the chain but kept his foot there. I tried to open it, but his foot was there, so I put my shoulder against the door and bulled my way in.

"I don't care what you say, I'm not runnin'," he said.

"You're getting up in the morning and you're freakin' runnin'."

"No, I'm not. Now get out!"

"What are you gonna do? You gonna hit me? You can't fight Holyfield but you'll stand up to me? Go ahead. Do something." I shoved him.

"Don't fucking touch me."

"Why? What are you gonna do? You don't wanna have camp no more, then just say so. But don't stand here and threaten me and tell me that you ain't gonna run because then you're tellin' me that I don't know how to be a trainer. You're tellin' me that what I do don't mean nothin', that you don't care about what we're here for. And I'm tellin' you it's not gonna go down that way. I'd rather freakin' get it over with now than to leave any questions. So if you wanna fight me, let's go. But don't tell me that you're gonna abuse me in another way by makin' me less than a trainer."

We stood there, inches between us, staring at each other. He put out his chest and said, "I'm warnin' you once more. You leave or we're gonna come to blows. Something's gonna happen."

"Do what you gotta do," I said. I braced myself. I really thought he was gonna get physical.

All of a sudden, he bent over, grabbed his sneakers, and rushed past me, swearing, "Motherfucker." He stopped outside the door, put the sneakers on—he didn't even bother to lace them up—and ran down the steps.

John Davimos was out in the parking lot. He saw Michael leave the building and take off running. He knew what was going on because Michael had called him, too, although when he realized I was inside with Michael, instead of coming in and getting involved, he'd stayed outside. We both knew Michael's threat not to run was really just a cry for help, that otherwise he wouldn't have called John and me to tell us. It was another in an ongoing series of tests. Would I stand up to him? How could he stand up to Holyfield if the guy who was telling him that it was going to be okay didn't stand up to him, if the guy leading him was afraid of the lion? He had to make sure that I was willing to face the lions, too.

"What the fuck happened?" Davimos said as I came down the stairs and out the door.

"I don't know. I guess he's doin' his freakin' roadwork."

It was tough keeping up with Michael's moods. A few days later, apropos of nothing, he said to me, "You never eat with me."

"Eat with you? You're lucky I train with you."

"You don't like to be around me?"

"I didn't think it was a big secret. I mean, it's not like you just discovered Capone's vault or anything."

"Why don't you come to dinner with me tonight?"

"All right, fine. You payin'?"

So we went out to dinner. Me, Davimos, Michael, and his guys. We sat there and ate and talked about the next day's training session. At one point our waitress didn't hear Michael call out to her. He decided she was purposely ignoring him. It made him so mad he stormed out of the restaurant. Flem went after him, but I just kept eating. After a while, life with Michael was like being in a combat zone, and you just learned to shrug things off. Bombs blowing up, bullets whistling by? No problem. Keep going about your business.

Davimos looked at me and said, "You're still eating?"

"Yeah. He'll be there in the morning."

Flem came back a while later. "I couldn't find him," he said. "He took off."

"Don't worry about it," I said. "Finish your meal."

When we got back to the hotel, Michael was back in his room. It was close to ten o'clock. He told Flem that after he left the restaurant he started walking back to the hotel. At a quarter to ten he realized he was still a mile away. He didn't want to break his curfew, so he ran the rest of the way. When I found out about that, I was floored. I mean, think about that. This wacko *ran* back to his room so he wouldn't miss his curfew. That's heavy. It showed me that, despite all of the posturing and acting out, he wanted to win the fight. He didn't want to break the discipline of the curfew, because he thought there was some magic to it. The other thing it showed me was that he was looking for somebody, a parent, somebody, to take him and say, "It's gonna be all right, son."

Some days the responsibility of that was a heavy burden. I couldn't let this guy be weak, and that meant I couldn't indulge my own weaknesses. Every day it was a battle, every day it was another test, another challenge, to see if I was going to be there and stand up for something and tell him to stand up, or if I was going to flinch and run away and give in. It got to be very wearing, the physical confrontations, the near fistfights.

There were days when he wouldn't throw punches and I would physically get in the ring with him and say, "Throw fuckin' punches. Throw punches!" I had nightmares that he would get in the ring with Holyfield and not throw punches and the referee would stop the fight.

Desperation and inventiveness often go hand in hand, so here's what I did. We'd have a hundred or more people watching his sparring sessions—there were seats set up for them in the tent—and I went around one day, right before his last round, telling them that when they heard me say "jab," I wanted them to say it, too. I knew that the jab was going to be a big part of the fight.

So in the last round, the whole place was taking my lead and going, "Jab!" The whole crowd was going, "Jab, jab, jab, jab!" How could he not respond? He had to jab. He *had* to. Michael's guys, Flem and Wick and the rest of them, loved it. "You're scary," Wick said to me. "You're startin' to scare me."

Two weeks before the fight, an amazing thing happened: Michael became perfect. After all of our confrontations and problems, he suddenly became the most perfect student you've ever seen in your life. We were hitting the bag during a training session one day, and this guy, who had been refusing to box, refusing to train some days, said, "Tell me to be strong." As soon as he said it, I knew I couldn't stumble.

"You *are* strong," I said.

"Tell me what's gonna happen on the twenty-second."

"You're gonna be the next heavyweight champ of the world."

"Tell me how I'm gonna do it."

"You're gonna do it with the jab. You're gonna do it with a consistent jab. You're gonna do it with a hook . . . and you're gonna do it with determination. That's how you're gonna do it!"

He was tearing up the bag. *Bam, bam, bam, bam.* Faster and faster and faster. It turned out to be the best workout we ever had. The strange thing was, it made me really nervous. I walked back to my room afterward and took a shower. Then I went outside and got in the Jacuzzi and let the jets wash over me. He'd bought into what I was teaching him, he'd stopped fighting me, he'd gotten with the program. In a weird way he'd managed to flip things around. I remembered something that Cus used to say: "Nature is very smart and intuitive and it finds a way." Michael had figured out how to get out of the eye of the storm. He'd turned things around and now all the pressure was on me. It was as if he had said, "All right. I'm gonna do everything the right way now. I'm gonna do everything you say. No more excuses. No more finding reasons to lose. No more setting myself up. No more refusing to face what's coming. I'm gonna do everything right. Now it's on you, Teddy. It's on you."

He was right. If he hadn't turned the tables, I'd have been able to say, "The son of a bitch didn't listen. He didn't want to win." It would have given me a way out. But if he wanted to win, if he gave his all and he didn't win, then what would that mean? That I had lied to him? It wasn't something I wanted to think about too much.

From that day on, Michael never gave me a problem. If I told him to box six rounds, at the end of six rounds he'd say, "Do you wanna go another?"

Davimos came up to me a couple of days later and said, "Did you see the spaceship?"

"What?"

"The spaceship," Davimos said. "The one that came in and abducted him a few days ago and replaced him with this alien."

"He is like an alien, isn't he?" I said.

"I didn't say anything the first day because I figured the next day he'd come back to earth. Then the next day, I figured, 'Okay, the real Michael will reappear today.' Now it's three days, and he's definitely not himself. He's definitely an alien."

"The thing is," I said, "you're not giving him enough credit. He's a smart bastard. He's not gonna give me one more problem for the rest of camp."

"Nah, he could blow up tomorrow," Davimos said.

"No, I'm telling you, John. I know what he did. He reversed it. He found a way to transfer the responsibility. He's very smart."

Davimos thought about what I was saying and then looked at me. "That is what he's doing, isn't it?"

I nodded.

"Now you're the one who's afraid." He understood instantly what it meant.

"Yeah, now I'm the one who's afraid . . . ," I said. "The only thing is he's not gonna freakin' lose."

A FEW DAYS LATER, WE FLEW INTO VEGAS. THE FIGHT WAS A week away. Caesars Palace had a limo waiting for us at the airport. When we got to the hotel, there were all these half-naked Cleopatras and Roman gladiators lined up at the front entrance to welcome us. It was definitely a little bit different from the smokers in the Bronx, where it would be one wino lifting his bottle of Thunderbird in salute as I was walking my fighters into some bombed-out building.

All through training camp and even before, there'd been these omens that made me feel something out of the ordinary was going on—the fight in the parking lot in Mississippi, Michael coming back to me because of it, my father dying. When we got to Vegas we trained at this gym, Johnny Taco's, and when Michael got in the ring, I noticed a poster up on the wall behind him of Mike Tyson. It was strange because it was a poster I had never seen before. It had Tyson's record listed on it, which at the time of the poster was 35–0. Michael Moorer's record was 34–0. If he won the championship it would be the same as Tyson's at the time of that poster. It was an eerie moment for me: I was looking up at Michael in the ring, and there was Tyson's ghost floating over his head, this thing that was supposed to have happened for me but didn't.

I guess the suspense of not knowing what was going to happen, the anxiety, had started to get to me by then. All these omens I'd seen and it still wasn't enough. I said to myself, "Gee, I wish there was an even more direct sign that would tell me that everything's gonna be okay." That's how much pressure I was under. I just had to win the fight. As I walked through the casino, I decided to ask the spirits in a very Vegas way: I stopped at a roulette table. I didn't even know the rules. But I stopped at the table, handed the croupier a hundred-dollar bill, and received four green twenty-five-dollar chips. I said, "How does it work?"

"Whatever you want to do," the croupier said. "You can play red or black, or different columns—"

"No, I don't want to do any of that. I just want to put it on a number."

"What number?"

"Thirty-five." I handed him the chips, and he placed them on 35. There were other players at the table. They were playing much smaller, a dollar at a time. I didn't even know to look at the ball going around the wheel. I wasn't even looking or aware when the spin was over. Suddenly, they pushed me thirty-five hundred dollars in chips. The ball had landed on 35! I turned to the lady next to me and said, "I won?"

"You sure did."

"We're gonna win!" I shouted.

"You already won, honey."

"No, no, you don't understand . . . holy shit!" I didn't know what to do. A part of me wanted to cry. A part of me wanted to explain it all, to tell them, "This means we're going to win the world championship!" But I didn't. I just picked up the money and left the table. I went to the cage and cashed out. I thought it meant something, I really did. It was like, Everything is coming our way. So I took that money plus fifteen hundred more and put it on Michael, who was a two-to-one underdog, to win the fight.

* * *

Las Vegas, in the days leading up to a big fight, develops this supercharged atmosphere. You can feel the buzz in the air. But even with that charge, or maybe because of it, I was very concerned that Michael not lose his edge. I brought Bigfoot Martin along with us, which was an unusual thing. Usually when you break camp for a prizefight, you send the sparring partners home. But I made Bigfoot come with us because I wanted Michael to spar one more day. Nothing too hard; I didn't want him to be overtrained. Just three easy rounds five days before the fight to keep him sharp and focused. There were a million distractions to contend with: all the media people, the interviews, the TV spots, the fans wanting to say hello or get an autograph.

I tried to control as many things as I could. I had Michael staying in a room under an assumed name because I didn't want any strangers or enemies calling him up in the middle of the night and waking him. You actually worry about stuff like that. The other thing I did was have his guys Flem and Wick set up a security station down the hall from Michael's suite. They were there twenty-four hours a day. They did eight-hour shifts. Anybody who wanted to get into Michael's room had to get past them.

We also had all the food orders that went to Michael sent up to another room on the floor under a different name, again to make sure no funny stuff was going on. All those years with Cus, some of his paranoia had definitely rubbed off on me. But like they say, just because you're paranoid doesn't mean they're not out to get you. Somebody could do something as simple as putting a laxative in your fighter's meal so he got the shits for a couple of days and was weak. Stuff like that actually happened in the old days, and I wasn't taking any chances now. Flem, Wick, and Michael approved. They loved all the cloak-and-dagger stuff.

My greatest worry, of course, was not outside distractions, but what was going on inside Michael's head. The day after we got there, I went into his room and all the drapes were drawn. I couldn't see him—literally could not see him.

"Where the hell are you?" I said, waiting for my eyes to adjust.

I heard this small voice. "Here."

I didn't want to hear any small voices. Not when my guy was about to become heavyweight champion of the world. No small voices.

"Where? Where are ya?"

"Over here." Again the small voice.

"What the fuck are ya doin'?" I shouted. I went around the room yanking open the drapes.

"Whoa! Shut the— Ted, don't do that."

"Don't do what? Who do you think you are, Dracula?"

"C'mon, Ted. Stop!"

I opened up every drape I could find. I was like Mr. Sunshine. It was the middle of the day and he was in a black room, all by himself. "You haven't hidden one day," I said. "Even when you tried, I didn't let you. You did everything. Tell me how many days of sparring you missed?"

"None."

"How many curfews?"

"Never missed a curfew."

"That's right. So let's not hide now. There's no drawn shades here. We got nothing but great stuff to look at."

The sun streamed in and Michael squinted but he stopped protesting.

The main thing, leading up to the fight, was to keep him busy, keep him positive, not let him brood too much. I had him skip rope every day, shadowbox, break a sweat. I didn't want him working too hard. The main push was already done. I just wanted him to stay loose and fresh.

A few nights after we arrived, Mike Boorman, the PR man, a big, fat-cheeked Brooklyn guy, who had become a good friend of mine, and John Davimos and I went out to a restaurant to grab a bite, while Flem and Wick and the rest of them took Michael out to the mall. In the middle of our dinner, Flem suddenly came rushing in, out of breath.

"What is it, Flem?" I put down my burger.

He shook his head. "I'm embarrassed."

"What is it?"

"We lost him."

"Lost who?" I was so past it all at that point, I couldn't take it seriously.

"Would it be your fighter?" Boorman ventured.

At that point, Davimos chimed in, saying to Flem: "You're a security guy. How do you lose a two-hundred-and-twenty-pound fighter?"

"Well, you see . . . ," Flem began, winding himself up to tell it, the way a kid would do if he were explaining how he lost his homework. "We had just come back from the mall, and we were walking into the casino, and Michael was in a good mood. But as we were walking past the bingo hall, the doors suddenly opened and all the bingo ladies came rushing out, and there was all this commotion. A couple of them bumped into him, these seventy-, eighty-year-old women. One of them yelled at him, 'Get out of my way, you big lug. You knocked over my bingo card.' And Michael got so mad and upset, he took off. He ran away. I tried to catch up to him, but he was moving too fast. Last I saw of him, he was running down the strip." Flem hung his head.

"Mike, you finished with that ketchup?" I said.

"Yeah, Ted. You want one of my onion rings?"

"Sure."

Boorman held out his plate of onion rings. I took one. He looked at Flem and said, "I wouldn't worry too much, Flem. But I might keep that story quiet."

"Excuse me, Mr. Boorman?"

"You know, about the next heavyweight champ of the world losing a battle to a bunch of bingo ladies?"

"Uh-huh." Flem looked confused.

"But as far as finding him, I guarantee you, wherever he went, he'll be back by his curfew. Ask Teddy."

"I'd bet on it," I said.

And of course that's exactly what happened. No matter what, Michael made his curfew.

The interesting thing was, aside from that dinner and a few other occasions, once we got to Vegas, Michael wouldn't let me out of his sight. He wanted me around all the time. Boorman was the first to pick up on it. We'd finish an interview and be on our way out of the interview area, and if I was lagging behind Michael and his crew, he'd suddenly stop and go, "Where's Teddy? Where's Teddy?"

Boorman thought it was hysterical. "He's your best friend now, huh?"

"You understand what's going on, doncha, Mike?"

"Yeah. He's scared to death, and you're his security blanket. Did anyone tell him that you ain't gonna be throwing the punches Saturday night, he is?"

The day of the weigh-in, Michael was waiting for me in his room; we were supposed to shake out, just stretch and loosen up. I was late picking him up, and John Davimos came running up to my room, saying, "Where the hell are you? He's freakin' out, asking for you. What are ya leavin' him alone for?" It reminded me of that book *Lonesome Dove*, where Augustus, the old Ranger, rescues this girl from the Indians, and after that she won't let him out of her sight. She's totally dependent on him, to the point where she falls apart if he's not there. I didn't want that happening to Michael. If he wanted me around all the time, it was another kind of weakness, and that wasn't good.

I was thinking about that as we headed over to Michael's room. We walked in and he had all his guys around him. I said, "Okay, we're not gonna shake out today."

"Why not?" Michael said.

"Because you're ready."

He looked at me as if he weren't sure what I meant.

"You're more ready than anybody I've ever trained," I said. "In fact, I want you to know that I'm going to do something I've never done before. . . ."

"What's that?"

"I've gotta go do a live interview with an ABC affiliate from your hometown. Monessen. I'm telling them that you're going to be the next heavyweight champ of the world. I'm guaranteeing it. You know I never say things I don't mean. I'm going to go on there and guarantee this. And I'm right, ain't I?"

Again, he just looked at me.

"I'm *right,* ain't I?"

"You're right," he said.

I grabbed his cheeks, looked right in his eyes, and said, "I know I am."

A little while later, I went on the air and made the guarantee. I knew his friends from back home would contact him. Sure enough, the calls started coming in. "Michael, you know what your trainer just did? He guaranteed that you will win the title tomorrow night. If you don't win the title he said it means he's not a real trainer. Can you believe he said that shit?"

Boorman asked me about it. He said, "When did you think of that?"

"When I walked in and saw the look on his face."

Later that afternoon, with the fight less than thirty hours away, I said to Boorman, "Let's take him to a movie." We got a newspaper to see what was playing. There were movies that had gotten good reviews, love stories and dramatic films that were up for awards, but I said to Boorman,

"Let's find the movie that has the biggest body count." I don't remember the name of the movie now, but it was something with Ice-T in it. *Slim Jim Jack Fucks Up the 'Hood.* Something like that. All I know is that a lot of people in it got whacked. Boorman was sitting next to me, squirming and muttering the whole time, "When is this gonna be over?," while Michael was behind us with his whole crew, yelling at the screen, "Yeahhh. Fuck this guy up! Cap the motherfucker!" At one point Boorman tried to get up and go out to the lobby, but I grabbed him and said, "No, you're here to the end. Just like me. You're not leavin'."

After the movie, Michael and his crew went back to his room. Around ten o'clock I went over there and made everyone leave. After they left, I sat in a chair while Michael got ready for bed and brushed his teeth.

"What are you doin'?" he asked me from the bathroom.

"I was just gonna tell you a bedtime story."

"What?"

"A bedtime story. About a kid who came to camp not sure of why he came to camp and by the time it was over he knew why, he made up his mind why. He was gonna be the next heavyweight champ of the world. He went to sleep a regular contender and he woke up the champion of the world."

Michael came out of the bathroom. He had the toothbrush in his hand and his mouth was full of foam. He just looked at me and smiled a little. We had been through so much together by that point. He just smiled at me and said, "Awright, Teddy," and we said good night.

After I left his room, I went down to the lobby of the hotel to give a ticket to my brother Terryl, who I'd just flown out from New York. It was mobbed downstairs, the fight crowd out in full force. As I tried to find him, all these people were coming up to me and wishing me luck and shaking my hand. I was exhausted. I just wanted to get back up to my room.

I finally found Terryl and gave him his ticket. People were still coming up to me. All of a sudden, one guy shook my hand and it was different. He didn't say "Good luck," he said, "Congratulations." I wasn't really looking at him at first. But when I did take a look, I recoiled in shock. It was Donnie LaLonde. I let go of his hand like it was contaminated.

"You piece of shit," I said. I felt dirty because I'd shaken his hand. "I didn't know it was you!"

LaLonde was thrown by my reaction, but he kept plowing ahead. "I just wanted to say congratulations."

"Congratulations? Congratulations? Go fuck yourself!"

"But you're there. It don't matter no more, Teddy. You don't need to be mad no more."

I stared at him. I'd completely forgotten about my brother. "You fuckin' piece of shit. What you did hasn't changed because of this." I took a step toward him and he saw the look on my face and backed away.

"How can you still be angry?" he said. "You're there! You made it!"

"I'm there?" I said. Now it wasn't even about him having the nerve to show his face and think that he could be forgiven, it was about him not understanding. "I ain't there. We didn't win yet!"

"But you made it. Everyone knows."

"I ain't made it! We haven't won anything!"

Now you could actually hear his wife or his girlfriend, whoever she was, say to him, "Donnie, let's get out of here. You tried. Let it go." She took his hand, pulling him away. He kept looking back, saying, "It don't matter. You're there."

By then all these people had come between us, not even aware of what was going on, just well-wishers wanting to shake my hand. "Hey, Teddy, good luck." I was pushing past them, going after him, saying, "You fuck! I didn't win anything yet! It does matter! I haven't won anything!" My brother caught up to me and grabbed me by the shoulder. I kept yelling after LaLonde, "It does matter, you piece of shit! It matters!"

SATURDAY NIGHT. FINALLY. CUS USED TO DESCRIBE THE final days before a fight as being like waiting to go to the electric chair. There's the dread and anxiety, but at a certain point you also just want to get it over with already. In the dressing room before the fight, I had a list of things I wanted. One of them was a boom box. I wanted Michael to have his gangsta rap music. When we got to the dressing room, there was no boom box, so I sent Flem back to the hotel. "Get that freaking boom box!" I said.

It was funny, because during camp Michael and I had gotten into arguments about his music, all that "motherfucking bitch slut ho" stuff, which I hated. It amazed me that record companies produced music like that and that people bought it. I tolerated it as long as there were no women or kids around. One time Michael put on one of those tapes when there was a group of kids watching, and I said, "Shut it off. This is a professional place, and I won't allow it."

"Make me," he said.

I took the tape out of the boom box and stomped it with my foot. Michael got angry, then went into a sulk. I said, "C'mon, Michael, let's just do what we're here to do," but he kept sulking. Eventually, he put on a Whitney Houston tape instead and did his exercises, but he still wouldn't talk to me. Finally, after doing a series of sit-ups and push-ups, he said, "So what kind of fuckin' music do you like?"

"Similar to this," I said, nodding at the boom box.

"Yeah? Who? What's the name of the band?"

"Frank Sinatra."

"Man. That's old-school shit, Teddy."

"It's what I like."

"So what's a good record of his?"

"'Summer Wind' is my favorite, but they're all good."

That night, I went to dinner with Davimos at Sonny Bono's restaurant. In the middle of dinner, Michael came in, put a paper bag on the table, said, "I'll see you later," and walked out. I opened up the bag—it was a freaking tape of "Summer Wind." I found out later from Flem that Michael had driven all over Palm Springs until he found it.

The next day when we started our usual exercise routine, I popped in the tape. A lot of the people who had been there the day before and witnessed our argument had come back. When they heard Frank's voice, they smiled. It was like, "This is funny. This is worth our dollar."

Now, on the night of the fight, I was returning the favor: I wanted Michael to have his gangsta rap music. Flem came back with the boom box and I got a tape out. Michael said, "Nah, that's all right." I said, "No, no," and I put it on because I didn't want him being absorbed by silence. I felt the music would keep him from slipping into the darkness of his thoughts and his fears.

So the music was playing, and there was a TV on, a monitor in the dressing room showing the preliminary bouts. A couple of the guys said, "Hey, do you want to keep that monitor on?" It was showing the Junior Jones–John Michael Johnson fight. Jones was a big favorite, undefeated world champ, seven-to-one or something like that on the Vegas tote boards.

I was thinking maybe we shouldn't have it on; he's the favorite, just like Holyfield's the favorite, and if he wins, it might not be good. But in a couple of minutes of watching, I picked up what was going on. I took a gamble. "Leave it on," I said. "Junior Jones is gonna lose this fight. You wanna know why? Because this is a night of upsets."

Meanwhile, a procession of people were coming by the dressing room to say hello to Michael and to me—nobody was allowed in, but they were coming by anyway. I kept popping out of the dressing room to shake their hands and say hello. Then I'd go back. On the monitor, just as I predicted, Junior Jones was losing his fight, and I'd say, "See. It's in the air. It's a night of upsets!"

Six-forty-five. Just one hour before the fight now. Michael had already limbered up a little, done some jumping jacks and stretches. Officials from the Nevada Boxing Commission and a guy from Holyfield's camp stopped by to watch me wrap Michael's hands. One of our guys was over in Holyfield's dressing room watching his trainer wrap Holyfield. That was the protocol.

The commissioners also brought the gloves over, the ones that we had marked at the weigh-in the previous day. Holyfield, the champion, had gotten first choice of the gloves, as was the custom, after which we had gotten our turn. The brand of glove, Reyes, was negotiated at an earlier meeting. I thought the Reyes glove gave us an edge, because it was a punchers' glove, a little bit tighter and more streamlined than most other brands (although now, if I had my choice, I'd go with the redesigned Everlast glove). Once we had found a pair that fit Michael properly (which wasn't easy, because Michael had very large hands), I had signed the inside lip of the glove. These were all normal precautions to ensure that the gloves weren't switched. It might sound excessive, but in a big-money event, with gambling involved, you couldn't be too careful.

So I inspected the fight gloves, plus the backup pair, to make sure my mark was in them, then set about wrapping Michael's hands. His music was playing. Flem and Wick and some of the other guys were standing around along with the commissioners and a TV cameraman. Michael sat in a chair in the middle of the room, near the table with the medical supplies and tape. I put another chair in front of him, with a rolled-up towel on top of the back for him to lay his forearm across. He extended his right hand. We always wrapped his right hand first because that was his jab hand, the hand that started everything. I took his hand in mine and started winding one of the wraps around it. I said, "This hand's going to sing all night."

It's very intimate, wrapping a fighter's hands. You can feel it if there's tension in his hands, and see in his eyes and demeanor if he's drifting or if he's focused. Michael looked good to me. After I finished wrapping and taping his hands, we had thirty-five minutes left before showtime. Michael put on his cup and trunks. I helped him tie the cup on and tape it. After that, he did some more stretching, and then some shadowboxing, enough to work up a little bit of a sweat. With ten minutes to go, I put the gloves on him, taped up the gloves so the laces were secure, then put on the robe. I always did a checklist to make sure we hadn't forgotten anything. Did he have his cup? Was he wearing his trunks? That's not a joke. I'd seen fights where the fighter took off his robe and he was just in his jock; he'd forgotten to put on his trunks.

I did a checklist with my cut man, too. Made sure we had our End-Swells (flat metal devices used to compress bruises and keep swelling down) and Vaseline in a bucket of ice (you wanted the Vaseline nice and hard so that you could apply it in a thicker layer, rubbing both ways on the eyebrows to make sure that it got under the hair). Various coagulants? Check. Q-tips? Scissors? Adhesive tape? Gauze? Towels? Mouthpiece and backup mouthpiece? Check. Check. Check . . .

"It's time," somebody said, sticking his head in the door. "It's time."

THERE COMES
A TIME

AS WE CAME OUT OF THE TUNNEL THAT LED INTO THE boxing arena, I impulsively decided that we should run into the ring. Not jog, *run*. There was a camera guy backing up in front of us, and as the lights hit us and the music blasted, I shouted at the camera guy, "You better be moving." He almost fell over, trying to back up and stay with us as we ran toward the ring. Michael loved it. Loved the running.

We got in the ring and he was all charged up. We had gone over this moment so many times in training. As the challenger he was going to have to wait for Holyfield, which wasn't an easy thing. "Michael," I said, "I want you to think about one thing now: This is the last time you'll be coming into the ring first. From now on you'll be coming in second."

When Holyfield entered the arena, he had MC Hammer as part of his ring-walk team. I said, "And this is also the last time you'll see MC Hammer. Because after tonight he'll be retired. He won't be doing any ring walks anymore." I was just talking, but it turned out to be right. His career went into a nosedive. Hammer time was over.

As they were making the introductions, I could see that Michael was nervous. I thought, *I'm not going to disappear on him. I'm gonna show him that I'm right there with him. I'm not going to leave him alone.*

I had these two old-timers in the corner with me, Moe Smith and Ralph Citro, who was a cut man with the Kronk gym for years. I wanted guys who had been around and to whom it meant something to be there, guys that could be counted on. In Moe's case, he had been around boxing for sixty years, and he'd never been in a heavyweight title fight. I felt that he should be.

Mills Lane was the referee, which I was happy about. I felt comfortable with him. Like Michael Buffer, the ring announcer who was famous for his trademark "Let's get ready to rrrruuummmble!," Mills had his own signature phrase, which he would bark loudly after issuing the ring instructions.

"Let's get it onnnn!"

In the moments before the bell rang to start the fight, I reminded Michael once again that he was going to win this fight with his jab. Our whole plan was predicated on that, because I had noticed, watching tape of Holyfield, that he bounced, and when he bounced he wasn't set to punch. He had to stop. There was a split second where he was vulnerable. That was when I wanted Michael to catch him with jabs.

The first round went okay. Basically, when you're in the first round of a big fight like this, and there's been all this buildup and hype, you just want to make it through the round, get past the nervousness and realize that it's just a fight. You also don't want to get blitzed. You know, where the guy just comes at you with everything he's got before you're really into the fight or ready to deal with it. We got through the round okay, but the problem I saw right off was that instead of throwing the jab steadily, which was our plan, Michael was looking for one punch. I knew if I didn't see that jab, then I didn't have him. I didn't have his attention. On the other hand, I was also seeing that I was right about Holyfield. That we had gotten him at a good time. That he was vulnerable, and that this was the right night.

The second round, Michael went out and this time he did what we'd worked on. He threw the jab. He also hooked off the jab, which was another thing we'd worked on in camp. I felt that could be very effective for him, especially because he was a southpaw. But near the end of the round, which he was dominating, he got careless. He threw a big right uppercut, and he posed after he threw it. He stood up too much, didn't move after he punched, and Holyfield caught him with a short right followed by a left hook that put him down.

My family was in the arena watching. When Michael hit the canvas, Nicole burst into tears. Elaine had her eyes closed. She couldn't watch. But little Teddy said, "It's okay. He's up. He got up at the count of two. He's not hurt."

One of the questions about Moorer was his chin. He'd gotten knocked down in previous fights but he'd always gotten back up and won. When I saw him go down, after the little jolt of anxiety of whether or not he'd get up, I thought, *I need to remind him that every time he's been on the floor he's always gone on to win.* The other thought I had was that I needed to tell him why he'd gotten knocked down, what his mistake had been, so he could feel good about going back out there. Because the worst thing for a fighter is to go back out there not knowing why he got hit. It's like sending a guy into a dark room. He doesn't know what's there.

In retrospect, the knockdown was the turning point in the fight, because one of the judges scored it an even round on account of how dominant Michael had been up to that point. We didn't know it at the time, but that was our heavyweight title right there. That could have been a 10–8 round. A lot of judges would have just counted the knockdown and ignored the rest of the round. But that isn't what happened; two judges scored it 10–9 for Holyfield and the third judge made it 10–10. Technically, that's the correct way of scoring a round like that, but still you don't expect it.

In the third round, Michael went out very cautiously. He fought only when he was being forced to fight. I was yelling at him, trying to wake him up. If you're a gardener, you don't wait until the weeds are killing your bushes, you start pulling them before they take root and start choking your garden to death.

"I want you to use that jab and I want you to work off it," I barked at him when he came back to the corner. "But I don't want you to be satisfied with it. You go in there and you start backing this guy up and doing what we trained to do. Otherwise don't come back to this fucking corner! You hear me!"

As the fight progressed, the pattern continued, Michael coasting instead of hitting the gas. I'd get him to step it up for a while, but I was frustrated by my inability to get him to keep his foot to the floor.

I had told Michael in training camp that "you look at Holyfield's body and it can be intimidating if you allow it to be because it's so chiseled. But it's actually a negative for him."

"What do you mean?" he asked.

"He's so streamlined and tight that there's actually not much protection in his body." Holyfield had gotten hurt by body punches when he fought Michael Dokes. The perception was that wasn't the place to go. But the reality was that it was the place to go. I told Michael that, and whenever he landed a body punch in the fight, you could see Holyfield grimace. The problem was he wasn't doing it enough. Every time I saw Michael stop working, I said to myself, "How can I get him to do more?"

Holyfield looked lethargic to me. He wasn't the consistent offensive machine he usually was. But incredibly, at the end of the fifth round, Michael tapped him on the ass with his glove before they headed back to their corners. It made me crazy.

"What the fuck are you doing, tapping this guy on the ass?" I yelled at him. "He ain't gonna let up on you because you do that. Don't start looking for deals or begin lying to yourself."

As the fight went on, Michael kept letting Holyfield hold on the inside, kept letting him rest, kept letting him use his experience to conserve energy for the later rounds. Even though I thought we were winning most of the rounds, I was upset. We were trying to take a special fighter's title.

Sure enough, in the seventh round, Holyfield stepped it up. Even though Michael was still doing some good things, I got caught up in what he wasn't doing. Holyfield was too seasoned and too smart a boxer. If we left him in a position to be able to steal the fight, he would. Especially because he was the champion and we were in Las Vegas.

The eighth round produced more of the same from Michael. I could see all the opportunities he was missing. I was scared, frankly. I thought we were blowing it. When the bell rang, ending the eighth round, I put Michael's stool in the corner and climbed in the ring. As Michael walked toward me, I grabbed him and looked in his eyes.

"If you don't want to fight this guy, I will!" I yelled. I needed to get through to him somehow, so I sat down on his stool. It was impulsive. It wasn't premeditated or planned. Michael didn't know what to do. He just stood there, looking at me.

"Do you want me to fight him?" I said. "Do you? Do you want me to change places with you?" I had his attention now. "Look, Michael, I'm not getting up until you tell me you want to win the title. Do you want to win the title?"

"Yes."

"Then you gotta show it!" I got up from the stool and let him sit down. "Listen," I said, "this guy is finished!" I squeezed a wet sponge on Michael's head to cool him off. *"He's finished!"* I was right up in his face. "Michael, there comes a time in a man's life when he makes a decision to just live, to survive—or he wants to win. You're doing just enough to keep him off ya and hope he leaves ya alone. You're lyin' to yourself, but you're gonna cry tomorrow. You're lyin' to yourself! . . . And I'd be lyin' if I let you get away with it! Do you want to cry tomorrow? Huh? *Then don't lie to yourself anymore!* There's something wrong with this guy! Now back him up and fight a full round!"

Over in Holyfield's corner, he was being told things like "Trust in Jesus," and "Relax," and "Breathe deep." If you could have cut around the arena, the contrasting scenes that were going on at that moment were really something. Down in their seats, Elaine and Nicole and little Teddy were sitting in front of this big gambler, Roger King of King World (the syndication company behind shows like *Wheel of Fortune*, *Jeopardy!*, and *The Oprah Winfrey Show*), who had $200,000 riding on Michael. Elaine told me later that when King realized he was sitting behind her and my kids, he said, "That's why I bet on this fight. Your husband. I didn't bet on Moorer, I bet on him." He wound up talking to them throughout the fight, and when I sat down on Michael's stool, he said, "Now that's different. I've never seen that before." Meanwhile, Elaine was going, "Oh my God. He's lost his mind." And my nine-year-old son, little Teddy, was going, "It's okay. Dad knows what he's doing. He's trying to get Michael to fight." And on the HBO telecast, Jim Lampley was saying about me and Moorer, "I don't know how long that marriage can last, but it's an interesting one."

Despite my attempts to rouse him, Michael didn't pick up the pace in the ninth round. It was as if he refused to acknowledge to himself that the heavyweight title meant something. If he told himself it actually was important, he'd be too vulnerable if he lost. If he didn't acknowledge the importance, then he couldn't be hurt. That was why I told him that he was lying to himself. I knew it was going to hurt if he lost. I knew it. I felt that I couldn't let up. At the same time there was a temptation to let up, there was this little voice in my head saying: "They're not going to look at you, they're going to look at him. They're going to say, 'You did all you could. You can't fight for the guy. He's a mutt. It's not your fault.'" The impulse to hide behind that scared the shit out of me. If I did that, I was a co-conspirator—I was the real mutt.

So I kept pounding it into him. "I'm telling you, you're blowing it, Michael. You're blowing it! And you know what? You're gonna cry afterward. You're gonna cry! He's gonna lose his next fight instead of this fight!"

Some people might think I was too hard on him. But I knew it was all there for us. Holyfield was less than a hundred percent. By not going full out, Michael was allowing him to survive. Holyfield was grabbing him, and clutching, and Michael was going along with it, he was making that silent contract with Holyfield, he was embracing it. If Michael had kept pressing him, he would have knocked Holyfield out. As much respect as I have for Holyfield, that's the simple truth.

In the twelfth and final round, Michael continued to nail Holyfield with his jab and with the jab-uppercut we had worked on in training camp, but always just one punch at a time, landing then backing off, the way he'd done throughout the fight. When the bell sounded, my first thought was, *Did we do enough?* Everyone else in the corner was kissing him and hugging him, saying, "Hey, champ!" and congratulating him. The first thing I said to him was, "You could have done more."

In those agonizing moments while we were all waiting for the decision, that's what I kept thinking. *You could have done more.* What's funny is that down at ringside, my son, little Teddy, was like an echo of me. He was telling Elaine, "I don't know if he did enough." A nine-year-old boy analyzing it as calmly as could be.

The longest moment in boxing is the one right after you hear the words "The winner and . . . ," and you're waiting for the ring announcer to say either "new" or "still champion." That's an excruciating moment. At ringside, where my family was sitting, Roger King and this other gambler who had bet on Holyfield were arguing over who they thought had won. My daughter was so nervous she was shaking, but my son was very serene. He was listening to these two gamblers argue. King was going "And new!" and the other guy was going "And still!," and that's all my son could hear, "and new" and "and still" back and forth. So when Michael Buffer said, "The winner and *new* . . . ," Teddy turned back to the Holyfield bettor and said, "And new!" and that was it. Everybody started going crazy, hugging each other, jumping up and down. That's all I was waiting for, that word. But if you watch the tape of the fight, you'll see that while Michael was hugging Davimos and the Duvas and their partner Bill Korzerski, I was off by myself to one side, lost in my thoughts. Meanwhile, Jim Lampley, on TV, was saying, "What is Teddy Atlas thinking right now? Look at him, he's the only one not sharing in the celebration."

Amid the pandemonium—the crush of the TV crew, the cornermen, the security people, and the fans—I was thinking about my father. During the twelfth round, I had looked up—and I had never done this before—I had looked up and crossed myself. I had said, "Listen, Dad, please help us. This is what I wanted to give you. All those years I lived in Catskill, this is why."

In the midst of the bedlam, I thanked him. I said, "Thanks, Dad," and it was as if I had finally buried him, as if he hadn't really been buried until that moment. I said, "It turned out okay, didn't it?" Then I thought, *I gotta get my kids in the ring.* You see, my dad had looked out for me and given me this gift, now I needed to look out for them. I knew they wanted to come in the ring. When they were real little they had asked me, "Dad, when you win the heavyweight championship of the world, can we come in the ring?," and I had said, "Yeah, of course." So that was what I was thinking about. I'd never forgotten them asking.

Henry Gluck, the CEO of Caesars, made his way over to me and said, "Congratulations, Teddy." I responded, "Yeah, thank you. Listen, can I get my kids into the ring? I gotta get them in here." It wasn't easy with all the people and the security jammed in there. Gluck turned to one of the security guys and said, "Get Teddy Atlas's kids in this ring right now."

The security guys located my kids and started passing them up, handing them up into the ring. Nicole was crying. Little Teddy's eyes were red. "You did it, Dad!"

"No, we did it," I said, taking them both into my arms, hugging them to me tight.

THE DAY AFTER THE FIGHT, DOWN IN THE CASINO LOBBY, just before leaving for the airport, I was with Mark Kriegel, who had been filing stories on me and Michael for the *Daily News* and knew about the omens and odd coincidences leading up to the championship. He followed along with me when I went to the sports book to cash my winning bet on Michael.

"What the hell, Teddy?"

"You didn't know I made a bet on him?" The guy behind the counter ran my ticket through the computer, then handed me two packets of five thousand dollars apiece. I put the money in my gym bag. "I'm telling you," I said to Kriegel, "it was destiny. I knew we couldn't lose. Here, wait a minute." We were walking past the high-limit slot machines. I went over to the lady cashier and handed her a hundred-dollar bill. "I need a hundred-dollar coin," I said.

"Ah, you're gettin' cocky now after you won," Kriegel said.

"No, I'm tellin' you, it was fate. It was my father. Until I leave here, I can't lose. That's just how it is."

I went over to a slot machine and put the hundred-dollar coin in. Kriegel was the kind of guy who wouldn't bet two dollars on the sun coming up in the morning. Gambling made him very nervous. "You're a sick man," he said.

"You don't understand," I said.

I pushed the button and the wheels rolled. *Bop, bop, bop, bop. . . . Ding, ding, ding!* Just like that, two thousand dollars in silver coins dropped into the tray! Kriegel's eyes bugged out of his head.

"That's crazy," he said.

"If I didn't have to leave this place, I'd never lose." We had to get to the airport to catch our plane. Elaine and the kids were waiting for me.

Kriegel was shaking his head. "I gotta do something about this," he said, and started to take off.

"What? Where ya goin'?" I said.

He looked back over his shoulder. "I gotta see if I can get ahold of my editor, see if it's past deadline."

"What?"

"That story I filed today?" he said. "How can I not try and put this in?" And with that he took off, sprinting across the endless carpet.

PART OF THE PLEASURE OF WINNING THE TITLE WAS KNOWing that other people were with me, rooting for me, and that it genuinely meant something to them. That made me feel good. You usually don't think of those things, but for me that was a really unexpected and meaningful part of the whole experience. My old friend and guardian, Brother Tim McDonald, called to congratulate me afterward. He was living in Vancouver now, running a skid-row soup kitchen called The Door Is Open. When he found out they were showing the fight locally on closed circuit and charging seventeen dollars Canadian, he scrounged up enough money to go see the fight. This was a guy who barely had a red cent to his name because he always gave everything away. If I'd have known he wanted to see the fight, I would have flown him to Vegas. But I hadn't known.

The only place showing the fight in Vancouver was a topless bar in the red-light district. For obvious reasons, Brother Tim didn't want to be seen in a place like that, so he took this wool cap he always had and pulled it down real low, almost over his eyes, and ducked into this topless bar as inconspicuously as he could. It was easy to picture him, because I remembered that blue wool watch cap from when we'd taken our walks around the streets of Greenwich Village all those years earlier.

Once inside the strip club, he had to move up close to the bar because he was hard of hearing and needed to be close to the TV. Naked girls were twirling on a pole near him, and even the bartender was scantily clad. She approached him and asked him what he wanted to drink.

"Nothing," he said, averting his eyes.

"There's a two-drink minimum."

"All right. Two Cokes."

When the fight came on, Brother Tim tried to keep a low profile, but whenever something exciting would happen, his emotions would get away from him and he'd stand up and cheer. In between rounds, instead of breaking for commercials (because it was pay-per-view), the cable network showed the corner action. They'd cut from Holyfield's trainer talking about faith and trusting in Jesus to me saying to Michael, ". . . otherwise don't come back to this motherfucking corner." This went on round after round. Finally before the last round, Holyfield's corner was again going, "God is with you," and Brother Tim couldn't contain himself anymore. He jumped out of his seat and yelled, "No, he's not! He's on the other guy's side!" Of course, as soon as he said it, he remembered himself and pulled his head down, muttering, "Sorry. Sorry."

MICHAEL AND JOHN DAVIMOS CAME TO NEW YORK AND visited me a few days after the fight. Elaine made Michael chicken the way he always liked with plenty of garlic. Everyone was in great spirits. After lunch, Michael grabbed a basketball and said, "Let's go to the park." The way they were all smiling, I should have known something was up. But I went along with them, down the elevator and across the street toward the park. Suddenly, Michael said, "Hey, that's a cool car!" And we all turned and there was this beautiful, shiny red Lexus sports car parked at the curb. Michael walked over toward it, going, "Wow, I wonder whose car this is. This is a *bad* ride!"

Michael was such a car freak, it wasn't out of character for him to act like that. But then everyone else walked over to take a closer look. Elaine. Her sister. The kids. Davimos. Now that I think back on it, it's obvious that it was all planned out. Anyway, I noticed that there was a dealer's sticker on the side window. When I took a closer look I saw my name was on it. I looked up and everyone was grinning. Michael held out the keys for me and said, "Thank you."

Meanwhile, all these people and kids from the park saw what was going on and came over, and they all became part of the moment, congratulating me and Michael, shaking our hands, slapping us on our backs. "The world champs!" One of our neighbors from across the park came over and said to me and Elaine, "We're going to be sorry to see you guys leave." She just made the assumption that would happen, even though we didn't move for another year or two.

"C'mon, Teddy," Michael said. "Let's take your new wheels for a spin."

The two of us got in the car. It had that new leather smell. Everything was pristine and spanking new. I turned the key. The engine hummed to life. With everyone smiling, applauding, and waving, I drove slowly down the block.

I drove a couple of blocks, not really knowing where to go, and then we were passing by my friend Anthony Spero's place, and I thought, *Anthony would get a kick out of this.* I pulled over and jumped out, leaving the car running at the curb. Anthony was a good friend of mine, a boxing fan, who at that time was under house arrest for alleged mob-related activities and was wearing a bracelet. (He's currently serving a life sentence in Florida, which, in my opinion, is a travesty; I think the government set him up and I hope someday it'll be rectified and he'll get to come home. I'm not saying he's a perfect individual, but in my eyes he's a good man and a good friend.)

When he saw me coming up the walk, Anthony and his girlfriend, Louise, came out of the house. He couldn't go too far because of the bracelet, but he came a little ways and gave me a hug. Then Michael got out of the car, and I introduced them, and Michael went, "Hey, Anthony, what do you think of Teddy's ride?"

"What?" Anthony said.

"What do you think of my man's ride?"

At that point Anthony understood, and he said, "It's beautiful." Then he said to Michael, "You fought good. You're a good fighter." But he didn't leave it there. "You could be champion for a long time," he said. "You've got a beautiful jab. You just gotta be more aggressive with it. You should have knocked that Holyfield out."

It cracked me up. The heavyweight champion shows up at his door and Anthony, a big boxing fan, not only gets to talk to him but gets to give him pointers on top of it! It was like Derek Jeter showing up at your house a couple of days after winning the World Series, and after high-fiving him you mention that he should have stretched that one single into a double. Not to mention the fact that you're delivering this critique while under house arrest.

BEFORE TRAINING CAMP I HAD GONE TO VISIT MY FATHER'S grave. When I got back home, to acknowledge his help in winning the title and pay tribute to him, I went to a florist and bought five dozen red roses. My father had loved red roses and always had a bunch of rosebushes at the house I grew up in.

As I was coming out of the florist's with my five dozen roses—which is a lot of roses for one person to carry—this car full of young wiseass kids slowed down and one of them yelled, "Hey, Teddy! Those ain't for the champ, are they?"

I looked at them, ready to say something, but then one of them said, "Hey, we're just kidding! Congratulations!" And they pumped their fists and beeped the horn.

When I got to the grave, I laid out all the roses on Dad's grave. Then I wrote a note to him. Nothing long or involved. Just a little note. "Dad, thanks for helping us win the fight." I put it under the roses and left.

THE OTHER THING I DID, AND THIS, AGAIN, WAS TO COM-plete a circle, something that was begun in an earlier part of my life that I wanted to connect to the place I had come to now, was to go up to Catskill, because the kids up there, my old kids, wanted to see me. Greg, Gary, Rodney, Kevin, and George were there, as was John Chetti, who had become a youth counselor.

They handed me a plaque, another plaque—it had been many years since that first plaque—and this one said, "From your friends at the (old) Catskill Boxing Club, and the people who really know. Finally your time has come. We love you."

In a way, my winning the title with Michael was validation for them, too, because they had believed in me, they had supported me, and it af-firmed their faith in all the stuff I had taught them. It made them feel they had been right to put their trust in me. It made them feel—at least maybe a little bit—like they had won as well.

BIG GEORGE

I N BEATING HOLYFIELD, MICHAEL HAD TAKEN A huge step toward overcoming some of his demons and becoming the guy he—and I—wanted him to become. But defending the title would be a very different thing than winning it.

When I finally sat down in late May or early June of 1994 with John Davimos and Bill Korzerski to discuss the future, we carefully considered the factors involved in Michael's first title defense. Number one, of course, was money. Who could we fight that would make for the biggest payday? That was the first thing. At the same time, we had to weigh any short-term windfall against the possibility of losing. If we picked the wrong fight we could lose both the title and our economic hammer in a hurry. So we wanted to make sure we chose a fight we felt confident about winning. That meant not picking a guy whose style would give Michael trouble.

A bunch of names were thrown out. Tyson was in jail. Lennox Lewis was too dangerous. Oliver McCall wasn't enough of a draw. There were other guys mentioned, but all of them were discarded for one reason or another.

Suddenly, it came to me. "George Foreman."

It was as if a flashbulb had popped. Everybody stared at me, and you could see it in their faces. George Foreman! Of course! That was the fight! It gave you everything. There was the draw of his name. His ongoing comeback story. His big personality and ability as a salesman. And the best part: George was an old man, forty-four years old, a guy Michael matched up well against. It was a fight, at least on the surface, we should have no problem winning.

From that moment on, all our efforts went into making the bout happen. Supposedly—and sometimes it's hard to know what's true and what just fits into the lore—Foreman had been telling his people, even before we approached him, that he wanted to fight Michael. He had seen something in Michael while broadcasting the Holyfield fight for HBO that made him feel he could win.

A guy once said that there are no second acts in American life. I'll tell you one thing, he wasn't thinking of Big George Foreman. In his first life, Foreman had been an aloof, antisocial strongman, a bully who pounded his boxing foes into submission and looked for all the world to be invincible. But in 1974, in a fight famously promoted as the Rumble in the Jungle, in Kinshasa, Zaire, Foreman was knocked out by Muhammad Ali in what still stands as one of the biggest, most stunning upsets in boxing history. Three years later, having never really recovered from the loss, Foreman experienced a religious awakening and became an ordained Christian minister. He also became a family man, fathering five daughters and five sons (all of the boys named George, like him).

In 1987, ten years after his retirement from the sport, Foreman reinvented himself yet again and launched a boxing comeback. It took him a few years, building up his record against carefully selected opponents, but he fought his way back into contention, finally landing a championship bout against Evander Holyfield in 1991. Though Holyfield beat him convincingly, Foreman proved he was no fraud or novelty act. Even so, most people encouraged him to retire again. But Foreman was stubborn. He wanted redemption, and kept looking for another chance to win back the title.

After he did the TV color work on the Moorer-Holyfield fight, from what I heard, he basically called up the HBO people and said, "Get me this fight." They tried to talk him out of it. "Come on, George, you did it already. You came back. You had your shot. You fell short. It was a great thing. Because of it, you've got all these commercials and endorsements, you've got this TV gig with us. Why keep going? You're not getting any younger. You don't need to prove anything. You could get hurt."

"No, I can do it," he said. "I can actually finish it now."

What he had seen in Michael, I believe, was somebody he could beat mentally. You see, George was a guy who found out the hard way that it was tougher to quit than it was to fight. He had quit in Zaire. There's no doubt about it. He pirouetted around the ring and gave up. He got broken down by a man that he couldn't deal with, Muhammad Ali, and he had been forced to live with the indignity of that, the lonely truth of that, for all these years. He'd been forced to confront the kind of truth that visits you at three o'clock in the morning and comes out of the mouths of people who are not on your payroll and never seems to go away. He'd been up against that all these years, and now he saw a way out. Independent of us, he started up the machinery to get the fight. Meanwhile, at our end, we were seeing what we needed to see, and starting the wheels turning, too.

All of us were seeing opportunity, and it was great and very American that way. Everybody saw their end. We went from defending the title for probably a couple of million dollars to a $7 million payday because of George Foreman. In what would be an easier fight for us—at least theoretically.

And yet, even as the words were coming out of my mouth, as George Foreman's name was rolling off my tongue, there was something in my gut, a sharp stab of—I don't know what else to call it—fear. It didn't stop me from uttering his name, but there was this dark, ominous feeling that went along with it. I said to myself, "Do I really want this?" At the same time it made sense, as was obvious from everyone's enthusiastic response.

The negotiation for the fight went like most fight negotiations go, which is to say back and forth and on and off. Don King is always knocked as being a devious guy, which he is. But Bob Arum is just as scheming, though in a less flamboyant way; he's a hand-painted shingle to King's neon sign. I'll give you an example. The negotiation had been going on for a while. It was on, it was off, it was dead, it was back on. At one point, Davimos and Korzerski and the Duvas were on a conference call with Arum, and Arum said, "I just want you to know, you're going to have to call up your fighter and tell him you just fucked up his career—and if you don't tell him, I will—because Don King's got George Foreman on a plane as we speak, and they're halfway to Jakarta to sign contracts, and you fucked your fighter out of a tremendous payday. Don King's got George."

At which point someone from our side said, "That's funny, Bob, because our lawyer just spoke with Foreman ten minutes ago and he was in Houston. So unless he's using a *Star Trek* transporter, it seems unlikely that he's halfway to anywhere."

Arum didn't even blink. He said, "Forget that then. Let's move past that," and he segued right into whatever the next negotiating point was. Davimos and Korzerski and the rest couldn't contain themselves. They began howling with laughter. Arum was so utterly shameless.

In the end, the deal got made anyway. We got our seven million. As soon as we held the first press conference and got into the next phase, I had to face in a real way my worries about losing the title. More important, I had to confront my worries about losing the ground that Michael had already gained as a person and as an athlete. I realized then why I'd had that stab of fear when Foreman's name came out of my mouth. I knew what George had already been through. He could recognize weakness and fear in other men because he recognized it in himself. I always said that the old George Foreman, the forty-four-year-old man, would have knocked out the young George Foreman. He wasn't as good physically, not nearly so, but he was tougher mentally by far. He understood the difference between lies and the truth. He understood what the boundaries were. And his hard-won self-knowledge made him a much more formidable foe. He could look at an opponent with near X-ray vision and recognize the very same shortcomings he had once had himself before he had been forced to deal with them.

I went to the first press conference aware of all these things, wanting to make sure that we didn't lose a battle before the war had even really started. Sure enough, I was right: I saw Foreman was ready to start setting land traps already. Michael made the mistake, which I didn't correct, of showing up in dark glasses. Foreman immediately said, "What's the matter with you, boy? You afraid to show your eyes?" It was nearly an echo of what I'd said to Michael myself when he'd shown up in Palm Springs one day wearing sunglasses.

I knew I needed to do something. I went after Foreman on the spot. I called him a fraud, then I grabbed him and pushed him. I challenged him. It was on TV all over the country that night. The two of us scuffling on the stage at the press conference. People thought I was crazy. Out of my mind. Foreman, by contrast, didn't lose his cool. He knew how to play it. He restrained himself.

But I knew what I was doing, too. I was protecting my kid. I didn't want my kid to lose the prelim. It was like being in Rikers. Once you gave up the sneakers, it was only a matter of time before they took everything else. George grasped it all, how you can be the victim or the emperor of these things. And fortunately, or unfortunately, whatever your perspective is about a tough world, I understood, too.

When we held the next press conference in Vegas, what had happened at the first one was all over the newspapers and TV, this 150-pound guy shoving this 260-pound guy who was the former heavyweight champ of the world. It made the promoters very happy. They were all smiles. "We couldn't have paid for that kind of publicity." But that wasn't where I was coming from. It wasn't part of the promotion for me. It wasn't some pro wrestling stunt. It was real. Michael knew what it was. He understood.

Michael went to the next press conference without the sunglasses. He knew he needed to do that and that I wanted him to do that. But Foreman was the master of this universe. He used it against Michael. He said, "I see that I made you take your glasses off, boy."

Right after that press conference, I went back to my room and threw up. Mark Kriegel, the writer for the *Daily News*, who was following me again, as he had before the Holyfield fight, heard me in the bathroom, and when I came out, he asked me if I was okay.

"Yeah, I'm fine."

"It's because of Foreman, isn't it?" Kriegel was a good reporter with good instincts.

"My stomach's a little upset is all."

"You got a bad feeling about this one, don't you?"

I shrugged. His question made me uncomfortable. Because just as there had been an aura of destiny that made me believe we would win the fight against Holyfield, this one filled me with dread. Michael and I had needed to win the Holyfield fight for vindication and validation. Now we were champions. George Foreman, on the other hand, had been waiting twenty years to redeem himself. So when Kriegel asked me if I had a bad feeling, the truth was I did, I just didn't want to say it.

Unlike our previous training camp, this one, also in Palm Springs, was trouble-free throughout. Michael was a model of perfect behavior and hard work. But it only added to my apprehension because I knew the one way we could lose the fight was if Foreman suckered him.

I told Michael that the best thing that Foreman did was to throw a slow jab at you. He didn't throw it full. If he threw it full, you'd know what your line of distance was, you'd know the range where you were safe. But if he threw it a few inches short, the way he did, you'd get a false sense of security and be fooled into thinking that was as far as it went. Nobody else had really picked up on this. I had watched a lot of tape. I knew Foreman inside out.

"George is forty-four," I said. "This is his best thing. This is the only way he can beat you, by lulling you to sleep, by making you think you're safe when you're not. He'll throw this slow jab, he'll make you slow to his pace, he'll get you feeling comfortable, and then suddenly there'll be a right hand behind it. You'll never even see it coming. It won't even look like a big punch. It'll look like nothing."

Every day, I went over this, trying to drill it into Michael, trying to make him understand. After a few weeks, he said, "Teddy, not again. I got it. I got it."

"No. Get in the ring," I said. "We need to go over it again."

It reached the point where Michael would mimic me. He would say, "I know, he does this and then he does this, and then there's a right hand and you never see it. . . . I know, Ted. I *know*."

George was so good at running a con and making you dance to his beat that if you weren't absolutely vigilant, you were lost. After the scrap at the first press conference, I really didn't know what to expect from him in Vegas, so I went to that second press conference prepared for anything. I had somebody meet me on the way in and slip me a roll of quarters. I made a fist around the roll of quarters. Cus had always told me, although I knew it from the street, that a roll of quarters added twenty pounds to your punching power. I guess I felt I needed it against Foreman in case we got into anything again. I wanted to be ready. But George had instincts that were almost better than my instincts. He didn't do anything. He was friendly, charming, and funny. He already had what he wanted, so there was no need to do anything. I'm telling you, George was a master.

One thing that having the title and a bit more money did was give me an opportunity to show my appreciation to a lot of people who had been loyal to me over the years. I flew a number of guys out to Vegas for the fight, old friends of mine and guys from the neighborhood. I probably flew four or five guys out, all told. There was my friend Mikey Smith— Smitty—who was a kid I hung out with on the corner; another guy, Ronnie Scripps, whose late father was a bookie; Jimmy McMahon, who had been Nick Baffi's fighter, and who I'd managed until he retired because I'd made that promise to Nick when he was dying of cancer; and Larry Coughlin.

Of all my friends, there was probably no one as loyal to me as Larry Coughlin. Larry grew up in the projects, part of a large, hard-drinking Irish family. His uncle was a big shot in the transit union, and he got all the brothers and nephews jobs. Larry became a subway car cleaner. It was a pretty good job, but there was an accident in the yards and his left arm got partially crushed. The odd thing was that Larry acted like he'd lost the arm. The truth was, and it took me years to understand this, the arm wasn't that bad. Despite a bunch of operations and skin grafts, he could still move it. But psychologically it loomed very large for him; it was damaging. He always wore long-sleeved shirts to hide it.

As a result of the accident, he got what at the time we thought was a very large settlement. In fact, it was only about three hundred thousand dollars—half of which went to taxes and lawyers' fees. Larry took twenty thousand and bought his mother a nice little house in the South Beach area of Staten Island, and took the rest of it and put it in bonds and lived off the dividends (although eventually he went through the principal, too). I helped move him and his mom with a U-Haul. He was so proud to be able to get her out of the projects and into this little house. He moved in there, too, into the basement. It was a pretty good setup. He lived well. The most important things he had down there were this mini-fridge that was always full of beer, and a TV. The two of us spent a lot of time in that basement together, drinking beer and watching Larry Bird on the tube. He loved Larry Bird.

The problem was, I was moving a little bit, and he wasn't. He was in that basement, and his ambitions did not often lead him out. I didn't kid myself about him. He had a drinking problem and he wasn't comfortable socially. But he had an innocence and a spirit, and I loved him, and he loved me, and it was pretty simple in that sense. When his drinking got really bad, and this was when I was living in Catskill, I brought him up there and made him drink nothing but milk shakes. He dried out, and after a while he went back to his basement, the Bunker, we called it. Larry was almost like a cult figure to us. For a while, we called him Headband because he always wore a headband. Then he got called Bud because all he drank was Budweiser.

Anyway, Larry was one of the guys I flew out for the fight. He'd never been to Vegas. I mean, he'd hardly ever left his basement. So a huge five-thousand-room casino and hotel like the MGM Grand might as well have been a foreign country to him. I'd told him that he'd better behave himself, that he better be good, so that was on his mind. "Teddy told me I better be good." I wasn't being a hard-ass—it was lighthearted—but I sincerely didn't want him to get in trouble.

The first few days there, everyone was getting lost because the place was so huge. I was busy, but my crew would meet in different places, and I'd try to join them whenever I could. I'd see Larry, and Larry would hug me and say, "I've been good, Teddy."

"You need anything?"

"Nah."

I'd give him a few bucks anyway, and he'd say, "Thanks, Pops." He called me Pops.

"Stop the bullshit, Larry. You being good?"

Then he would see Elaine, and he'd say, "Tell Teddy I'm being good."

Early on, Larry made a discovery. He sat down at one of the bars in the MGM that was right along one of the central thoroughfares. Now Larry wasn't much of a gambler, but he sat down at this table that had a video poker game built into it. He took out five bucks and fed it in, and he started playing on that five bucks, a quarter at a time. Now, five bucks can last you a long time that way, and while Larry was sitting there, a cocktail waitress came over and asked him if he wanted a drink. Naturally, he said yes.

A couple of minutes later she brought him back a Bud—and didn't charge him for it. Ten minutes later, he ordered another one. Again no charge. He didn't know that in Vegas as long as you're gambling, they don't charge you for drinks. Larry thought he'd found Shangri-la. He was looking around, and he was like, "I ain't telling no one about this." And he wasn't moving. Not for anybody.

Some of the guys found him there. They'd been looking all over for him. I'd asked Smitty to keep an eye on him.

"C'mon, Larry, we're going to the Steak House."

"I'm staying here."

"C'mon."

Nope. Not moving. Larry didn't know what the explanation was, but he'd found a seam in the fabric of the universe, here in this little corner of Las Vegas, and he wasn't budging. "I ain't fuckin' this up, and I'm not gonna let anyone else fuck it up for me either." He didn't know when the seam might close, and he wasn't taking any chances. So he just stayed there. Five hours. Seven hours. Nine hours. Twelve hours. He stayed in that spot and the waitress kept bringing him drinks.

Word got back to me. Larry was in this spot, and he thinks he found the one place in the universe where liquor flows eternally, and if he moves he ain't ever gonna get the same deal. Meanwhile, everyone else was making their plans for dinner, for shows, for music, whatever, because apart from the guys I'd flown in, there were about 130 other friends and relatives of mine who'd come for the fight. They started making every plan around where Larry was, because that was the only thing they could count on in Vegas. Where are we going to meet? That corner bar where Larry is. For the entire week, everyone would meet there, where Larry was sitting. And anytime someone would see Larry, he'd say, "It's okay. I'm good. I'm behaving. Tell Teddy I'm behaving."

Fight night finally arrived, and from the moment we got into the ring, the bad feeling I'd been carrying around got worse. For one thing, Foreman jogged into the ring the same way we had for the Holyfield fight. He had never jogged into a ring in his life. As if that weren't bad enough, he was wearing the same boxing trunks that he had worn against Ali in Zaire in 1974. I had to use all my discipline to push away negative thoughts when I saw that—because what those trunks indicated to me was that here was a man who was facing down his past. He wasn't running from his ghosts. He was confronting them head-on. I was scared. A guy who was able to face the truth that way was a dangerous guy. That was why I had thrown up on the day of the press conference. I had recognized that about Foreman.

Even so, as the fight got under way, it seemed as if Michael was too young, too fast, and too skilled for Foreman to keep up. I had been hoping the Holyfield fight and all that we had gone through would complete Michael. He was a better person now, a more confident man. But were those qualities going to be his ally against Foreman? I knew in general they were, but would they be for this specific fight? The truth is, the careful way he'd fought against Holyfield, as frustrating as it was for me, was the way he should have fought against Foreman. But I couldn't tell him that. My job had been to make Michael more whole, and now that he was, I couldn't steer away from it. I couldn't tell him not to be Secretariat, to pull back and not be a champion horse. I let him gallop. For most of the night, it looked like a smart move. He took the fight to Foreman in every round. He was dominant.

Still, I knew, as a strategic approach, it was dangerous. There came a moment in the eighth round, where my corner, I think it was Mo, said to me, "Great job, Teddy. This one's in the bag." I went nuts. "Shut up! Don't you say nothing about this fucking fight being over. Don't fucking say that!"

Mo apologized. "I didn't mean anything by it."

"This fight is far from over! Don't you understand?"

He didn't say another word. It was so obvious to my corner that I was scared. "This fight ain't nowhere near over," I said. "This guy's been waiting twenty years for one moment. It ain't about the rounds. He didn't come here to win a decision!"

They got very quiet. In between the ninth and tenth rounds, I told Michael again, as I had been telling him throughout, that he was doing great, that he was a champ. I also warned him for the thousandth time that Foreman was looking for that one punch, and that it was going to be a right hand.

"The only way he can do it, Michael, is with your cooperation. You have to keep moving to your right. He can't pull it off if you keep moving to your right."

In the tenth round, it was almost as if I could see the future before it happened. I could see the thoughts form in Foreman's mind. He threw a left hook, and I understood exactly what he was thinking. I screamed, "No!" It was just a throwaway hook. It wasn't going to end the fight or even hurt Michael, but it was thrown to stop Michael from moving to the place he needed to move. It was thrown to make him move the other way. And I screamed "No!" because I saw it and understood immediately. It was like a hunter shooting in front of his prey to make it move into an open field where his partner had a clean line and an unobstructed shot.

It was weird to watch Foreman's reaction. His face lit up. He smiled almost. Then he did just what we had gone over in camp every day. He followed the left with the right—*bang*—and just like that the fight was over. The moment the punch landed and Michael went down, I was going up the steps to get into the ring. My guys grabbed me. They didn't understand.

"It's over," I said.

"No, he's going to get up," they said. It looked like nothing. Which is what I'd been saying to them all along. That it was going to look like a nothing punch. They were actually waiting for Michael to get up, thinking he would survive the round. I knew better. There was no getting up.

"This is over," I said. "He did it."

They didn't understand. It didn't look like anything.

"He'll get up."

"No. Foreman did what he wanted to do. Michael ain't getting up."

I got angry afterward at people who said that Michael quit. They didn't understand. Neither did the people who said Foreman got lucky. He didn't get lucky. He spent twenty years preparing to throw that punch, learning what he needed to get to that precise moment in time. When it landed, it was like pulling a plug out of a circuit. It was over. Foreman knew it. I knew it. And Michael—Christ, the force of the punch split his mouthpiece in half. It drove his tooth through his lip! I'm not a protector of George. He doesn't need me standing up for him. But I believe in giving credit where it's due. He came prepared physically and mentally to be tortured and to endure, to be ready to do what he needed to do after all that punishment from a younger guy who could punch. Was that lucky? No. That was preparation. That was work. That was sacrifice.

After the fight, I got on the service elevator with Michael and Mike

Boorman. It was just the three of us in this big steel box. Michael was holding a towel to his bloody split lip. I had called ahead to a plastic surgeon because if Michael decided that he didn't want to fight again, I didn't want him to have a scar. Suddenly Michael said, "Where is everybody?" Boorman looked at him, at this guy who normally had this huge entourage, and he said, "This is everybody." Michael nodded, taking that in, understanding what it meant.

Obviously there was a lot of depression after something like that. In the aftermath, all of my friends, people who had come out to Vegas, didn't know quite what to do. The next day, Mikey Smith got so drunk that he climbed this huge fake tree that towered over a boulder and a waterfall right there in the middle of the MGM lobby. Larry Coughlin was still in his spot, drinking beers, and watching Smitty, who was supposed to be looking after him, climbing this tree. What the fuck was the guy doing?

Meanwhile, people were checking in and out of the hotel at the front desk. There was this one mother with two small children. She had all her bags and she was giving them to the bellman, and the kids were going, "Look, Ma, it's a show!," and they were pointing at Smitty. They were smart kids and they figured it must be a show. The woman was distracted, but the kids kept pulling at her sleeve, telling her to watch, and she finally looked over just as Smitty fell out of the tree, crashed down about fifteen feet onto the boulder, hit his head, and then bounced off into the waterfall and lay there.

Now the kids were cheering, and Larry could see the mother trying to get them away, trying to shield them from this ugly scene with the drunk and the boulder that now had blood on it. She was saying, "C'mon, we gotta go." And the kids were going, "No, I want to see the man. I want to watch him do that again." And the mother was trying to pull them away before some other nut climbed the tree, before some other Smitty came along.

After they were gone, Smitty finally got up and staggered out of the waterfall, dripping wet, with a knot on his head the size of a baseball and growing larger by the moment. People were looking at him and gasping as he just calmly walked over to where Larry was and sat down.

The barmaid came over. She said, "You better go to a hospital. That looks bad."

Smitty shook his head and told her to get him a beer. Eventually, Jimmy McMahon, who hadn't even met Smitty before this trip, talked some sense into him and got him to a hospital to get checked out.

As for Larry, well . . . a couple of years ago, I came home from a trip, and when Elaine saw me she couldn't even speak. I asked her to tell me what was going on, and she burst into tears and said, "Larry's brother Brian just called—" I didn't let her finish. I grabbed her mouth. I shouldn't have done that, but I didn't want her to tell me the rest.

I guess I had known on some level that Larry was capable of killing himself. But not really. Maybe I had gotten too soft. I thought he was more resilient. In my mind, Larry was Larry. I knew he was hurting, but that was part of his life, part of who he was. It was normal. I didn't think he'd ever do anything.

Forty-five minutes before he hanged himself in his basement apartment, he had called and left a message on my answering machine. It was tough as hell to find that out. I know if I had been home, I would have stopped him. But I wasn't, and it still haunts me. It's been a couple of years now. Sometimes a week will go by and I'll be okay, and then all of a sudden, three days in a row, I'll be mad at him. I'll say, "Goddamn you, Larry, you motherfucker," and then I'll be mad at myself, mad that I didn't pay closer attention.

AND ONCE AGAIN

AFTER THE LOSS TO FOREMAN, MICHAEL WENT BACK to his house in Boca Raton, and I went back to Staten Island. It was a tough time. A lot of people were saying things that weren't fair—that Michael quit, that he lost to an old man, that kind of stuff. On top of the normal depression of losing, Michael had to deal with that, and basically he decided to retire.

In Florida, with time on his hands, he began drinking again. There were occasions when he would call up Davimos and ramble on incoherently about what he should do. One time, he called while he was shooting a gun at the ceiling. Davimos phoned to tell me, and he was panicking. It was scary because Michael's girlfriend had been there and she had run out of the house, and the cops were on the way. I got him on the phone. I could hear the sirens in the background. I said, "Michael, if you don't put that gun down and not shoot it in the next minute or two, you're gonna get yourself killed." I was scared. Especially him being down in Florida. Luckily, nothing happened.

Around the same time, I was receiving some interesting business offers. Lennox Lewis's people called me to see if I would be available to train him. From an emotional standpoint and an economic one, Lewis was certainly an attractive prospect. He was coming off a loss to Oliver McCall.

Even so, you didn't have to be Angelo Dundee to recognize that he was a much better bet to come back than Michael. A lot of friends were telling me that I should go with him. But despite the fact that Michael couldn't give me a definitive answer about his plans, I told the Lewis people no.

The thing was, I knew that Michael didn't really want to retire, that it was a knee-jerk reaction and a sign of him sliding back a little. We had lost some of the ground that we had gained during the Holyfield fight, but I felt in a profound way that he was my responsibility. I had made money with him. More important, I had made demands of him that I could make only as long as I could stand and deliver on them myself.

I decided that I had to find out what Michael was going to do and help him do that. Loyalty demanded that. At the same time, I felt I couldn't sit back and wait. I had to talk to him. It was delicate, though. It had to be something that he wanted to do for himself. Also, though I wanted to go talk to him, I realized that it shouldn't come in the form of Davimos or Duva buying me a ticket and sending me down there. It had to be me just doing it. Especially with Michael being as vulnerable and fractured as he was. That was important. I called him up and told him I was catching the next plane.

I could hear in his voice that it meant a lot.

He said, "You're coming down?"

"Yeah. Give me your address."

"No, I'll pick you up at the airport." It was like his father was coming home.

And he was there at the airport waiting for me. I could see how glad he was to see me by the way his face lit up, but in the next moment it was as if he said to himself, "I better act a little bit ornery." It was like a switch went on. There was the spontaneous love and comfort in seeing me, and then all of a sudden it was like, "Oh, I better show him that I'm fractured, and that he's gotta deal with that."

All of a sudden it was, "I ain't fuckin' fighting."

I didn't even let him go there. I said, "Shut up. I want to eat something."

He was completely disarmed. "You want to eat?"

"Yeah. I haven't eaten anything. I'm hungry. I don't want to talk to you about this now."

When we got to his house, we ordered Domino's Pizza. There was no point in arguing about his diet at that point. Even though I knew that was what he was living on. We ate the pizza, then he took me on a tour. I had never seen the Florida house, and he was proud of it. Proud of what he had accomplished that enabled him to get a big house like that. He showed me his cars, including his twin Mercedes-Benzes.

"I still don't believe you bought the second one," I said. "You're an idiot. You already have the same exact model, and the second you drive it out of the showroom, it's worth half of what you paid for it."

He got so mad. "Oooahh, you always have to say stuff like that."

"Well, you always have to act like a moron."

It was our routine. People would say, "There they go again." Like we were Abbott and Costello. Only sometimes there was a serious edge to it. Like now when he started his thing again about "I'm not coming back."

"Be quiet," I said. "I'm not here to tell you that you gotta fight."

As soon as I said that, I could see the disappointment. He got scared. Is Teddy gonna leave me? He's just going to let me hang here?

I knew I had him then. I knew right there what the answer was. I didn't know when I got on the plane, but I knew right there. This guy wanted to fight again.

"If you tell me you're retired, you're retired," I said.

"Well, that's what I'm going to do," he said.

"Fine, you just better be sure that's what you want. Because I'll tell you what you're not doing. You're not calling me in a year and telling me, 'Let's do it again.' That's what you're not doing. You make your choice now and you live with it."

That was the point at which he began to break. "So what should I do?" he asked.

"No, no, no, no. I'm not going to tell you what to do. I'll point out to you what's there to be done. And if you want to do it, then it's your decision."

He looked at me, wanting me to continue.

"Look, you grew after that Holyfield fight," I said. "And the fact is, it might have hurt you against Foreman."

All the edge in him was gone now. He just looked at me with those big brown eyes wanting to hear more.

"You felt like a champion," I said. "Maybe it was my fault. I let you feel like too much of a champion, because from a strategic standpoint you went after him too much. But who could hold you back, who would want to hold you back from becoming what you always wanted to be? It's a lot more than having a belt or two over your shoulders. It's about what you felt. It's about feeling it and being it. And you were being it. I'm proud of that.

"Then what happened, happened. Because of a mistake on your part and because of his experience. The good part of that fight for you was good. That shouldn't be erased. That shouldn't be forgotten. That shouldn't be mixed up with the defeat."

"But what should I do?" he asked.

"No," I said. "That's not how it works." To me, it was like showing pictures to a kid. What's really in the picture, what's hidden there? Is there a horse? Do you see any pigs? He was the one who had to find the answer. "Look, I know what's going on," I said. "People are saying you lost to a forty-four-year-old guy. Why hide from that? You lost to a special guy, who had a special mission, and you made a mistake. But for nine and three-quarters rounds, you weren't just winning, you were kicking the shit out of him."

For the first time since we'd started talking, he smiled. "I was, wasn't I? I was busting his ass."

"Let me tell you something," I said. "If that weren't the case I would have come down here anyway, because it's the right thing to stay partners with somebody you did something with and be able to tell them, 'No more.' If you weren't good enough, I would tell you to stay away. I would tell you to take your money, put it in T-bills, stop being a jerkoff buying these freakin' Mercedes-Benzes, and walk away. But the fact is you dominated him every second of every round the way a good fighter should, a fighter with a future, a fighter that's more than a one-trick pony. And because of that it's not complete. You haven't fulfilled your destiny. Michael, you always trusted my judgment as a trainer. I'm talking to you as your trainer now. You could still take those steps toward where we want. I can't tell you we're going to get exactly where I thought we could. But we can still get somewhere in that direction. Isn't part of living finding that out?"

After all the depression and drunkenness and all the crazy shit he'd done, now he grabbed me and looked at me and said, "You really think we can get the title back?"

"It doesn't matter what I think, Michael. That's what I'm saying. You know what I think."

I saw him make the decision. "Let's do it," he said. "Let's get it back." "I'll call Davimos and tell him to set it up."

FOREMAN HAD PROMISED TO GIVE US A REMATCH, AND THAT was what we wanted, obviously. But King was trying to move his guys in, and the whole corrupt machinery of boxing was in play. We moved forward as if the rematch would get worked out. We weren't stupid or naive enough to think that Foreman and his people might not fuck us, but we also knew we had to act. There was a certain date the fight was going to happen, if we could set it up, and that was only a few months away. So my call was to start training camp. Michael had gotten heavy. There was a lot of work to do on his body and his psyche. We went to Woodland Hills, California, and we spent three weeks there. He dropped about twenty pounds and training went well. Meanwhile, I was keeping in touch with Davimos about the negotiations. We were going to get three million for the fight, and Foreman wanted eight to ten million. When HBO wouldn't come up with the money, I offered to give up my end of the purse, about $300,000. Michael offered to give up some, too. It went back and forth, on and off, and finally the call came, the last call: it was gone.

I took an hour by myself to think about what I was going to tell Michael. I didn't want to lose him. I finally went to his room, and as soon as I walked through the door, he said, "It's off, isn't it?" He could tell just from looking at me.

"Look, Michael," I began, "there was never a guarantee that this was going to happen, but that doesn't mean that what we did here doesn't matter. This was about us, it wasn't about George Foreman. . . ."

As I was talking to him, Michael turned away from me. I thought he was giving me a problem, and I grabbed his shoulder.

"Look at me when I'm talking to you," I said, spinning him around. I was expecting attitude and I was stunned when I saw his face. He was crying.

"Michael, I thought—"

"It's okay, Teddy," he said. The tears slid down his cheeks. "I'm going to be all right."

All the people—people in his own camp—who thought he didn't care. I'd been right all along. He was just trying to protect himself; all the bullshit, it was just because he was afraid to admit or show how much he cared.

"Mike—"

"It's okay, Teddy. . . . Go ahead and talk, because you're going to have to talk anyway. I know. That's what you do." He was standing there in sweatpants, not wearing a shirt. The TV was going in the background. "I know you do it because you care," he said. "I know, and I want to hear what you have to say, but I also want you to know I'm okay. I ain't gonna fall back."

I almost laughed—it was a good moment. It showed how well he knew me. And he was right. I was going to talk anyway. I said, "It's just part of the test, Michael. That's all it is. I mean, beating Foreman? I wanted you to have that. But whoever you wind up fighting, the most important thing is that you've honored your commitment to come back and be whole again and be champion again. I'm proud of you for your three weeks here. It's not going to register in your record, but it's going to register down the road."

We broke camp after that and went home. The Foreman fight, instead of taking place in the ring, took place in court. But before that could happen, we set up another fight for Michael, on HBO. It was a nontitle fight against a Jewish heavyweight named Tim Puller, and on the same card, Lennox Lewis was set to make his comeback fight. We trained in Tampa this time, and it was a very different atmosphere. All Michael's guys were gone. Only Flem was left. It was different, but it wasn't bad and it was what it needed to be.

My relationship with Michael at that point was—there's no other way to describe it—like father and son. There was one episode that encapsulated it perfectly. Our day's training was over, and just as at the other camps, I'd retreated to the pool to read a book in the late afternoon sun. I was sitting there on the chaise, sipping iced tea, when suddenly this shadow fell over me.

"We have a problem, Teddy." It was Michael, with Flem standing off to one side behind him.

I shaded my eyes. "No, we don't. I'm reading a book. It's a beautiful afternoon. We don't have no problems."

Michael rubbed his hands. "Yeah, we do. Oh, boy, Flem, I can't wait to see what Teddy's going to do to this guy."

"What guy?" At that moment, a waiter came by and refilled my iced tea.

"Come on. You gotta get dressed and come with me."

"I ain't going nowhere." I took a sip of my tea.

Now I noticed that Flem was holding a small glass of water.

"You're gonna teach this guy a lesson," Michael said.

"What guy?"

"The guy I bought the clippers from."

You have to understand, Michael was like Felix Unger from *The Odd Couple.* He was a cleanliness freak, obsessed with germs and personal grooming. When he brushed his teeth, he brushed his tongue. When he shaved his head, he put alcohol all over it to make sure it was sterilized. Earlier that afternoon, he had gone into downtown Tampa and bought a brand-new top-of-the-line electric clipper for $120. Someone else would have just brought it home and used it. Not Michael. He took it apart, took out the clip, and dipped it into water.

"Show it to him, Flem."

Flem showed me the glass of water he was holding.

"So you got a glass of water," I said.

"No, look closer. See the hair?"

I saw little microscopic hairs floating on the surface.

"That's nasty," Michael said. "*Nasty.* These damn Koreans. They sold me used clippers. I can't wait till you go up to them and tell 'em who the hell they're dealing with."

"I ain't going."

"You gotta go."

"I'm not going."

"You gotta."

We went back and forth like that idiotically. In the end I realized that it was a losing battle, that with Michael this was part of the deal, and if I didn't give in he would make me pay some other way. I put on my T-shirt.

Michael said, "Teddy, what are you going to do if he says, 'Fuck you, nigger, I ain't giving you your money back.'"

"I'm not gonna do a thing," I said, "because it will be obvious at that point that he isn't talking to me."

"Come on. Come on. You're gonna go crazy. I know you will."

I could only shake my head as I laced up my sneakers. We got in his truck and drove downtown. Before we got there, I laid down the law. "Listen to me. I'm telling you right now, Michael, when we go in, you keep your mouth shut. Let me do all the talking. Do not say a damn word."

He wasn't listening; he was rubbing his hands together, saying to Flem, "Wait till Teddy takes care of this guy."

We drove over to the place, a Korean variety and electronics store, and Michael jumped out of the truck. He told Flem to give him the glass of water, and when Flem handed it to him, he held it out in front of him at a distance from his body, like it was a urine sample.

"Remember," I warned him. "Keep your mouth shut. I'm not playing with you."

I opened the door of the store. There was a guy to one side, behind a counter. "Is that him?" I asked.

"Yeah."

"All right, now be quiet."

I walked over to the counter, with Michael and Flem behind me. The guy behind the counter was in his twenties and had a wide, flat face and a full head of jet-black hair. I looked at him in a certain way, very cold, and put the clippers down on the counter. I opened up the box.

"These are used," I said. "I want my money back."

He looked at me, and started to say something, but I stared at him so cold and so hard that he changed his mind. I kept staring at him, and finally he rung open the cash register. He used his two forefingers to slide six twenty-dollar bills out from under the spring arm, then he handed them to me.

I turned around and said, "Let's go."

Michael started in with the guy. "Man, you nasty," he said. He couldn't let it be. "You *nasty.*"

"Michael." I tugged his arm.

"You thought you was gonna get away with it, didn't you?"

"Michael. Shut up. We got our money. Let's go."

I had to drag him out the door. He was growling and cursing the whole way.

MEANTIME, WHILE WE WERE IN TRAINING, FOREMAN FOUGHT Axel Schulz, who was the number-one contender. We watched the fight on the TV in the hotel bar. It was tough. We were the ones who should've been fighting Foreman. We would have been if he and his managers hadn't screwed us. Even so, we were cheering for him. If he won he'd have to give us a rematch. But Schulz was not being cooperative. A crew-cut German, not great in any one area, but pretty good technically, with a good chin and some confidence, Schulz was making the fight close. We were on the edge of our seats, watching. At the final bell, it was too close to call. A lot of people thought Schulz actually won, but the judges gave it to Foreman. In my mind, it was a fair decision.

At the last second, the guy we were supposed to fight in our comeback bout fell out. They got another fighter to fill in, Melvin Foster, who was trained by Victor Valle. I didn't like the change and balked. They begged me to go forward. They flew guys out to Sacramento to talk to me. It was like the Camp David Summit. Eventually, I relented, but then I had only two days to get Michael prepped for Foster. Two days! I brought film in. We had to cram to adjust to a completely different style. But we did it. We won a unanimous decision.

The toughest part, really, was the first round. Anytime you have a fighter coming off a knockout, the first round is tricky. When Michael came back to the corner after the opening three minutes, I didn't criticize him at all. I just allowed him to sit. I said, "Welcome back. Now you know you're okay. Let's just fight a regular fight." George Foreman was the commentator again, and he said something nice. He said, "That Teddy Atlas is a pretty smart guy. He knows what a fighter's thinking. He knows just what to say." Everyone was startled by that. People said to me, "He gave you that compliment even though you went after him?" But George was a smart son of a bitch. He was like the Godfather. It was always business with him. It was never personal.

Despite our hopes for the rematch with George, it never happened. He wanted to go his own way, and as a result he was stripped of his title. Then King and Bob Lee tried to do an end-around, and have Schulz and François Botha, who was a King fighter, fight for the vacated title. They told us maybe we would be next, but who knew? So we took them to court. We had lots of ammo, evidence of payoffs and graft, things like that. Pat English, our lawyer, put a very good lawsuit together. (It prompted a federal investigation that eventually led to an indictment of Bob Lee, who is currently in jail as a result.) Ultimately, a settlement was reached, in which we dropped the lawsuit in return for a title shot against the winner of the Schulz-Botha fight. But when Botha tested positive for steroids, King and Lee tried to void the agreement, so we had to bring a second lawsuit, which we won, and which resulted in Michael getting his shot against Schulz.

The Schulz fight was a challenge, more because of the circumstances than because of his abilities as a fighter. The biggest obstacle was that we had to go fight in an outdoor stadium in Dortmund, Germany, and try not to get robbed. That might sound like an exaggeration, but it's not. We had to exert all our muscle and influence to get the right judges. That was the key to that fight. We won because we won the fight before the fight. We wound up getting two honest judges, and that was the difference in a split decision. That's what boxing is about sometimes, I'm sorry to say.

My method in the corner on that fight was the opposite of the Holyfield fight, where I was always going to the whip. Michael needed something else. In one round, I said, "All right, Michael, I know you've been wanting to hear it and you never hear it—I care about you. Okay? I care about you. You're important to me."

He looked at me, because he had always told Elaine, "You know, I love him, but he's too tough, he'll never say he loves me. How come he can never say he loves me? I know he does. How come he can never say it?"

Now, in the middle of this fight, when I needed him to care, I said, "All right, I care about you." I couldn't say the other word, but I said, "I care. Now it's time for you to care. You've got to be able to say, 'I care. I care about winning that title. I care about putting myself out there and daring to be champion again. I care.'"

He looked at me and he said, "All right."

After that, Michael picked up his pace and did what he had to do. He won back the title. Outdoors. In Germany. In someone else's backyard, with thirty-five thousand fans rooting for his opponent. Following a loss in which he had been devastated by a forty-four-year-old fighter who had God on his side. I allowed myself to feel pretty good about that. In some ways I appreciated it more than winning the title from Holyfield.

* * *

WHEN WE DEFENDED OUR IBF CHAMPIONSHIP FOR THE FIRST time, against François Botha, it was part of a night of champions that also featured Holyfield defending his WBA title against Mike Tyson. It marked the first time that I would be involved in a Tyson fight since I'd left Catskill. To make it even more interesting, if we beat Botha, we were going to fight the winner of that fight for ten million dollars.

I came to the press conference at the Rainbow Room prepared for anything. I brought a few guys with me that I trusted would be with me if I needed them. Tyson was known for trying to disrespect people in these situations, trying to break people, trying to intimidate people—even doing more than that, like he did with Lennox Lewis later on. He used to go up to people and tell them that he'd "rape" them. I wasn't going to put up with any of that. If we got into it as a result, so be it. If I went down, I wasn't going down without inflicting some damage. So I was there with my friends, Bobby, Louie, and Eddie. We were well dressed and well behaved, quiet, not looking at anybody. King recognized the situation. He came right over on the stage and put his hands out and said, "Teddy, nice to meet you." I didn't say a word. I shook his hand. You could see he understood the playing field.

Tyson had this guy Crocodile who had just gotten out of prison. He used him to intimidate people. Crocodile was talking all this shit, jawing at Holyfield, and at one point he stopped and looked at me. I thought he might be wanting to start in with me. I stared right back at him—and if there's such a thing as sending mind messages out, I sent them. The telepathic message he received was roughly: "Don't continue looking at me, and don't even think about saying anything, because if you say anything to us, I will be up and I will be on my way to you." Apparently, it worked. He looked away. And Tyson took note.

Once we got to Vegas, other stuff happened, although not, for the most part, with Tyson. There was a writer who showed up at the Grand for the fight, a guy I'd done a lot for when he was a kid, who was now putting out a crummy boxing rag that Don King was funding. He wrote some nasty, slanted stuff about me. When I saw him, I lost it. I'm not proud to say that, but this guy was a real jackal, so I'm not sorry, either.

I also think I was in a slightly deranged state of mind with Tyson around. Anyway, I went after him. The funny part was that I was on my way to do a live interview with CNN at the time. My friend Mike Boorman was coordinating it. He was up on the podium they'd built, waiting for me to get over there from the weigh-in. The interview was all set up, Boorman was on a walkie-talkie, and a guy was walking me over. Suddenly, across the floor of the convention hall, I caught sight of this piece of shit "writer"—I hesitate to even use the word, because he wasn't a real writer.

The CNN guy said to Boorman, "You got Teddy Atlas, right?" Boorman was looking down at me as I walked across this vast carpeted floor. He knew the whole story about me and this guy, and he had begged me not to do anything. Begged me. "Please, Teddy! The guy's not worth it." But he also knew me. So he was holding the walkie-talkie, saying to the producer, "Yeah, I see Teddy. He's on his way. He'll be here in sixty sec—" All of a sudden he stopped. "Uh . . . we might have a problem."

"A problem? A problem? What kind of problem? We're on the air in two minutes."

"He just made a left instead of a right."

"What?"

"Look down on the casino floor, at one o'clock."

The CNN producer looked down—and watched as I suddenly veered off in a direction that did not lead to the podium. I beelined toward this writer and cracked him one in the jaw. The CNN guy went, "Oh my God!" Meanwhile, security was racing over, the cameras were rolling, and as they pulled me off this piece of trash, some of my guys, who were trailing me, got into it. I tried to keep them out of it, because it was just about him and me, but I couldn't stop one of them, Bobby, from hitting the guy a few times. Boorman said to the CNN producer, "It doesn't look like Teddy's going to be available. You want me to see if I can get someone else?"

When I showed up for the glove selection twenty minutes later, my shirt was torn, I had blood on my hands, and I was still a little keyed up. Now, Frans Botha happened to be trained by Panama Lewis, a guy who was a real lowlife. They were probably not the best kind of people for me to be mixing with in the kind of mood I was in.

Lewis was infamous for having given Aaron Pryor water that was allegedly juiced during his fight against Alexis Arguello, enabling Pryor to win. Also, and more seriously, he had removed the padding from Luis

Resto's gloves in a fight where Resto nearly killed Billy Collins. The young and until then undefeated Collins saw his boxing career ended by this abominable act—and a year or so later, having become an alcoholic, he died in a car wreck. Lewis spent a year in Rikers for that and got thrown out of boxing for life—or at least boxing's version of banned for life. In actuality, the only thing he couldn't do was work his fighter's corner during a fight. Otherwise, his restrictions were few. So here we were, picking out gloves for the fight, Lewis and this wannabe wiseguy manager, and me and Lou Duva. A number of press guys had followed me in from the lobby, literally smelling blood.

Almost immediately, things got contentious; I don't even remember over what. In the middle of our heated exchange, Panama Lewis turned to Lou Duva and said, "Hey, Lou, you better calm down. You might have a heart attack."

Something snapped in me when he said that. I grabbed the neck of his shirt. *"Oh yeah? You'll be the one fucking dropping dead! You'll be the one!* You apologize right now! *Right now!* We don't fucking talk this way *because we're fucking gentlemen here! We're gentlemen!"*

Everybody was watching, their jaws hanging open but not a peep coming out. How they could keep a straight face with me yelling at the top of my lungs, "We're fucking gentlemen here!," I don't know.

I picked out a pair of gloves and signed them. Usually, the other camp would get the first choice of the backup gloves, but I was so geared up I didn't wait. I picked out my backup gloves, too. Not one word was uttered in protest. Afterward, Lou Duva said to me, "You could have put a freakin' horseshoe in one of the gloves, and they would have said, 'You want to put one in the other glove, too?'"

It wasn't as if there were no repercussions from my encounter with the writer. The whole thing had been videotaped. It was on all the news channels that night. A friend of mine, Mitchell, who owned a couple of gyms, told me how he was in his gym when the news came on TV. They said, "Stay tuned for the big melee at the big fight in Vegas." Mitchell was watching it with a few friends. When they showed the video clip, he said, "Hey, that's Teddy in the middle of that . . . and there's Bobby." They watched Bobby hitting the guy. Mitchell said, "Jesus. I hope his parole officer don't see this." Bobby hadn't gotten permission from his PO to make the trip.

The MGM management came to the decision that they wanted to remove me from the premises, and there was talk of pressing charges. The Duvas, Davimos, and, most important, Michael stood up and said, "Fine. You won't have a fight tomorrow if Teddy Atlas is not in the corner. Is that what you want?"

The hotel was packed. The fight was sold out. In the end, they backed down and discussed instead kicking out some of my Staten Island guys. When they came and told me, I said, "No. I ain't doing that to my guys. My guys risked themselves for me and I'm not doing that to them."

"We knew you were going to say that, but do you think maybe you could just keep them in the background a little? We don't want someone coming with a warrant or something."

I left it up to my guys, except for Bobby. We decided maybe it was a good idea if he wasn't at ringside. I didn't want him to get arrested. Bobby stayed in the back of the arena during the fight.

BOTHA WAS A GUY WHO HAD A SOFT LOOK. HE WAS ONE OF those guys who, no matter what shape he was in, would never look taut or cut. But it was deceiving. It didn't mean what you thought it did. To look at him, you weren't going to be intimidated. His punch wasn't going to scare you, either. But he was a guy who could give you trouble if you took him lightly. He didn't have great talent in any one area, but he was very busy, he threw a lot of punches, and he could keep you off balance. He could out-hustle you. When you factor in that Michael could be lazy— and you had to be honest with yourself when you were looking at your fighter—it spelled trouble. I knew that Michael wasn't lazy, that it was other things. But the bottom line was that sometimes he didn't work hard enough. He let guys steal rounds from him. Some fighters have to get hurt before they come to life. Michael was one of those.

I didn't want Michael to get hurt. At the same time, I was worried that this guy could lull him to sleep and steal the fight. During camp, I'd been afraid to make him watch tape of Botha because he wouldn't see the things he needed to see, he'd just see the obvious things, the awkwardness, the softness.

Sure enough, that was what happened in the fight. Michael almost knocked him out in the third round, but Botha survived—he had a good chin—and Michael stopped pressing the attack. Meanwhile, Botha kept busy in his awkward way. He wasn't right in Michael's face. He wasn't snapping his head back with jabs and putting a trickle of blood in his mouth. But he started sneaking away with rounds. Each round began with Botha looking thoroughly exhausted, his hands held low like he didn't have the strength to keep them up, yet he kept throwing. By the tenth round, my spies told me that we were actually behind on the cards. It's not supposed to happen, that you know that, but it does. Although when you think about it, what other sport is there where you don't know what the score is?

Anyway, the point was I had to make a move. What should I do? Michael came back to the corner and sat down. I told Mo to give him water, and while that was going on, I walked all the way across the ring and got Mills Lane. I said, "Mills, do me a favor, I need you to come here for a minute." I really respect Mills. He's an impeccable ref. And I could see with someone else, he probably wouldn't have done it. Even with me, he was a little leery, but he followed me. I got him to the corner. I said to Michael, "See this man?"

Michael looked up, and there was Mills Lane, the highest-profile referee in boxing.

"I've just instructed him—listen to me clearly—to stop this fight after this round if you don't start fighting. You hear me?"

He nodded.

"All right, Mills," I said, and at that point he knew he had been used. He was, like, fuck, I'm getting the hell out of here.

Michael dropped Botha the next round. The guy barely made it out of the round. I didn't know if it was enough. I thought we might still be behind.

"Listen, Michael," I said, when he took the stool, "there's a saying. You know the saying, 'It's in God's hands'? Well, it's not true. It ain't in God's hands. It's in your hands. Your hands! Now you take those two hands and you go out there and you fucking knock this guy out. Don't leave it in anyone else's hands. Not the judges. Not God's. Yours!"

And the next round—the last round of the fight—he went and knocked him out.

I went nuts. I literally jumped over the top rope. I flew into the ring, right into Michael's arms. He caught me. My son told me later that he couldn't believe it. He said, "Dad, I never saw you act that way." It was really strange because I had never showed emotion. In the Holyfield fight I didn't show anything. The Foreman fight was what it was. The Schulz fight I was very happy, but not over the top. Not like this. Mike Boorman said, "I didn't think a white man could jump that high." There was so much that Michael and I had been through, that had built up—and I guess I just finally let it out.

The night wasn't over, though. Because now Tyson was coming into the ring. A lot of people, fight experts, sportswriters, were actually fearful for Holyfield's life. For his life! And we were supposed to fight the winner. Obviously, we were going to watch. But first, we went back to the dressing room. I noticed Michael's face was real swollen. He had gotten hit a lot. I didn't like the way he looked. The whole thing here was my fighter—that was my primary concern. I said, "We're taking him to the hospital."

There we were, all together, like a family, and we were going to make sure he was okay. It was funny, you could see how much that meant to Michael. As much as he fought and argued and acted out, he admitted to me years later that his happiest times were being with his fight team. Even though it was bought love to a certain extent, there was still genuine love and care. It was a place where he could get things he never got in his life. Love. Care. Discipline.

Me and a few of the guys were about to take him to the hospital to get X-rayed. Meanwhile, little Teddy was still out in the arena, so I told a couple of my other guys, I think it was Maurice and Tank, "Go get my son." Teddy was sitting in the front row, ringside. He was twelve years old and cute as hell. Maurice and Tank went out there and said, "Your dad wants you to go back to the dressing room."

"No, I want to stay here and watch the fight with my friends."

"We've got to take you back. Your dad's going to the hospital with Michael, and we can't leave you out here."

"I'm with my friends," Teddy said. "I'm all right."

At that point, Tank looked at who Teddy was sitting with, and it was Magic Johnson and Babyface. Magic Johnson smiled at Tank and said, "He's cool. We'll watch him. We'll bring him back later."

Tank and Maurice came back to the locker room empty-handed.

"Where's my son?" I said, starting to get upset with them.

"Ted, don't get mad," Tank said. "You're not going to believe this, but he's with his friends."

"His friends! What friends? What are you—"

"Magic Johnson and Babyface."

"Magic Johnson and Babyface? They're looking out for him?"

"Yeah."

I shrugged. "All right."

We left Elaine and Nicole in the locker room with the guards. The Tyson-Holyfield fight was about to start on the closed-circuit monitor. I got in the truck with Michael and Maurice and Tank and Flem John Davimos and we went to the hospital. I thought Michael's jaw was broken. It was all blown up. He wound up having to get an MRI, but it turned out not to be broken. The whole time we were in the hospital, we were trying to find out about the fight. One of the nurses got something off the radio. Third round and Holyfield was winning. *What?* I mean, following his loss to Michael, Holyfield had fought a terrible fight with Bobby Czyz, he had gotten knocked out by Riddick Bowe, and most people thought he was shot. But he still had character. He wasn't that shot. And the character of the man was too much for Tyson. Fifth round, we got another report. Tyson got knocked down. We were going crazy. Meanwhile, Michael was inside this tube that was making these science-fiction sounds, these *pings* and *doinks*. When he came out, we told him: "Holyfield's kicking the shit out of Tyson!"

We put the radio on in the truck, on the way back to the arena, and we heard, "Fight's over." Except they didn't say who won right away. Did Tyson catch him with a punch? No. Eleventh-round TKO. Holyfield won. He was a champion again. Unbelievable!

If Tyson had won, we were supposed to fight him for ten million. With Holyfield, we'd get eight. Losing the two million—which would have meant an extra two hundred thousand in my bank account—didn't make me unhappy. It would have been a rough thing for me, if we'd gotten Tyson. I mean, I was getting ready for it a little bit, by bringing my guys to the press conference. And Tyson kind of showed what it would have been like by not even looking at me. We had exchanged one look, though, and I'm sure he could see I was the same guy, that living was very important to me, but that dying the right way was also important. If it had come to pass, if we had wound up fighting him, it would have been a very difficult thing for me to deal with. The truth is, I'm glad it never happened.

COMPLICATED
BUT SIMPLE

ALL ATHLETES HAVE JOCK SNIFFERS HANGING AROUND them, guys who try to pal around with them and be part of their world. Michael certainly had his share, especially after he became champion. Roger King, the head of King World Syndications, who'd had a chance to invest in Michael at the beginning of his boxing career and didn't, now started inviting Michael to clubs and gambling resorts, impressing his friends because he had the heavyweight champ in tow. Not only that, but if there was any trouble, he had the champ to protect him. This was the same King who had been sitting behind my family during the Holyfield fight—the big gambler.

I'd met him a couple of times and thought he was a piece of shit. He was a degenerate guy with a terrible reputation. He thought that having all the money in the world exempted him from acting like a human being or showing respect for anyone but himself. He indulged himself in any way that he pleased. He once, after a night of gambling and drinking, threw up at a casino bar and asked an employee to help him procure a prostitute. He would fly Michael to gambling joints in the islands, where he'd lose half a million dollars without blinking. Meanwhile, Michael would lose fifty thousand, trying to keep up—and that money meant much more to him. But Michael was dazzled by King's show-offy excesses.

I wasn't. When he showed up at Michael's dressing room, drunk, with a whole posse of other rich white assholes, I wouldn't let them in. I said, "Unless he's looking to shell out some money for the reconstructive surgery that he's going to need afterward, I advise him to stay outside." He stayed out.

For the Botha fight, he was sober. He knew I wouldn't let him in otherwise. He had actually gone out of his way to be helpful leading up to the fight, getting us into a smaller hotel than the MGM so we could be away from Tyson and the whole crazy atmosphere. He showed respect by having Davimos ask me if he could come in. I said he could come in and spend one minute if he was sober. He came in and said good luck. Someone said it was a put-down, the way I treated him. But it wasn't. I was just protecting my fighter and the sanctity of the dressing room.

One night I got a phone call. This was after the Botha fight, around the time of the holidays. It was Michael and he was drunk. I could tell because he was slightly giddy. He put Roger King on the phone. Big mistake. Now, Michael's contract was running out with Davimos, and with the Duvas and Korzerski, and King got on with me and basically said, "I'm going to be heading up Michael's new management team. Don't worry, you're still with us, Teddy, but everyone else is gone." He went on to say we're going to do this and we're going to do that, and I interrupted him. I said, "You're going to do another thing, too. You're going to get another fucking trainer."

"Well, Teddy, we would never do that."

"No, no," I said. "You've just done it."

"I think you're misunderstanding—"

"I understand perfectly, you piece of shit. You think because you got fucking money that I'm impressed. You think you can take this kid who fucking hardly knows who he is and drink champagne with him and get him all screwed up so he does something like leave the guys who've been with him his whole career, and then you can come to me and think you're doing me some kind of favor? You think I'm still going to want to train him?"

"Teddy, I don't know why you're talking to me this way. Everyone respects you—"

"No, you don't. You don't fucking respect me. You think I'm a piece of shit."

"No one has ever talked to me this way. I don't understand . . . we respect you. I'm here with Robert Shapiro, and—"

"He's a piece of shit, too," I said. Shapiro was one of the lawyers with O. J. Simpson's Dream Team. "All of youse can go fuck yourself," I said.

He was stunned. He said, "I got on the phone, talked to you respectfully, and—"

"No, you didn't. You got on the phone telling me that you think I'm a piece of shit. Because the second you said you were taking away these guys who've been with him his whole career, who brought me into it, you were insulting me. Forget about what I did. I did my job. But these guys were there way before me. They took risks when nobody thought two things about Michael. They stayed with him through all kinds of shit. Where were you? Now he's a champion for a second time, and you're going to tell me, who you don't even know, that I'm lucky that you're going to keep me on board when you're fucking everyone else? Well, I'd have to be an even bigger piece of shit than you to do that."

I heard his voice now, but it was fainter, like he was holding the phone away from him, "Michael, I can't talk to this guy."

Michael got on the phone, all worked up. "Teddy, what are you doing?"

I said, "What are *you* doing? . . . You think you're going to be disloyal to these people? You think you're just going to walk away from these people and I'm just going to go along with you?"

"But you're my guy. You brought me to a title. You and me can do a lot of things together. . . ."

"I guess I didn't teach you anything, did I, Michael? I thought I did, but I guess I really didn't teach you much, did I?"

"But, Teddy—"

"No, Michael. You either understand what's right or you don't. If you don't know the difference, I don't care how many times you win the title, you ain't no champion."

I hung up.

A few weeks went by. Everybody knew what was going on, of course. Davimos and all of them thanked me for being loyal.

"I don't know what to say to you, Teddy," Davimos said. "You need the money more than I do."

It was true. Davimos had been born rich. Elaine and the kids and I were still living in the same apartment in Staten Island that we'd been in since before little Teddy had been born.

Unless Michael changed his mind, I was walking away from the Holyfield fight, which was worth $800,000 to me. There was also an interim fight against a young unbeaten heavyweight named Vaughn Bean, which Michael needed to win or it would jeopardize things with Holyfield. But I didn't hear anything from Michael, and at a certain point we didn't know where it was going to go. It was getting closer to the Bean fight, which we had lost control over. I decided to write a letter to him. It was a hard letter. I said tough things, but caring things. Apparently he showed it to a girl that he was with at the time. He asked her what she thought. The girl said, "Whoever wrote this letter is a very unusual person." What did she mean by that? "Well, he only cares about what's right. And about you. He doesn't care about anything else."

It was as if he needed someone to tell him. He couldn't recognize that for himself. He needed an excuse. He wound up calling me and coming back. He signed the deal, ensuring that Davimos, Korzerski, and the Duvas would make the money they deserved. For me, however, the worst was just beginning.

Somebody had to pay a price. That was just the dynamic of it. Michael was embarrassed by what he'd done, the side of himself that he'd shown and for which I'd held him accountable. It was complicated but it was also simple. Michael had always wanted it to be about family and love. He had always been testing to make sure that you weren't there just for the money. I'd passed the test, but he hadn't. He'd been exposed because I hadn't gone along with him and sold out to Roger King. It filled him with shame and self-loathing, along with resentment toward me for pointing out his weakness. The result, the only way he could make things right, was by acting so terribly that I would be forced to abuse and punish him. I know it sounds crazy, but I think that was the unconscious logic. *I'm going to be as awful as Teddy thinks I am so that he can feel justified in hating me.* The other thing was that if he was abusive to me and everyone else, then in a way we'd all be selling out by staying. If we were being abused and staying, it must be for the money. It was very twisted.

We started training camp for the Vaughn Bean fight, and it was the worst, most fucked-up camp I'd ever been involved in. One session, he took off his headgear and threw it at me, and I picked it up and threw it back in his face. Another time, we got into something in his truck, and I smacked him. It got to the point where we were driving in separate cars, never eating together, seeing each other only in the gym. The amazing thing is he still kept his curfew. But it was awful. The whole experience made me feel selfish and small. I sat in my room one night, nearly crying, wondering why I was treating him so badly. I knew that I had to hold myself accountable, that it wasn't all on him, but I couldn't figure a way out of it.

The next day, I took a walk with him after our training session. We went down the road, beyond the hotel.

"Michael, listen, this has gone too far. This isn't good, the way things are with us. I know you made a mistake when you went with these people, and when I wrote you the letter, you realized it. I pointed out some things to you, some flaws in the way you acted, and that made you feel exposed. I understand that you're acting the way you've been acting almost as a kind of protection. You're pushing all this off from what it is. I understand. You think I don't care no more. You think that because you made a decision that was based on money, or appeared to be based on money, and not on loyalty, commitment, and principle, that I've written you off. But you're being a moron. Don't you know anything about me? Don't you know that what we've done together is something that can't be lost or minimized that easily? Don't you understand that just the act of me being here means that I still care about you?"

He stopped and looked at me. I could tell he wanted to get past what was there between us, but that he was struggling with it. There was another thing, I realized, that might be involved. "Maybe you think I care more for Davimos, that I somehow took his side in this," I said. "That's not why I did what I did. If I made that stand and was willing to risk everything for John, don't you friggin' understand that it would be no less for you? It's always been you that I cared the most about. But I wasn't going to let you do something that I wouldn't let someone do to you. How could you stand here with me and respect me and trust me, if I let that happen to John? Could I be any different for you?"

It didn't matter. He couldn't get out of the place he was in.

"Okay," I said. "The final thing I'm going to tell you is that I'm going to do everything I can to keep the title for you, so you can fight for the eight million against Holyfield. I'll do everything I can, and then I'm gone. I will not spend one more second talking to you the way I have had to talk to you for the last few months. I will not flush away everything we've done with this kind of shit. I won't do it."

We went three more weeks and it didn't get any better. Everyone knew I was going to leave, that this was my last fight with Michael. Boorman almost cried. He begged Michael to talk to me. "Please. He's not kidding around. He's going to leave." Davimos was trying to get me to hold off making it public, asking me to think about it, to reconsider. "Please, Teddy, wait until after." They didn't understand. I had spent plenty of time thinking about it. The press couldn't wait to get to me. The first time they put a microphone in front of me, I said, "It's my last fight with Michael Moorer."

The night of the fight, Michael was so lethargic, even the TV commentators, who knew about his tendencies in that direction, were stunned. His opponent, Vaughn Bean, a turban-wearing black Muslim, was undefeated, but against a string of nobodies. He was small for a heavyweight, and though he had some skills, and an all-star corner that included Joe Frazier, Michael Spinks, and Butch Lewis, he was a guy that Michael should have dominated. The fact was Michael went into the fight in decent shape physically. It was his head that was all messed up.

There was a point in the fight where I knew I had to do something again. I'd had a feeling that I might, and the day before, when Flem had said, "You need anything, boss?," I had told him, "Yeah, bring a cell phone." He looked at me, like, what the hell? Anyway, we reached this moment in the fight, and I told Flem that when Michael came back to the corner, I wanted him to hand me the cell phone. Flem was nervous. He didn't know what the hell I was going to do. But as soon as Michael sat on his stool, he handed me the cell phone. I pulled up the antenna and put it to my ear. I said, "Yeah? You've been watching? I don't know. I'll ask him." I handed the phone back to Flem. "Michael, that was your ex-wife, Bobbi. Your son is home crying. He just heard the commentator on TV say that you don't want to be champion no more, and he's crying. He wants to know why Daddy doesn't want to be heavyweight champ no more."

Somehow Michael managed to eke out a win. I think he won by a point. If he had lost that fight, he would have missed out on the Holyfield fight and the $8 million payday that went along with it. It was a big thing. A very big thing. That money would have meant a lot to me and my family, too. It would have put me over the top. I wouldn't have a mortgage today. But Michael was stubborn. He couldn't find a way to come back to me. He called me one time, it was getting closer and closer to the fight and having to go to camp, and he called me from a bar, drunk, at three in the morning. He started to say something about wanting me to come back. I told him to call me in the morning when he was sober.

He never called back.

Part of it was that he had beaten Holyfield already. I had helped him defeat that dragon, and he had enough confidence to think that he could do it again, without me. I'll tell you one thing: if it was Tyson he was fighting, he would have called back. I guarantee you that. Michael would not have gotten in the ring with Tyson without me.

FOR YEARS AFTER THAT HE WAS DEAD TO ME.

He used to call when I wasn't home to talk to Elaine. He'd beg her to intervene. She would sneak these calls with him. I found out and it almost caused a serious problem between her and me. That's how bad it was. I told her he could be fucking lying in the street and I wouldn't slow down. I felt I had the right. He had ruined our destiny.

Some sportswriter read me a quote from Michael's new trainer, Freddy Roach, before the Holyfield fight. Roach said, "I'm not a dictator. I don't want a prisoner here. I let Michael be Michael." The writer asked me what I thought of that. I said, "What do I think? I always understood that it was my job to never let Michael be Michael."

It didn't surprise me when Michael lost the rematch. Do I think the result would have been different if I'd been in his corner? Yeah, I do. I know it sounds self-serving and conceited, but that's how I feel.

The thing was, no matter how many times I ignored Michael's calls over the years, he kept calling. He even cried one time. Eventually, he wore me down. I guess I was getting soft, because I was on a plane flying to Seattle to train this heavyweight, Kirk Johnson, and I took out some paper and started writing. Ten or twelve pages later I had a letter written. I just felt I had to explain how hurt I'd been to my core, to at least let him know why he was being held accountable, and not just suffering as some kind of innocent, which I thought might be how he thought about it.

He read the letter while I was in Seattle, and he called Elaine. He said, "I've been sitting in my truck for five hours. And I've read his letter seven times, and I can't cry no more, and I can't leave the truck. And I don't know what to do because I lost the only man who ever loved me. The only person who ever loved me in my life. And I don't know what to do."

I let him come back. I allowed him into my life and into my family again, just a little bit at first, but a little bit more as the years have gone by. There came a point when he asked me to train him again. I knew better than to go there. That part, at least for me, was over.

THE
FOUNDATION

IN A WAY, MY EXPERIENCE WITH MICHAEL, DESPITE its many incredible highs, ultimately led me away from my life as a trainer. I still loved the sweat and the discipline and the commitment. I loved helping a fighter achieve a level of accomplishment in the ring. But the emotional toll of investing so much in people who were almost certain to betray me finally started to outweigh my passion. I began to get involved in other pursuits that, more and more, took me away from the gym and training. It wasn't a conscious decision, just something that evolved over time. I got involved in broadcasting, doing the boxing commentary on ESPN *Friday Night Fights*. I spent more time with Elaine and the kids. And I started a charitable foundation in my father's name, the Dr. Theodore A. Atlas Foundation.

In a way, the genesis of that idea came from the writer Mark Kriegel, who said something to me that got me thinking. Remember this was someone who had spent a fair amount of time observing me, and what he said was, "You think that if somebody's written about and remembered in the newspapers, or they're recognized publicly, it means their life has been worthwhile. It makes everything okay."

I turned that over for a good long while, and thought, *Maybe he's right. Maybe I do think that.* I know that when Jack Newfield wrote something about my dad in the *New York Post*, it meant a lot to me. It made me feel good to see my father acknowledged in print that way. Even with all the difficulties we'd had, I'd always felt it important that my dad not be forgotten. I didn't think he ever got paid enough on this planet for what he did.

Although winning the heavyweight title had validated a lot of what my father had done for me and meant to me, my acknowledgment of that was a mostly private sentiment. I realized I wanted a more public expression of my regard for him and what he had accomplished in his life. Maybe I needed a way to communicate with him that I didn't have when he was alive, a way of making him take credit for things and receive praise for things that he would never take when he was alive. A foundation, I decided, would serve that purpose.

From a practical standpoint, I wanted to do something that would serve people, as he had, in a very direct way. I wanted what I was going to do to be free of bureaucracy and the kind of little humiliations that charities often put people through. It wasn't enough just to create a foundation. It was going to be a foundation the way I wanted it. It wasn't going to be for one specific cause, like muscular dystrophy or diabetes or cerebral palsy, it was going to help people who needed help in a variety of circumstances, people who might otherwise fall through the cracks. My father was a general practitioner, and that's what we would be. We would make house calls. Not only for medical problems, but for any kind of problems that required a helping hand.

Once the philosophy was in place, I needed a structure and a way to raise money to accomplish the good deeds I envisioned. There were a number of people who got involved in this project with me and volunteered their time. There was Judge Mike Brennan and his assistant (who's now a lawyer) Kenny Mitchell; there was Tom Conway, who coached basketball at St. Theresa's; and there was John Rowan, who was a graduate of the Naval Academy and also a lawyer. Later on, others joined, including Kathy Zito, who does so much stuff now that it would take a whole chapter to cover; David Berlin, a lawyer who does pro bono work; Sean Sweeney, Paul Quatrocchi, Neil Murphy, Joe Fama, Kevin McCabe, John Hanson, Joanne Felice, Sue Hession, Roberta Davola, John Vatucchi, John Cirillo, Dan Tomei, and Joe Spinelli, and Steve Zawada, my old probation officer, who became a private investigator and checks out people we intend to help to make sure they're legit.

Our first meeting, we didn't have any place to convene, so my friend Neil Murphy, who, along with my friend Mike Peterson, owned a bar called Bottomley's, down near Stapleton, let us have the upstairs room there and served us free pizza and beers. We pretty quickly agreed that an annual dinner with celebrities as the attraction was the simplest way to raise money. I was able to reach out to people like Willis Reed, Phil Simms, Bill Parcells, Pete Rose, and Harry Carson, and also guys from the boxing community, like George Foreman and Larry Holmes and Lou Duva (who brought in the comedian Pat Cooper), as well as some Hollywood people, like Willem Dafoe and Stephen Baldwin. We were off and running.

The first year we held the "Teddy" dinner at the Statten Catering Hall and had three hundred people and seven celebrities. The next year we had five hundred. The next year seven hundred. We finally had to leave the Statten. We had so many people in there it got to be a fire hazard. (Of course, with the fire marshals as our guests, nobody was saying anything.) In 2004, in our new home at the Staten Island Hilton, we had eleven hundred people and seventy-five celebrities. My committee said, "Teddy, please, we gotta have fewer celebrities. They're taking away too many seats from people who will pay. It's losing us money."

Over the years, we've raised about 1.5 million bucks and given it to people in need. This past year alone we raised $500,000 and we also opened a food pantry that dispenses food to the hungry. Since everyone working for the foundation is a volunteer, there are no administrative costs; every dollar we get goes to people who need it. After 9/11, we raised over a quarter of a million dollars for victims who had fallen through the cracks. We couldn't cover the whole city, but we got a list of everyone on Staten Island, the families of restaurant workers, messengers, window washers, and others, who had been killed or disabled when the towers came down. The firemen and policemen, God bless them, had organizations that took care of them, but there were other victims of 9/11 who needed help and weren't getting it.

The Red Cross fund was supposed to help those families, but something went wrong. The money didn't go where it was supposed to go. I don't want to use the word "stolen," and I'm not knowledgeable or in the know enough to say where the money went. I'm just saying that I know when a duck is a duck and when a duck ain't a duck.

Attorney General Eliot Spitzer held a meeting at the Staten Island

Hilton to address some of the people who were waiting for help. We found out about it and went down there with our checkbook. There were all these parents and grandparents and families crying—literally crying—saying where's the money? We've been waiting for months, we went down and filled out a stack of papers, and meanwhile they make us feel worse because we got to prove that we're victims.

It was terrible, absolutely heart-wrenching. They were asking for answers. A few of these politicians were decent, but a lot of them weren't, and these poor people were being handed a load of bull. All of a sudden, one of the family members got up. He was crying. He said, "I don't want to be bullshitted anymore. Don't tell me you're going to do something when you're not."

Kathy Zito and Sean Sweeney from my foundation went up to this man and said very quietly and nicely, "Look, sir, just give us your name. We've got a list already, and we can give you a check right now for a couple of thousand dollars."

He was still upset. He said, "Please, I don't want no more bullshit. Everybody's been telling me that for months now and I don't want—"

Kathy started to write a check out, and he looked at her, calming down a little, his face still wet with tears. "What are you doing?"

"We're giving you a check," Kathy said.

He started crying all over again. "I don't understand. How are you doing this?"

"We already have your name on a list. We did all the work. And we're giving you a check."

At that point, he turned toward the front of the room, where all the politicians were, and he started yelling, "How come they can do this? Why can they do this and you can't?"

Other families started coming over to us. I think we wrote out thirty thousand dollars in checks that night. I wish we could have done more, but the point is, we've been able to do things that a lot of foundations have trouble doing. Part of the reason we've been able to do that is because we're small. As my father used to say, "Bigger hospital, bigger problems."

People can face huge problems way beyond their control, but certain things aren't impossible to solve. There was a five-year-old boy with lymphoma cancer. His parents ran out of money and couldn't pay their health insurance. They started paying with their credit cards but soon maxed them out. They'd heard about the foundation and gave us a call. We picked up the cost of the insurance, and a few weeks later, to lift the kid's spirits, we took him to a Yankee game and made arrangements for him to meet Derek Jeter, A-Rod, and other players down on the field before the game.

Another example: A house burned down. Mother and father with four children. They were renters, but they didn't have any renters' insurance. Thank God they got out. But they lost everything. They got out with the clothes on their backs, didn't even have time to put on their shoes. We got a check for three thousand dollars in their hands the next day. Drove to where they were in the motel and handed it to them. The person who delivered the check from the committee—I can't remember if it was Kathy or Tom—spent an hour with them while they cried together. What did it give them? It gave them a little stability. The kids could get shoes and not miss another day of school. It's not a long-term solution, but it makes a difference. It serves as a bridge, and a bridge is important.

When I look at some of these big foundations—the United Way, the March of Dimes, and others—I don't see much of the money they raise actually finding its way to the people or causes they're supposed to be helping. Does that mean I would turn down corporate sponsorship if we could get it? Absolutely not. If we got corporate sponsorship and then had to hire somebody to bring it to the next level—where we were raising a million a year—I would do it. I would still keep a couple of my guys and keep that grassroots, human part of it. But I realize that we need to keep growing each year. That's just the nature of these things. No matter what, though, I'll never let this foundation lose sight of its purpose, which is to help people.

George Foreman came to the dinner one time, and he said to me, "I go to these thousand-dollar-a-plate dinners where we all wear tuxes and pat each other on the back and we don't know what the hell we did there that night. Here, we know what we did. We hear about it, and we actually see the people we've helped."

There was one dinner where some of the money we raised almost had to go toward paying the funeral expenses for our emcee, the comedian Jeff Pirrami. I'm not kidding, the guy nearly got himself killed. What happened was that Pirrami, who's from the Don Rickles school of comedy and calls everyone "a fat rat bastard," insulted the wrong guy. This was one of our last years at the Statten, and we were filled to the rafters. Now our crowd is as diverse as you can possibly imagine. We've got lawyers and bar owners and cops and construction guys and Wall Street guys. The whole world comes. At one table in the back was a gangster we'll call "Benny" and his crew. A lot of guys are thought of as gangsters, but this guy was the real thing. He'd killed people. Even though he wasn't a big guy, he was a rough customer. Most of them are just rough with a gun, but this guy would kill you with his bare hands. He never went to these charity events normally, but he knew me and he knew it was for a good cause and he wanted to help me out. "I want to support Teddy." So he bought a table.

He was sitting there with his wiseguys and wannabe wiseguys, and of all of them, he was the one to win a raffle prize of a couple of Knicks tickets. Benny got up and said, "This is great. I'm gonna take my grandson to the game."

The rest of his crew, they were all trying to kiss his ass, so they said, "Hey, Benny, siddown, we'll go up and get it for you."

"Nah," he said. "I'll get it." He'd had a little wine, he was having a good time, why not take a little stroll up to the front? What a fucking mistake. He started walking up, and it was chaotic, stuff was being auctioned off to raise money. I was focused on that and not really paying attention.

Pirrami was doing his thing, running the auction and keeping people entertained. Suddenly, as Benny crossed the room in front of him, he said, "Hey, get a load of this little no-neck wannabe gangster with the two-dollar rug." And here was the thing: Benny really did wear a hairpiece!

"Hey, pal," Pirrami continued, "what's that thing on your head? A Chia pet?"

Now the audience was laughing. Benny stopped dead in his tracks. Like I said, I was distracted and didn't notice, but my son told me right afterward—and even though he was only eleven or twelve years old, he noticed everything—"Dad, there's a man who just got really mad."

"Oh, yeah?"

"Yeah. It was the guy who won the Knicks tickets. He was walking up to the stage and Jeff made fun of him."

"Uh-huh."

"He stopped right in front of the stage and he cursed. He said something in—I think it was Italian. *'Morte.'*"

Death.

"And then he ripped the tickets to pieces. They were good tickets, Dad! He ripped 'em to pieces, threw them on the floor, and spit on them. And yelled *'Morte!'*"

I was listening to this, trying to make sense of it, but also distracted by a million different things. Somebody always needed me for something.

The dinner ended, and everybody was gathering up their coats and saying their good-byes. The place was a madhouse. People were coming up to me, slapping me on the back, shaking my hand. I became aware that there was somebody standing near me, waiting to talk to me. It was Jeff Pirrami. As soon as I took a look at him, I thought, *Boy, he looks pale. I don't remember him looking that pale at the beginning of the night.* I also noticed that he seemed quiet. This was a guy who you usually couldn't shut up. He was always loud and funny.

"Jeff, are you all right?" I said. The first thing that came to my mind was that the car we had to pick him up and take him home—and that's the only thing we did for him—hadn't shown up. "Whatsa matter?" I said. "The car's not here?"

"No, the car's here. . . . But so is the gangster."

"What?"

"How was I supposed to know he was a real gangster?"

I was looking at him, trying to take in what he was saying, but there were all these people hovering around, tapping me and trying to get my attention.

"He's got about twelve guys with him outside," Jeff said, looking like he was about to throw up, "and he just told me that I'm a lowlife piece of shit that doesn't deserve to live, and he's gonna put two in my fuckin' head and leave me in the Dumpster."

Despite all the commotion I was focused only on him now. "Who said this?"

"Benny X."

"Oh, shit. Benny X said that? He is a real gangster. He will put two in your head!"

"Jesus, Teddy!"

"No, no, I'm just saying—look, he's not gonna—nothing's gonna happen to you."

"You sure? He didn't look like he was joking."

"Yeah, I'm sure. I mean, anything happens to you is happening to both of us."

"This is how you try to make me feel better?"

"Don't worry about it, Jeff. Nothing's gonna happen."

"I don't want to die, Teddy."

"You ain't dying. C'mon. Just shut up and come with me." I grabbed him, and as I grabbed him I noticed that his whole body was shaking. I tried to ignore it. I took him outside and, sure enough, there was Benny and his crew of guys. As soon as we walked out, he said, "Teddy, this fuckin' lowlife scum has got no respect for women or children or nothin'. He's a fuckin' piece of shit—"

"Benny, hold on a minute . . . Benny, why'd you come tonight?"

"For you!"

"Right. And I appreciate it, Benny. I do. I appreciate very much that respect. But you didn't come for me. You came to help me—to help these kids out, for the charity."

"That's right," he said. "Because it's a charity you run, and I know what you do. That's why I'm here."

"Well, that's why he's here, too, Benny. He came for the same reason. He does it different than you, Benny. The way you do it is, you do a great thing—you buy a table. He comes and freakin' entertains people. People come to see him make fun of people. But he does it so I can raise money for the same people that you're helping me raise money for, Benny." I knew the key with him. I knew you had to play the game a little. I said, "He don't know who you are, Benny. He's got no idea who you are. By the time he's done with you, he's on to the next guy."

"But he—"

"Benny, he didn't mean nothing by it. He never woulda said nothing if he knew who you were."

Benny held up a finger and looked at Jeff. "If it weren't for this man . . ." He had found his way out. "If it weren't for this man, I'd leave you in the fuckin' Dumpster. I'm giving you a pass because of this guy. You understand that, you fuckin' piece of shit?"

"So we're okay, Benny?" I said.

"Yeah. We're all right. You know I respect you."

"And I respect you."

He came over, looked at Jeff like ice, then hugged me. I walked Jeff to his limo. When we got there, I opened the door and watched him get in. I stuck my head in, just to make sure he was okay. There was a bar along one side. I opened a bottle of scotch and poured him a glass. "Here," I said, handing it to him. "Drink this."

He drank it.

"You all right?" I asked.

He was still shaking. He looked up at me. Now he knew he was going to live, and it was like I've always said, you are who you are. He was a comedian. "You know," he said, "if he wanted to fuckin' kill somebody, why didn't he whack the lousy rat bastard who sold him that cheap toupee?"

I laughed out loud. I couldn't believe it. Now he was being cocky. "Listen," I said, "Benny's got a better sense of humor than he displayed tonight. He's still in the parking lot. Let me fuckin' tell him what you just said—he'll get a kick out of it."

"Get the fuck out of here! Are you crazy? Shut the door, Teddy. Jesus!"

I was laughing as I shut the door. I heard him yell at the driver, "Go! Go!" And they peeled out.

I didn't talk to Jeff again until close to the next dinner. I had to call him up and make sure he was coming. Almost the first thing out of his mouth was: "Is he gonna be there?"

"Who?"

"You fuckin' know who!"

"No, he's not gonna be here."

"You're lying. He is gonna be there."

"Jeff, don't worry about it. It's all done. It's in the past."

"It's easy for you to say. You aren't the one he was gonna kill."

He required a bit more reassurance, but I finally wound up persuading him it was going to be all right. Then, on the night of the dinner, just before he arrived, I went over to talk to the guys that did the security. They were all court officers and good guys, but that hadn't stopped Jeff from making fun of them like he made fun of everybody. They were itching to get him back. I walked in and heard one of them saying, "You better okay it with Teddy," and another one saying, "No, we want to do it."

I said, "Do what?"

They looked at one another, then one of them showed me a bullet-proof vest. Everybody knew the story of Jeff and Benny by now.

"What the fuck is that?"

"A flak jacket."

"Yeah, I know what it is. What's it for?"

"We want to—When Pirrami comes in, he's gonna be here in about an hour, he always gets here early, we want to go up to him and say, 'Listen, we can't guarantee your security this year. We want you to wear this. And we're gonna be around you all night.'"

"Get the fuck outta here," I said. "He's overweight to begin with. He's three hundred and fifty fuckin' pounds. He'll drop dead of a heart attack. Do you understand?"

"Teddy, please."

"Are you guys gonna replace him when he drops dead?"

"Pleeease . . ." They were begging.

"No. I ain't fuckin' letting you do it. I'm sorry. I wish you could, but you can't."

"Aww, shit. I told you we shouldn't have said anything. It's off, guys. Fuckin' Teddy said no."

They were just dying to get a piece of him—just a little bit.

But you know Jeff was more affected than I imagined. The first year back, he wasn't as funny as usual. Before he went onstage, I gave him a little pep talk, the same way I did with fighters. "Listen," I told him, "you're gonna be fine."

"Yeah. You fuckin'—No one was gonna put two in your fuckin' head."

"Seriously," I said.

"Where is he?" he asked. The place was starting to fill up, and Jeff was looking around nervously.

"Look, I'm telling you. He ain't here."

"You're lying."

"Just, you know, keep the strong jokes to the right side of the room."

"Oh, fuck! I knew it."

"No, I'm only kidding with you."

It took Jeff a couple of years to get back to his old self. It did. The thing with Benny screwed him up badly. But he wasn't a quitter. He knew we were doing good work, and even if it meant putting his life on the line, he wasn't going to let that stop him.

STICKIN' AND MOVIN'

EACH YEAR AS THE ANNUAL "TEDDY" DINNER AP-
proaches, my life grows even more hectic than usual. Elaine
has said to me on more than one occasion, "Now I know how you must
have felt trying to get your father's attention when you were a kid."

During most of the year, I fly out of town every Thursday to wherever that week's location is for *Friday Night Fights*. It might be in Las
Vegas, Florida, New Jersey, Sacramento, Connecticut—all over the
country. Two years ago they asked me to do *Tuesday Night Fights* as well,
which meant I was either on the air or in the air practically from Monday
till Saturday. Luckily, for the most part, I like what I'm doing.

It was over twenty years ago that I did my first few television broadcasts with Spencer Ross on Sports Channel New York. Later, I did one
fight on ABC's *Wide World of Sports*. I also did some radio work for
Westwood One with Larry Michaels, and three years of calling HBO
fights on the radio. But my career as a broadcaster didn't really take
flight until I landed the TV gig on ESPN seven years ago. In the beginning there, I put in marathon hours preparing for each show. When I got
behind that microphone, or in front of that camera, I wanted to know
that I was prepared. Cus always told me that the first sign of a pro was
preparation, and I took that to heart. In fact, sometimes I overprepared.

I was lucky, the first five years, to have a great partner in Bob Papa. (My new partner, Joe Tessitore, is also terrific.) Bob shared his wisdom and knowledge with me whenever he thought I needed it, but he was also incredibly respectful of the work I put in. He knew the kind of hours I spent—watching videotape, making notes and phone calls, reading background materials—and he said, "You know, Teddy, you don't have to do so much, you could just wing it. I mean, I've never seen anyone who from the moment the first punch is thrown knows how the fight will turn out." Then he looked at me, and said, "But you wouldn't dare not do all the work, would you?"

"I would be too scared," I said.

I wanted my audience to feel that when they were watching one of our broadcasts they were getting a light shined in places that might have otherwise been dark. I wanted them to not only hear about what was happening, but find out why it was happening. That was the challenge I set out for myself: to let the viewer in on what fighters were thinking, what pressure was causing them to do, and how they were dealing with it.

At the same time, I didn't want them to rely just on my opinion. That was why I needed to watch film and talk to people. I wanted to be armed with as many facts about each fighter as I could gather so that when I explained tendencies, strengths, weaknesses, it had a foundation. The other thing I tried to do was get ahead of the fight—to explain what was going to happen before it happened. If I could help a viewer understand why, the next time he might be able to see it on his own without me. The best compliments I've gotten are when people come up to me at a fight or on the street and say, "You've taught me. You've made it more interesting for me. I never realized these things were going on."

This past summer when I did the Olympics for NBC for the second time, I worked harder than I've ever worked. People ask me what the Olympic experience was like, what Athens was like, and it's hard for me to tell them much because most of the time I was in my hotel room preparing for the next day, although I did manage to at least see the Acropolis, the Parthenon, and the statue of Athena while I was there.

The Olympics were something I wanted to do very badly, in the same way that I wanted to train a world champion. It meant I'd reached a certain level in my profession. The next pinnacle. Beyond the Olympics, I suppose the next peak would be calling the really big fights on pay-per-view and HBO. (In April 2005 I did actually call my first and ESPN's first-ever pay-per-view fight broadcast from Las Vegas.) Beyond that I'd like to do a show about the psychological dimensions of sports—maybe even taking it into the broader realm of social and moral issues. I realize that it's not likely that I'd get an opportunity to do something like that on television at this point, but a sports talk show on radio might work. I could see that happening.

One of the best things about broadcasting is that it gives me a platform, a forum. As most fight fans, I think, are aware, I'm not timid about saying what's on my mind. It's gotten me in trouble on occasion, but if I see something going on that isn't right, I'm gonna talk about it. It's important to be able to stand up for a fighter who got screwed, and be able to say, "These friggin' crooked bastards. You know, they used to get away with this quietly, but they ain't getting away with it quietly no more."

Everybody knows that there are a lot of things wrong in boxing. I've been saying for a while now that we've come to the point where we need some kind of outside intervention, the involvement of a federal commission and some kind of national system. The alphabet soup of sanctioning groups is a corrupt joke. I once asked Max Kellerman while we were on the air, "Max, you know what the WBA stands for?"

"What, Teddy?"

"We Be Asking."

"How about the WBC?"

"We Be Collecting."

"I'm almost afraid to ask about the IBF."

"That's easy. I Be Felonious."

It's not an exaggeration, either. Bob Lee, the president of the IBF, was indicted for taking bribes from promoters and managers in exchange for rigging rankings and sanctioning bouts. Bob Arum and Cedric Kushner, two of the promoters who testified to paying the bribes, were later fined by the Nevada State Athletic Commission. (Despite overwhelming evidence, Lee was convicted only of money laundering and tax fraud, though he was sentenced to twenty-two months in jail with parole.)

A couple of years ago I was asked to go to Washington to speak in front of the Senate. Because of my schedule with ESPN, I couldn't make it on the day they'd set aside. What they did instead—and as far as I know this was the first and only time they'd ever done this—was have me address the Senate over a speakerphone. There I was in my home, on the telephone, and in the Senate chambers a speaker system was broadcasting my voice. I went over a checklist of things that boxing needed, including universal medical standards and federal rules and bylaws that each state would be required to enforce. I said that we needed a way of making sure that fighters knew what the actual monies were when they signed to a fight, instead of the way things stood now, where a promoter or manager could use fancy accounting to cheat them out of their share of the purse. I pointed out that the landscape of boxing as it was currently constituted encouraged corruption, that there were certain states where the promoters actually *paid* the fight judges, which is insane—it's the equivalent of George Steinbrenner paying the umpires who work Yankee games.

Why aren't other sports run like boxing? Because if they were, the credibility of those sports would be shot. Because somebody with some sense would stand up and stop it from happening. In boxing, those voices of reason and sanity are almost never heard. There is no one at the watchtower. In fact, there is no tower.

That's only a slight exaggeration. Senator John McCain has been speaking up for a while. In fact, he's been promoting a bill to empower a national boxing commissioner or czar, which is something I've been suggesting for a long time, too. The Senate Commerce Committee actually approved the bill by a voice vote, but as of this writing the bill has yet to be passed on the floor. The opposition to a reform that seems only to benefit boxers and boxing fans is odd, but perhaps it's no coincidence that Don King curried favor with Dennis Hastert and other Republicans now opposing the bill by taking a prominent role in the 2004 elections. King also donated heavily and made campaign commercials for President Bush, whose signature would be required to pass the bill.

The funny thing is that if a boxing czar actually were established and put into place, I'd be scared to death. You know the old saying, "Be careful what you wish for." Well, in this case, I'd be terrified that we'd get the wrong person. Cus always talked about that. He said, I'd never want to see that happen because I don't trust the government. They screw up everything. It could be worse than before, because instead of pockets of corruption you might have a single corrupt guy running the whole thing. But in the end even Cus admitted it would be worth the risk.

Assuming it did happen, and they were looking for a guy, I have some ideas. My top choice would be Joe Spinelli, the former New York inspector general, who was an FBI agent for ten years and was the first guy to bring Don King under investigation. He has a passion for boxing and an understanding of it, plus he's incorruptible. Another guy I'd feel good about is Tom Hoover, who played for seven NBA teams and was an inspector with the New York State Athletic Commission of Boxing. He's a good man who knows boxing, and he's tough. He's the kind of guy who would physically throw someone out of his office if he thought they were hurting the sport. Pennsylvania Boxing Commissioner Greg Serb would also be a good choice. My wildcard pick would have been somebody like the late Jack Newfield, who wrote extensively about the corruption in boxing and was a guy of great character and principle.

Some people have asked me if I would consider doing it. My answer is that a lot would depend on the amount of authority they gave to the job. If the czar was just a bullshit figurehead with a title, I'd turn it down flat. But if the job entailed real power, I do feel that I could do a lot of good in a spot like that.

As I get older, I'm beginning to come face-to-face with the things I've accomplished and the things I haven't accomplished. When I look to the future these days, I think about what I'm going to leave behind.

I'd love for my foundation to eventually open up homes for kids in all of the New York boroughs. A place where kids off the streets and kids who were being abused could go and be part of a cooperative living situation that centered around a boxing program and could give them what a proper home would give them—care, direction, instruction, discipline, accountability, and dreams. I'd like to see that grow—which is why I need to see my foundation keep growing—so it isn't just one house like that, but six, seven, eight houses in different areas of the country helping kids who need a safe, healthy environment that would give them the physical and emotional things they need.

I've been lucky in so many ways. Who would ever believe that a guy who was educated on a corner in Stapleton and in Rikers (and later in a gym in Catskill) would have one kid graduating from college and—my daughter—in law school?

I wish my father and mother were still around so they could see Nicole and Teddy when their graduation days come. I know this is going to sound funny, but I also wish Cus could see them. As much as there was good and bad about him, I wish that he could have been around as a grandfather type of figure, maybe taught Teddy a few lessons in the gym. I also wish he could have maybe seen me as a commentator. I think he would have gotten a kick out of that. Boy, he used to hate boxing commentators. Howard Cosell would get him so furious, he'd turn the sound off. I'd come in the room and the sound would be down, and I'd say, "What's wrong with the TV, Cus?" And he would say, "I can't listen to him. He doesn't know what he's talking about. Sit down and don't touch that knob."

As long as I'm going in this vein, I also wish Cus and my mom and dad could have seen this house that I built for the kids and Elaine. It's a funny story about the house. The truth is, I waited too long to build it, and when I finally got around to it, I took a huge gamble. I can say that now because it worked out. We went ahead and built a beautiful sixty-eight-hundred-square-foot house eight years ago when I had no big-time fighter and no real money coming in, and if I hadn't been hired by ESPN subsequently, who knows whether I would have been able to keep it? But I just felt like I had to do it. We had been in a small apartment all those years, and if I waited any longer the kids would grow up without ever having what I felt they should have.

As it turned out, it was one of the best things I ever did. Now we've got this great house on Todt Hill in Staten Island, and the kids were able to spend a few years in it before going off to college. It was like a big Christmas gift to them, and to me, too, to be able to give them something so tangible after all the years and all the paydays I've walked away from.

I never had a real family. I mean, I had my mother and father and my brothers and my sister, but we didn't know how to be a family. We didn't know how to take care of each other. I think that's why I have these alternate charges of electricity that run through me. Some people might go numb in that kind of circumstance; with me it just pushed my feelings to extremes. I can be sensitive and compassionate and giving to the point where it's almost too much. If somebody has needs and problems, I get moved and affected so much it almost controls me, that's how much I feel compelled to help. At the same time, if somebody acts disloyal, if they betray me, and then they try to avoid taking responsibility, if they hide behind the excuses of convenience or weakness or selfishness,

I'll go to a place of wanting to hurt them. I'll be ready to give up everything to right what I consider a wrong—even though I know that my response might not be socially acceptable.

I'm very aware of the extremes within me. The caring and the anger. I've gotten better over the years at modulating them and controlling them, but I won't pretend they don't still exist.

I guess in some ways my whole life has been a journey and a search for family. I wasn't some kid from the streets. I was a doctor's son who grew up in a nice house in a good neighborhood. It just goes to show that you can be lost and alone and neglected in any kind of surroundings. Even though I was never able to get what I needed from my siblings or my parents, I've managed to get there in other ways, with the family I've made for myself, with Elaine and Nicole and Teddy.

For that alone, I consider myself a very fortunate man.

ACKNOWLEDGMENTS

Mom and Dad, I wish we could have shared more together. My children, Nicole and Teddy III, thank you for giving me something I never understood—unconditional love. My wife, Elaine, thank you for reminding me that loyalty does exist. Peter Alson, I'm glad you asked to do this project because you're not only a tremendous writer but the right person for this. Thanks for a great job. Cus D'Amato, I'm only angry you didn't get to train my son. Thanks for helping me have a career in this sport. Jack Newfield, rest well and thank you for worrying about me and then calling in the cavalry when necessary. Joe Spinelli, Kevin McCabe, and Tom Hoover, thank you for being part of the cavalry. My foundation committee, thank you for keeping my dad's name alive and working. George Horowitz, CEO of Everlast, thanks for saying yes each time the foundation asked for help, and for becoming a friend. Larry Coughlin, I wish you were here, but thank you for always standing with me. Chris Reid, I'm sorry we didn't get that title shot a bit earlier, but thanks for being the most loyal fighter I ever knew. All the celebrities that have attended my charity dinner: thank you for caring and making it work. Michael Moorer: you disappointed me once, but thank you for giving me the chance to train the heavyweight champion of the world, for an experience and partnership my children will never forget, and for teaching me to forgive. Nick Baffi, thanks for being my friend and guide during those years in Gleason's Gym. David Berlin, thanks for the free legal work on behalf of the foundation and your friendship. Don Elbaum and Russell Peltz, thanks for sharing your great knowledge of the sport, and making me look a little smarter. Dr. Charles Melone, thanks for fixing my fighters' hands and reminding me that *real* doctors still exist. Tyrone Jackson, you never won that world title, but to me you became a real champ by becoming a father and husband to your family. Anthony Spero, thank you for showing me that some people know how to act once they've made a choice—right or wrong—regardless of the consequences. Dennis Hamill, for all those articles in the New York *Daily News* that helped promote the foundation even when nobody knew. Cormac Gordon, for pushing the foundation in the *S.I. Advance,* so that it could continue to grow. Jerry Izenberg, for writing that story and giving me a way to tell my dad I loved him, and good-bye. Mark Kriegel, for spending that week in Las Vegas and chronicling each day leading to the title. Now it's always there to remember. Brother Tim McDonald, for giving me faith in people, and rooting for me and praying for me. ESPN, and Dick Ebersol at NBC, for giving me an opportunity to leave training and do television. The New York Yankees and Robert Bernstein, for saying yes to the foundation's requests to allow two cancer patients into the dugout with the players before a game, and making them forget they were sick. Bob Papa, my first TV partner, for helping me learn. Jeff Pirami, for emceeing the foundation dinner each year, and not getting killed. My brother, Tommy, for telling me you loved me, even while you've been in a place that has none. Judge Radin, for not putting me in jail, and giving me a chance to write this book. John Davimos, you let me down, but you gave me the opportunity to train Michael Moorer, and I'll always be grateful. Gaga, my grandmother: I'm sorry we didn't have more time to play bingo together. Mitchell P., Bobby R., Louie, Gary P., and Eddie F.: Thanks for having my back and risking yours. Dan Halpern and David Hirshey at Ecco and HarperCollins, for not only buying this book but for letting me trust that it would be okay. All my kids from the Catskill Boxing Club, for giving me a reason and a purpose during those early years, and teaching me to be a father. Rudy Greco, for helping my brother Tommy. Kevin Monahan, for getting me the opportunity to cover the Olympics for NBC. Nelson Cuevas, for running the Apollo Boxing Club all those years so that kids like Mane Moore and Gary Young could grow up and develop. Jeff Mitchell: Thanks for coming to Las Vegas and Germany to support me and my family at these title fights. Fred Chetti, for standing up for me when I left Catskill, even when it wasn't convenient. All the people at Ecco and HarperCollins who did different work to make this happen. Ron Borges: thanks for your support, loyalty, and friendship. Sean Timpone, for teaching me to respect life, not just live it. Mike Boorman: Thanks for being my cornerman and friend in Vegas and Germany. All the boxing fans who have always given me their support and have also tolerated me on TV, thank you. Peter Alson's mom, Barbara Wasserman, thank you for transcribing hours and hours of audiotapes so that Peter could write this book, and for doing it for nothing else but the spirit of helping a son, and for doing it with a special level of care. Eddie Argenio, for the tremendous support and loyalty you gave to the foundation every year. It will never be forgotten. To all the people who buy a ticket or ad to make a donation to the foundation and help many of the less fortunate in an important way. John Rowan, for helping me get the foundation started. I hope we're making you proud up there. Bob Jackson, Norm Stone, and Johnny Val, for looking after my son in the gym. Holt McCallany, for your commitment to the foundation and my family. Joey Trembone, for showing me what a real fighter is, without my ever seeing you throw a punch. John Cirillo, thanks for your pro bono work each year as you send out p.r. information on behalf of the foundation. All the guys at the Mercantile Exchange, for your loyalty and support to the foundation and now the Food Pantry. Bill Mikus, thank you for looking out for me and my family. Scott Waxman, without you this book would not have happened. Thank you. Lorraine Brancale, for having two sons who care about others and for always making me laugh, thanks. My current partner at ESPN, Joe Tessitore, a gentleman. The production team at ESPN, who travel with me and do magic to make me look good each week: Rob, Rick, Johnny, Roger, Brian, Mike, Saul, Joe, Dennis, Nick and Wayne, thanks. Allan Scotto, thanks for your loyalty and your care for boxing.

Peter Alson would like to thank the following people for their contributions, counsel, and advice during the writing of this book: Elaine Atlas, Holt McCallany, David Berlin, Pat English, and Brother Tim McDonald.

Thanks are also due to John Stravinsky, who first mentioned to me that Teddy was looking for a collaborator. To Elizabeth Shienkman, who graciously stepped back when that was the only way possible for me to take on this project. To Dan Halpern, our thoughtful and literate editor at Ecco, whose enthusiasm for this project has meant so much. To David Hirshey, Rob Grover, and everyone else at HarperCollins who had a hand in helping.

Though there is no possible way to express the true measure of my thanks to my mother, Barbara Wasserman, I will try: Mom, no exaggeration, without your help, this book would not have gotten done; from your help with transcribing to your patient counsel to your encouragement, you were nothing short of incredible. Thank you.

And to my wife, Alice O'Neill, who is always there for me, and whose support and patience in often trying circumstances mean the world to me.